More advance praise for *Practical Continuous Improvement for Professional Services*

Your book is a welcome and needed guide for the quality improvement process in professional service firms.

 —Richard Millet, Executive VP and Chief Practice Officer
  Woodward-Clyde

This book develops a quality model for professional service firms in the vein of the Malcolm Baldrige National Quality Award and ISO 9000. I recommend it for quality professionals and senior managers who are looking for new ideas to revitalize a stagnant quality improvement process.

 —Robert S. Irwin, P.E., Vice President, Quality
  Sverdrup Facilities, Inc.

This book provides a complete guide, from definitions to an overview for executive management. The explanations for the tools required for successful implementation are clear and practical, and can be put into immediate use.

 —Richard L. Meagher, President
  Harza Engineering Company

The message that professional practices should apply techniques of TQM/CI to create a culture of continuous improvement is one which I wholly support. It provides a ready source of ideas as a reference book to anyone seeking to improve their performance.

 —Sir Jack Zunz, F. Eng., HonFRIBA

The excellent organization and "down-to-earth" writing style provides crispness and clarity, and the strong focus on metrics for management processes, coupled with an excellent array of examples, provides a real contribution to achieving TQM. Effective strategic planning, problem solving, and training are well defined, with an excellent perspective on partnering. This book is a valuable contribution to improving quality in the American services and A/EC industry.

> —John Jackson, Vice Chairman
> Management Analysis Company

TQM concepts have now been embodied. The author's style provides the reader with a more sensitive understanding of the value of the quality process. The text provides a step-by-step guideline which leads to realistic quality goals.

> —Francis J. Geran, P.E., Senior Vice President
> URS Consultants, Inc.

Practical Continuous Improvement for Professional Services

Also available from ASQC Quality Press

Quality Handbook for the Architectural, Engineering, and Construction Community
Roger D. Hart

Total Engineering Quality Management
Ronald J. Cottman

Quality Management for the Constructed Project
ASQC Construction Technical Committee

Construction Quality Program Handbook
Eliot S. Mickelson

Process Reengineering
Lon Roberts

Mapping Work Processes
Dianne Galloway

To request a complimentary catalog of publications, call 800-248-1946.

Practical Continuous Improvement for Professional Services

CLIVE SHEARER

ASQC Quality Press
Milwaukee, Wisconsin

658
.562
.S53
1994

AEC 8704

Practical Continuous Improvement for Professional Services
Clive Shearer

Library of Congress Cataloging-in-Publication Data

Shearer, Clive, 1944–
    Practical continuous improvement for professional services / Clive
Shearer.
        p.   cm.
    Includes bibliographical references and index.
    ISBN 0-87389-281-X (acid-free paper)
    1. Total quality management.   2. Quality control.
    3. Communication in management.   I. Title.
    HD62.15.S53   1994
    658.5'62 — dc20   94-28615
                                                                 CIP

© 1994 by ASQC

10 9 8 7 6 5 4 3 2 1

ISBN 0-87389-281-X

Acquisitions Editor: Susan Westergard
Project Editor: Kelley Cardinal
Production Editor: Annette Wall
Marketing Administrator: Mark Olson
Set in Palatino by Linda J. Shepherd.
Cover design by Paul Tobias.
Printed and bound by BookCrafters, Inc.

ASQC Mission: To facilitate continuous improvement and increase customer satisfaction by identifying, communicating, and promoting the use of quality principles, concepts, and technologies; and thereby be recognized throughout the world as the leading authority on, and champion for, quality.

For a free copy of the ASQC Quality Press Publications Catalog, including ASQC membership information, call 800-248-1946.

Printed in the United States of America

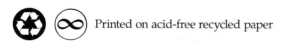 Printed on acid-free recycled paper

 ASQC
Quality Press
611 East Wisconsin Avenue
Milwaukee, Wisconsin 53202

Contents

Part IV Professional Service Applications

Appendices

Figures

Preface

Why This Book Is Different

Volumes have already been written about total quality management (TQM) and total quality service. So much so, that many managers have had enough of the fad and are waiting hungrily for the next flavor of the month, sprinkled liberally with new jargon to match the anticipated taste. This is a reflection of the human condition: People are always waiting for the ultimate dessert.

Well, in a way, this book is it! The term *TQM* will be used, but in a context that may not be expected, because this book focuses on a new model that delivers practical continuous improvement, and has little to do with the intangible concept of quality. Continuous improvement is the ultimate dessert, helping organizations to stay slim, fit, and healthy, no matter what the next fad happens to be. This is because continuous improvement encompasses everything, accepting the healthy and nutritious ideas and spitting out dangerous, time-consuming, and low-productivity ideas. Continuous improvement is timeless!

So the time for theory is over. If readers know the sayings of the masters, well and good. Deming's 14 points will not be explored, nor will Juran's three aspects of quality. Their ideas are invaluable, but this book translates ideas into action. This author divides TQM ideas into hard and soft aspects, and a great number of quality books focus on the soft side. Yet the core, the hard side shown in Figure P.1, is the solid bedrock of continuous improvement. The soft aspects are no less vital,

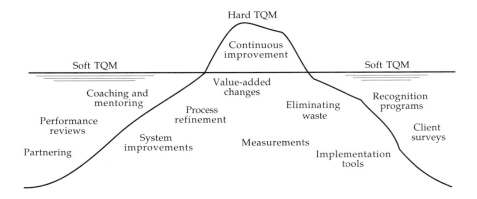

Figure P.1. Hard and soft TQM.

but they require the bedrock to realize their full potential. This is the future of TQM, and the Shearer model—the backbone of this book—describes how to accomplish this potential in the service world.

How to Get the Most Out of the Book

Part I. The book starts with an overview of TQM in the professional service context. For those experienced with TQM, a word of caution: Proceed with an open mind. Some commonly held truths have been adapted to the professional service world.

Part II. The Shearer model is introduced, and provides a blow-by-blow, nuts-and-bolts account of how to establish continuous improvement, using the ideas expressed in Part I. Part II of the book will be most valuable to those establishing TQM, as well as to team facilitators. They may use it as a step-by-step, meeting-to-meeting guide through the many traps and pitfalls that await the unwary.

Part III. Here readers will find the tools that are most practical and useful. These tools, used with discretion and purpose, will help to unlock the power of the continuous improvement process. Some of the tools are well known, some have been adapted for the professional service environment, and some were created by this author. Because communication in professional services is so vital, clarification and decision-making tools are included in the toolbox. Descriptions have been kept as simple and user-friendly as possible.

CEOs, presidents, principals, and team facilitators should be familiar with the tools at the start of TQM. Team members usually learn the tools on an as-needed basis, so this part of the book may be used by the team facilitator as a text to teach the tools of the trade.

Part IV. Here again, the Shearer model outlines how all encompassing and valuable TQM can be to professional service firms. This part is written for CEOs, presidents, and principals, but all stakeholders may draw inspiration from the seven aspects of global continuous improvement.

Summary

The Shearer model gives a readily understandable and practical, no-holds-barred approach to implementing professional service continuous improvement. Readers are urged to use the book, much like the Yellow Pages, and this author would be delighted if each copy acquires a dog-eared look in the process. Use it; use it well; and keep focused on getting better!

Professional Service Truths and Realities

This book breaks open some of the misconceptions about TQM. Not every truth has a practical use, and many change in meaning and depth when exposed to the light of reality. The following list of truths and realities gives readers a foretaste of the path this book will tread.

TQM Truths	TQM/CI Realities
1. TQM can't be applied to professional services.	1. TQM can easily be adapted to the professional service environment.
2. Clients care about quality.	2. Clients care about getting what they want.

TQM Truths	TQM/CI Realities
3. TQM only works when the leadership cares about it.	3. TQM only works when the staff believes that the leadership cares about it.
4. Success depends on the leadership supporting quality teams.	4. Success depends on the leadership supporting an effective TQM structure.
5. Empowered teams are the key that unlocks TQM.	5. Internal and external partnerships are the keys that unlock TQM.
6. TQM must focus on quality.	6. TQM must focus on continuously improving all aspects of a professional practice.
7. Quality is free.	7. Once established, continuous improvement gives back more than it takes.

PART I

A New Perspective on TQM

CHAPTER 1

Why Professional Services Are Different

Overview

Readers are asked to approach this chapter with an open mind as commonly accepted theories are translated into a usable professional service format. For those who already have knowledge of TQM, or have begun to practice it, or are less than fulfilled with their TQM program, this chapter will fill in many gaps that traditional TQM does not seem to satisfy. *The term TQM/CI has been created to show the integration of TQM with continuous improvement.* With a focus on continuous improvement, the tough, determined little TQM caterpillar moving along on 1000 legs can become a beautiful butterfly and take off.

The Five TQM/CI Payoffs

Continuous improvement is not new. It has been going on since the birth of civilization, as humanity has progressed from the plough and wheel to satellites and the moon. Evolution, as investigated and researched by Charles Darwin, is a process of continuous improvement on a global scale. Management practice is finally catching up!

It is important to make the clear distinction between a company that has a quality system, from a company that practices TQM/CI. *Total quality management* or *total quality control* can be misleading phrases outside the manufacturing world. In professional services, the focus on the word *quality* has led to misunderstandings. Many firms reject traditional TQM by thinking: "We are a quality firm anyway, so we don't need it;" or, "We have a good quality assurance manual, managed by a QA/QC specialist, so we don't need it;" or, "Our staff is made up of quality people, so we already have total quality management;" or, "We've had a quality program for years, this is just the same thing with jargon."

All are hung up on the word *quality*. Figure 1.1 sums up the five payoffs of TQM/CI.

Payoff 1: Quality Results

Most organizations already provide quality results for external clients. But TQM/CI stretches across the board to encompass all internal, as well as all external clients.

Payoff 2: Greater Productivity

Quality results are not really the prime issue. The prime issue is the difficulty firms face in getting those quality results. Most professional service firms already have quality, but go through battle zones, crises, and high stress to arrive at that quality. It is far better to achieve breakthroughs in productivity by improving the way that the work is done, by improving the way people communicate, and by facilitating operational consistency. Not only will productivity increase, but quality results will also flow much more easily when stress, frustration, and bottlenecks have been eliminated.

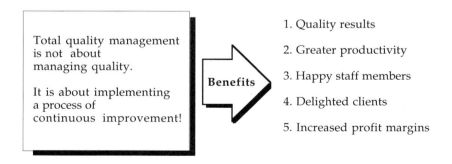

Figure 1.1. The five payoffs of TQM/CI.

Payoff 3: Happy Staff Members

Unhappy people just don't do good work. They won't go the extra mile unless pushed; they won't be conscientious; and they won't care about the success or failure of their organization. Yet happy people may still not do good work if they are

- Incompetent
- Poorly trained
- Inadequately coached on the job
- Hampered by an inefficient system
- Frustrated by frequent miscommunications
- Ignored when suggesting improvements

Naturally, if these conditions persist, even happy people may become unhappy people with the consequences noted. And very unhappy people can

- Disrupt others in their work
- Become bottlenecks
- Be catalysts in morale disintegration
- Project a negative image to clients
- Sabotage the organization

When there are lots of unhappy people in an organization, call 911. Sadly, these emergency calls are usually not made—the leadership sails on—unaware that its ship is slowly sinking. Case histories where loss of market share, coupled with the defection of competent personnel have led to fire sales, takeovers, and closures are not that uncommon. Many of these occurrences stem from unhappy people working in a tense, pressured environment.

Competent staff members usually remain as happy as the day they came on board when they are

- Coached by their managers
- Involved in professional development programs
- Delighted by system improvements
- Pleased by smooth communication channels
- Listened to by peers and managers

Workers cannot be both loyal and unhappy at work for very long. Loyalty must be projected from both sides. Given the right environment, mutual loyalty will flourish.

While it is true that many people have personal problems unrelated to their work, perhaps they can find some alleviation from their personal stress by being in a supportive, cheerful, and productive professional work environment. In fact, these types of environments can actually help with their personal healing by fostering feelings of self-worth, partnership, and loyalty.

Accordingly, happy staff members, working in positive environments, tend to be more productive, and tend to care more about quality inputs and outputs. By being involved in improvement structuring, they are empowered to add value to their work and to their lives. They strive for success. The success of their organization, their leaders, their peers, their staff, and themselves thrives in a continuously improving environment.

Payoff 4: Delighted Clients

Clients come first on most managers' lists, except for those unfortunate managers who see themselves as number one. If clients come first, why are they placed at number four on this list of continuous improvement payoffs? Clients can be any of the following:

- Delighted
- Happy
- Satisfied
- Dissatisfied
- Unhappy
- Angry

Most organizations get along with the majority of their clients being satisfied, a few unhappy, and the occasional angry client. With the marketplace heating up, and competition becoming more fierce, this form of complacency is no longer good enough—especially when competitors are starting to have a few delighted clients, many happy clients, and none unhappy. And competitors are working hard to move most of their clientele into the delighted range.

How is this done? By continuously improving operations to achieve consistent, easily attainable quality, with staff members who are happy in their work because they believe that their organization is the best. So this item is number four on the list, because clients can't be consistently delighted without the groundwork previously described.

The interaction between staff members is another aspect of delighted clients. Each team member is an internal client to be served with the same dedication and attitude as paying, external clients. This is discussed in more detail later in this chapter.

Payoff 5: Increased Profit Margins

"Profit is the king." "Only the bottom line counts." Statements like these have been, and continue to be, the basis of the capitalist world. Yet there is a possibility to break away from a profit-at-all-costs attitude and look at a broader perspective. Amazingly, continuous improvement embraces the seemingly incompatible goals of greater quality and greater profit.

How can this be done? Most firms already produce quality results. As mentioned, the problem is the effort they put in to achieve those results. Continuous improvement will cut the cost involved in rework, revisions, overtime, and overhead, while concomitantly enhancing overall quality. When systems are being improved and clients are trusting and loyal, the work volume will allow a company to refine client lists, thus eliminating difficult clients and slow payers. Increased profit margins are the final payoff of continuous improvement.

Traditional Management Compared to TQM/CI

Figures 1.2–1.6 facilitate a brief comparison of management styles. While by no means exhaustive, these examples are presented simply to whet the appetite for TQM/CI and to help illuminate why it is so very different from business as usual.

Setting Goals

Figure 1.2 shows a side-by-side comparison of traditional management with TQM/CI. Traditional management often sets numerical goals to motivate staff to accomplish excellence and achieve results. Deming wisely said that one can only get what the system will deliver, and a numerical goal, by itself, won't guarantee success.

In most manufacturing scenarios the product is designed on the basis of consumer feedback and market research. Only after production do the individual customers decide, in the store or via a catalog, if they want to buy the product. In the professional service scenario, the client orders a custom service, and the client usually has a very clear and detailed set of goals and specifications that must be met. So goals in the professional service world are simply unavoidable.

Accepting the reality of client-established goals still leaves a host of operational, marketing, human resource, and project management systems that can be continuously improved. Results-oriented goals often place an artificial lid on achievement.

For example, in the first case, a 15-gallon gasoline tank cannot hold 20 gallons. If existing systems can't contain the desired goals, a lot of wasted energy and often number manipulation result.

In the second case, a 20-gallon gasoline tank can hold a lot more than 15 gallons. If management says that the goal is 15 gallons, most people will stop filling at 15 gallons with no questions asked, because they achieved their goal. Meanwhile a lot of potential travel distance goes to waste. The exception is the milestoned numerical goal. This compares the distance to travel with the energy required and is tracked at gas station after gas station. This is the route to continuous improvement and better results.

Traditional management	TQM/CI
Focus on goals ◆ To motivate: productivity goals ◆ To get results: client goals	Focus on goals ◆ To accomplish potential ◆ To improve
Work process tracked to meet goals. Goals are the limits.	Work process is milestoned to facilitate continuous improvement.
Waste is "the cost of doing business."	Waste is measured and reduced.

Figure 1.2. Setting goals.

In any case, it is not the goal that is important, it is the planning for the goal, the preparation for the journey, the start of the journey, the vehicle that is selected for the journey, and the learning that takes place during the journey. When done with an open mind, systematically and thoroughly, each future journey becomes increasingly easy.

The Role of the Players

Figure 1.3 examines the role of the players. It compares the traditional style of management, where the staff is blamed for quality deficiencies, to a TQM/CI company, where the management is recognized as being responsible for quality improvement.

The concept of partnering, explored in Part IV and threaded throughout this book, is a philosophical return to the way things were when informal and verbal agreements were the norm. Just as one can partner with a client, a contractor, a supplier, a subconsultant, and even a public agency, one can partner with staff. Consensus on roles and responsibilities is essential in this approach, and sets the ground for continuous improvement. This leaves intact the individualism that is especially important in professional service firms. So the ideal concept is the recognition of the individualism of the staff, while harnessing its talents into a team partnership.

Western culture tends to reward individual performance. Even on sports teams there has to be a most valuable player. The bookstores are full of books about leadership, with far fewer volumes on teamwork. It is tougher to get team consensus than to act as a leader.

Traditional management	TQM/CI
People perform better when they have goals.	People do best as individuals in partnership.
Failure leads to blame.	Failure leads to learning.
Strive to avoid blame.	Strive to improve the process.

Figure 1.3. The role of the players.

Fortunately, people in professional service organizations tend to be quite good team players as their work is structured around the team concept. That is why they are so amenable to TQM/CI, without requiring weeks of training.

Finally, when blame is avoided, losing a game can motivate a team to great heights. Learning from failure is an opportunity to solidify a team.

Process Comparison

Figure 1.4 compares traditional management to TQM/CI processes. There is nothing wrong with meeting a budget or schedule, or with fulfilling promises. There is no need to eliminate action lists and reports. But the way that they are traditionally used can do with a large dose of improvement.

These tools, like all the tools mentioned in this book, are there to facilitate a process and are not ends in themselves. For example, forms may be

- Evaluated to see if they add value to the process

- Evaluated to see if simplification is possible

- Combined with other forms, if this makes sense

Many forms can be adapted to serve as data collectors to assist in continuous improvement.

Crisis management can be a very damaging way to run a business. Take for an extreme example a project manager who is under crisis

Traditional management	TQM/CI
Use action lists, forms and reports to ◆ Meet a budget ◆ Meet a schedule ◆ Meet a quota or goal ◆ Check off items	Use check lists, milestones and reports to ◆ Verify conformance ◆ Beat expectations ◆ Track improvement
Meet budgets, schedules and goals with crisis management.	Improve processes and systems to better serve clients.

Figure 1.4. Process comparison.

pressure to meet the budget and schedule. Without a care for subconsultants or contractors, calculations could be hurried and not checked, code provisions ignored, uncustomized standard details and boilerplate specifications used, coordination with other disciplines bypassed, and documentation ignored. The budget and schedule goals would be met, but at what cost? Permits may not be granted, subconsultants would be frustrated, the contractor would scream, and the owner would sue. "Well I met my goals didn't I?" would be the project manager's defense.

TQM/CI Traps

In moving toward TQM, there may be some doubts and perhaps some difficulties. This book takes an honest look at what can go wrong with TQM/CI. Figure 1.5 gives a sample of pitfalls that can occur within all types of organizational cultures.

1. Covering a symptom with a bandage may not cure it. Yet so many quality teams form to examine symptoms and solve them. Meanwhile, the drama continues as the chronic root causes remain undetected. This is a very common pitfall for TQM do-it-yourselfers and those poorly trained in the process. It is like trying to assemble a jet fighter without plans, tools, or a parts list. The result might look more like a tractor with wings. TQM/CI requires a guide as well as a commitment.

Traditional management and TQM/CI issues

1. Solving symptoms, not chronic problems

2. Political issues and hidden agenda

3. Interdepartmental competition

4. Starting before structure is in place, roles clarified, and people trained

5. Expecting quick returns/profits

Figure 1.5. TQM/CI traps.

2. Politics can sound the death knell for any organization. Empire building and the fear of loss of control are difficult barriers to dislodge when deeply embedded in the personality of managers. This is a reality that must be faced, and some solutions are explored in Part II.

3. Staff members who are recently graduated or who are perceived to be slower or less skilled than others are often moved to other projects or departments so that they won't get in the way of meeting a client's goals. Project managers who remove these people may then meet their schedules and budgets, but the project managers who acquire these less-experienced staff members have to spend the time to coach and train, causing these managers to miss their schedules and budgets. This stems from the power struggle that project managers face to get the current, fastest, most reliable team members assigned to their jobs. This is compounded by the practice of setting fee estimates and budgets by assuming that only the most experienced will work on a project. When it is everyone for him or herself in the race for bonuses, promotions, and recognition, companywide guidelines for coaching, training, and sharing less-glamorous assignments are ignored.

4. Enthusiasm often leads to impatience. This occurs when firms see TQM/CI as just another program, the flavor of the month, or the life jacket that will rescue them. It isn't and it won't. Just as a physician knows that a blood transfusion must be infused drop-by-drop to prevent cardiac arrest, so is continuous improvement a step-by-step process of implementing positive incremental change that needs to be injected with care. This can lead to remarkable recoveries, dramatic gains, and breakthroughs.

5. Some firms, in the belief that TQM will help the bottom line, have pursued it solely to make more money. Payoff 5 explained that increased profits are a natural by-product of TQM/CI, but when money is the sole motive, staff will feel used and will cease to care.

Four Leadership Failings

There are four kinds of leaders who fail the TQM/CI challenge.

1. Those who pay lip service to TQM, agree to implement it because they think people want it, but have no real belief or understanding

of it. No matter how well TQM starts off, it can fail when these leaders become impatient, look at the implementation costs, and wonder "Why do we need more meetings?"

2. Those who are committed to TQM. They believe in it, understand it, and support it. But they never show up at a team meeting. One reason is that they can't be bothered; another is their decision to delegate TQM. A third reason is their honest belief that by not showing up they are empowering their staff. This can result in team members becoming discouraged and believing that they are operating without support. There is the ancient Zen story about the master who asks his student to demonstrate the sound of one hand clapping. These team members may begin to wonder if they are the one hand clapping.

3. Then there are leaders who get involved as quiet observers at all team meetings. When changes are suggested these leaders jump into the ring to cite numerous reasons why they will not work. These leaders were involved just to see what was going on, but were not committed to change.

4. There are also the leaders who see continuous improvement meetings as just another vehicle to dominate the proceedings. These leaders make suggestions and denigrate, or ignore the suggestions of others. Slowly but surely, the tender seed of management-staff partnering is destroyed before it ever had a chance to be nurtured and take root.

Professional Service Cultures

Various cultures around the world communicate and interact differently, and this is related to the structure of each society. This applies no less to organizational cultures. Figure 1.6 reveals why some organizations are not structured to easily implement continuous improvement.

Management by Decree

Leadership is attractive to so many because of the perception of power that rides in its train. There are four uses of power.

1. The power to get positive things done (positive-proactive).
2. The power to get negative things done (negative-proactive).

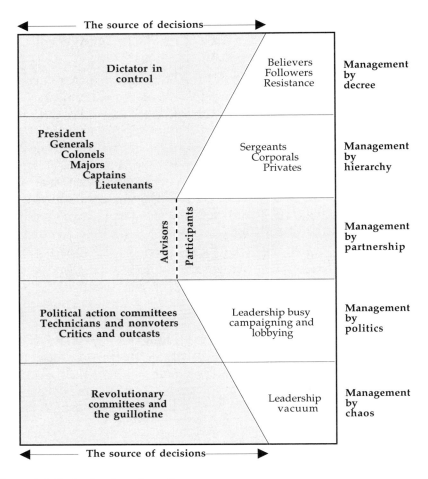

Figure 1.6. Professional service cultures.

3. The power to block and prevent positive things from happening (negative-reactive).

4. The power to block and prevent negative things from happening (positive-reactive).

Whether an action is seen as positive or negative depends on an individual's perceptions. There are vivid political and military examples in history that illustrate the power of those perceptions. A course of action may be seen as very positive by one leader, while being perceived as very negative by another.

In the management by decree culture, the believers are those staff members who sincerely trust that their leaders are doing positive things for the organization. The followers also endorse the leadership, but not so wholeheartedly. Perhaps the followers believe that, at best, their leaders are preventing negative events from occurring, or the followers may just be opportunists. The resistance is peopled by those who see the leadership as negative, or those who are disillusioned by their own lack of influence in the organization. They may gripe, complain, and snipe. In some cases, faced with a boss who has an impossible personality in a sweatshop environment, they may have good reasons for being resisters.

It is interesting to examine the pros and cons of management by decree. When the dictator is wise, benign, and possessed of a sound business mind, and when mutual trust and loyalty have been established, this culture can be a productive and low-stress environment. If however, the dictator is capricious, egotistical, and domineering, this can be a Soviet Gulag. High stress, burnout, and staff turnover will result. Even high salaries won't keep the top talents here for long.

Management by Hierarchy

This is the military model. Roles are clearly established, and the pecking order is very rigid. Professional advancement up the organizational ladder can be accomplished with the right stuff, but should one fail to possess state registration as a professional engineer or architect, or if one is not a highly degreed professional, the officers' ranks will be forever closed.

The pros in management by hierarchy are that everyone knows how things work and a sense of order and control prevails. The cons might include a dampening of innovation when systems are static and unchanging. Also, rapid advancement is rare and results in resentment by those who were overlooked when it does occur.

Management by Politics

This is a much looser structure than the military model. The leaders are frequently out and hard to access, much as political leaders are not always in Congress, being busy campaigning and lobbying. This often results in power struggles, intrigue, and cliques forming to control resources. These cliques are like political action committees. They form around project managers, department heads, and division or branch offices, and are empowered in proportion to the clique's influence. Technicians tend to become pawns in this power game, so that the cliques that are able to obtain the best and brightest on most of their projects have the most muscle and show the best results. The nonvoters are those who either choose not to play, are not asked to play, or have for various reasons dropped out of the cliques. In subtle situations, it may take a new employee several months to discern where the power lies. Blame is endemic, which is ironic because if most of the people are so bad, there must be something wrong with the leadership who hired them. There is no attempt to correct any deficiencies by coaching or training.

Office politics, however, is a way of life in almost every organization. If the game is played in moderation, and empire building is contained, the organization can be quite healthy.

Management by politics can foster strong team spirit within cliques, and the competitive drive can be positive. On the other hand, interteam rivalry can result in low organizational efficiency and lost market opportunities. When things are not going well due to internal or external conditions, the structure can move to chaos, with blame, mistrust and destructive rivalries forming.

Management by Chaos

An extreme form of politics results in a category all by itself. There are two cases of management by chaos.

1. The leaders are absent so often that they are virtually off the map. This can occur through lack of interest or after being stripped of power in a coup. This does not necessarily mean that the leaders are physically absent. Procrastination, lack of attention, focus on the unimportant, and lack of participation in meetings may indicate that there is a leadership vacuum.

2. Another example occurs when a current leader is about to retire. Withdrawing from leadership tasks over a period of months or years can, if not carefully managed, lead to a chaotic situation.

When either of these situations occur, the cliques transform into revolutionary committees to attempt to fill the leadership void. It is as if the corporate electrons have been heated up and the resulting activity and maneuvers can be quite frenetic. Empowerment may be total, and it is often undisciplined and counterproductive. This occurred during the French Revolution where the people took total power and the guillotine was feared until the next dictator, Napoleon, took charge. So management by chaos is not a steady state, and its inherent instability will inevitably result in change, for the better or for the worse.

The pros of management by chaos include the fact that positive change can emerge from chaos. So there is always the hope that things may get better. On the other hand, heads might roll!

Empowerment

Before describing management by partnership in Figure 1.6, it will be well to review empowerment. Empowerment implies a giving up, a transfer, or at least a sharing of power by leaders. Yet leaders are often wary of relinquishing any control.

In the manufacturing industries, designs are pre-established by a small group, very much like a professional service firm project team. Then it is up to the self-managed, empowered work teams to find the most effective way to get the product into the hands of the customer. In this scenario, employees may be trained in problem solving, given TQM tools, and even taught basic accounting procedures. They are able to eliminate waste in production and pare back activities that do not add to quality and the bottom line. With proper training, and with established experience and trust, this works exceptionally well.

In the professional service environment, which has no assembly line, totally empowered, self-managed work teams may result in chaos and TQM/CI cannot be implemented in chaotic situations.

Middle management and project management are involved in implementing policy and running projects. They are immersed in day-to-day control, and may perceive that they have a lot to lose by granting control to empowered people. When the top leadership wants continuous improvement, and the staff wants more participation, it is the middle and project managers who feel the squeeze, as shown in Figure 1.7.

Figure 1.7. Empowerment resistance.

Consider some of the different controls that these managers employ. They include quality control, financial control, project cost control, and budget control. These controls enable the organization to steer around and avoid collisions with poor quality, financial mismanagement, project overruns, and time crunches. Handing over total empowerment to the staff might be like giving the controls of all the aircraft above an airport to the passengers, and shutting down the flight control tower. The results could be painful.

The teams might have great pilots, but who is looking at the big picture? What direction should they fly? What ground speed should they maintain and at what altitude? Who gets which runway first? In the professional services environment, this translates into overlapping contacts with clients, unclear staffing assignments and conflicts over the allocation of resources.

On the other hand, empowerment within a structure, with a flight control tower and ground rules, can work exceptionally well. These structures, controls, and ground rules facilitate the culture of partnership. They are described in Part II.

Management by Partnership—Total Quality Management

In the TQM/CI environment shown in the center of Figure 1.6, the leadership remains intact and in charge, and the staff remains cohesive and involved. The boundary between the two becomes blurred and even evaporates when they are engaged in the partnership of process improvement. Sometimes the leaders are advisors and the staff are participants and implementers, and sometimes the staff are advisors and the leaders are participants and implementers. All this takes is trust—on both sides.

This cannot occur in dictatorial environments where decrees flow down from the top and are implemented with no questions asked. The staff has no say, there is no feedback, and continuous improvement cannot occur. It is interesting to note that a number of dictatorial organizations claim to have implemented TQM. Even benevolent dictators might say the right words and have statistical proof of improvements, but this all stems from the dictators proclaiming the changes, which are then rubber-stamped by the believers and followers who have played no role in proposing solutions.

Nor can TQM/CI be implemented in organizations that are managed by chaos. They must first regain stability. In reality, the stability that often follows chaotic conditions is management by decree.

Organizations that are managed by politics can introduce TQM/CI and make it work. The cliques need to pull together and achieve a sense of partnership by realizing that unity is strength. Team building, empowerment within a structure, the redemption of outcasts, and the introduction of a disciplined and cohesive management structure can make this type of organization a winner on the way to continuous improvement.

Organizations that are managed by hierarchy have the best chance to introduce TQM/CI and make it thrive. This is because they already possess discipline and structure—two of the keys to continuous improvement. What they require is the careful dismantling of their rigidity in order to establish a flexible partnership.

Readers will now see why the much-touted concept of cultural change is not practical, since it implies that dictatorial and chaotic firms can readily change their culture through training. Fortunately, most professional service firms are hierarchal or political, which means that they can more easily shift to embrace TQM/CI. This is a cultural modification, rather than a change. Figure 1.8 gives a brief look at some of the modifications needed to move into a TQM/CI culture.

Organizational Culture Quiz
The commitment to TQM/CI often facilitates the shift from management by hierarchy or management by politics to management by partnership. This shift is more a gradual softening than an abrupt change.

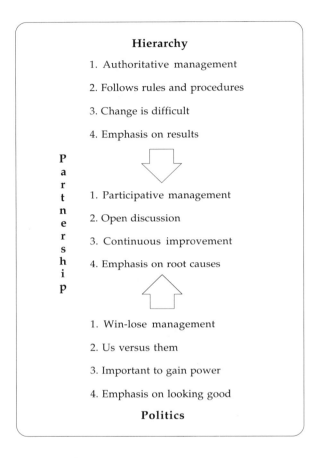

Figure 1.8. Culture modification.

The following test will help readers to gauge their corporate culture.

1. Are key decisions made only by management at the very top?
2. Are almost all corporate decisions kept confidential?
3. Do suggestions and recommendations from the staff and from first-line managers enter a black hole, never to be seen again?

Two yes answers indicate a probable management by decree culture.

4. Must all decisions made at a lower level be cleared by the manager at the next level?

5. Must memos be reviewed by senior management before being circulated, and are many staff members copied for information only?

6. Are there multiple titles such as technician, lead technician, supervisory technician, project manager, senior project manager, associate, senior associate, assistant vice president, vice president, and senior vice president?

Two yes answers indicate a probable management by hierarchy culture.

7. Are common sense solutions withheld because it is known that management won't buy it?

8. Do rivalries, competition for offices and resources, and internal connections exist?

9. Are there cover-ups, accusations, and finger-pointing?

Two yes answers indicate a probable management by politics culture.

10. Are top managers out of the office most of the time, rarely seen or heard from by anyone?

11. Is the office divided into several rival camps, engaged in trench warfare while senior management remains aloof?

12. Aside from the core of old-timers, who are bullet proof, does it seem like most of the staff changes over every few months?

Two yes answers indicate a probable management by chaos culture.

13. Does management and staff regularly sit down, in partnership, to discuss system and process improvements, problems, and solutions?

14. Do all levels of management keep their staff informed, getting regular feedback and sharing decisions?

15. Are staff members unafraid to share improvement suggestions, and thanked in public for their contribution?

Two yes answers indicate a probable management by partnership culture.

Professional Service Roles

Leadership Styles

This vast topic could be the subject of a lifetime study. By focusing on continuous improvement, the subject becomes much more manageable. There are leaders who

- Get things done by themselves
- Get things done with others
- Get things done by delegation
- Empower others to get things done
- Procrastinate so nothing gets done
- Refuse to delegate so they fast-track to burnout
- Are so controlling that everyone feels pressure
- Are visionary but impractical
- Are visionary and translate vision into practical action

This is just a sample of the leadership menu. Imaginative readers can cook up many more varieties.

Leadership Ingredients

What does a TQM/CI leader look like? The Shearer TQM/CI model, introduced in Part II, presupposes that the executive leadership will have certain qualities. The following list constitutes this author's top 10 leadership ingredients.

1. Self-confident—is aware of personal strengths and weaknesses
2. Open—is flexible and visionary
3. Honest—has ethical principles and is willing to admit to mistakes
4. Trusting—values and believes in people
5. Firm—will defend a valid decision when necessary
6. Reliable—is consistent
7. Stable—has no mood swings and makes no snap judgments
8. Loyal—stands by the staff
9. Sensitive—empathizes with the moods and feelings of others

10. Team player—believes that strength derives from the binding together of disparate talents into a unified force; coaches the team so that all players improve

This is a very demanding list and very few leaders are worthy of top marks in every category. Yet it is important that firms with TQM/CI have a leadership with at least a sprinkling of all of these ingredients. The most practical way to achieve this is to look at leadership as a team. When clients want to put a project together, their requirements very often demand diverse talents. While there are firms that can do it all in-house, they still rely on the abilities of staff members, in different departments, to get the job done.

So while accepting the need to team on projects, why not team on leadership? Put a group of committed leaders together, each being at least a team player, and their combined talents usually meet most of the requirements for TQM/CI.

Values, Emotion, Self-Esteem, and Partnerships

Many leaders endorse the concept of leading by values rather than by feelings. They perceive that feelings are too emotional, and emotional decision making just leads to trouble. Yet expressing feelings can be powerful. Who wants to work for a robot? That is why sensitivity is on the leadership list.

Notice that high self-esteem was not included. Too often this translates into egoism, which is different from self-confidence. The leader with high self-esteem may lack the openness and flexibility required to give new ideas an objective judgment. Working with people and standing behind them is vital in building up true team partnerships.

Must TQM Always Start at the 'Top?'

One of the most commonly heard cliches linking leadership and TQM is that "it must start at the top," and that without the people at the top leading the way, it cannot take root. In professional service organizations, where one encounters many brilliant people, it is not that simple. There may be a seismologist in the kitchen getting herself a cup of coffee, while talking to a gas desulphurization specialist. At the same time a small group may be gathering in the hallway to discuss the weekend. The group consists of a computer modeling software designer, a geophysicist, and a risk analyst. All may be PhDs. Meanwhile a senior architect may be discussing a land use issue with an attorney, an economist, and a hazardous waste management specialist. How much weight will these talented people put in a leader's pronouncements that the firm will now endorse TQM/CI? If they don't want to play the game, there may be no action after the kickoff.

On the other hand, what if these individuals decide that their destiny lies down the TQM/CI path? Can they get it going and sustain the effort without the endorsement and wholehearted backing of the top leadership? No, this too is destined to fail; however, given the realities of the typical professional service firm, each of the following scenarios can result in the successful launch and sustained flight of TQM/CI.

Scenario 1. Key managers hear about TQM/CI, become interested, and are convinced that it is the right approach for the future of a department. The leadership acquiesces and agrees to a trial. The Shearer model, with its structured approach, is used to provide the leadership with positive proof of the validity of the process. The leadership becomes motivated to facilitate the training and education for other departments within the firm.

Scenario 2. A leader becomes interested in TQM/CI, but knows that other leaders are not convinced that it is the right approach for their firm. They agree, however, to facilitate training. The training sparks with one or more of the key managers who agree to implement TQM/CI. They form teams who, through measurement, provide proof of the validity of the process and the bottom line results. The data convince other leaders, and it is implemented throughout the firm.

Scenario 3. A project manager or marketing manager, using the concepts and the tools as much as possible within the context of the work environment, may reveal the reasons for his or her success. This individual becomes a change agent by getting the attention of key managers and of the leadership.

These three scenarios show that initiation is not so cut and dried in the professional service world. Here, the success of TQM/CI is dependent on the interplay of all the players, but the game can start at almost any level, since in professional services, anyone who projects positive ethics and influences is, de facto, a leader.

Leaders Who Fear Change

Some leaders fear TQM without realizing how they can gain from continuous improvement. Part of the fear is the belief that loss of control will result in a drop in standards, thus leading to chaos. This mind-set occurs most markedly in the management by decree culture, where the managers tell the workers what to do, how to do it, and when to have it ready. This mind-set also occurs in the management by hierarchy culture, where workers are told what to do, and when to have it ready, but not necessarily how to do it. This enables managers to place total blame on their workers when things go wrong, so creative ways to improve the system never emerge. "We have always done it this way" is the motto, and this results in stagnation. Stagnation often appears to be stable, as the decay is slow and not evident day-to-day. This mind-set can be modified by determined leadership in the hierarchal culture. This has been proved by gains made by several branches of the U.S. government that have embraced TQM.

Empire Building

Empire building in the political culture becomes a problem when leaders are primarily engaged in turf management. TQM/CI cannot easily gain a toehold in such an environment, because the three *p*'s of protectionism, paranoia, and parochialism build an impenetrable barrier to open change. There have been cases, however, where TQM was introduced into these environments, albeit with a hidden agenda. The TQM champions thought that they would use TQM to increase their power base. Surprisingly, these managers' machinations can be subdued and overcome—not by force, but by themselves. Political power bases can be sublimated into a positive competitive drive, so that the empire is enlarged to embrace the entire organization.

Traditional Bottlenecks

The pressure to reduce nonbillable time stems from the old worker-bee days where the boss sat in a glass-walled office at the back of a long open room filled with workers. If everybody was not busy for eight or more hours every day something was very wrong. Sadly, some bosses still abide by these dictums and wonder why everybody isn't billing out at 100 percent. Yet in today's highly competitive markets one may not be able to bill for coordination meetings, team member reassignments, marketing, proposal writing, invoicing and collections activities, responding to client requests for information, extended phone calls, and paperwork processing. When the minutia that infests every office is not systematized, or when effective delegation is not practiced, bottlenecks result. These clogged-up business arteries can be dangerous to the firm's profit margin and corporate well-being. Key decisions are delayed, grand opportunities are missed, quality control becomes a cursory inspection, mistakes multiply, and morale drops. In other words, there is no harmonious interaction between people, systems, or processes.

The Orchestral Model

Figure 1.9 illustrates the way that this can be overcome. The traditional hierarchy has a small group of leaders at the top and layers of staff below. In this model the staff brings problems to the attention of management, and management devises solutions for staff implementation. Revisionists counter that one must turn the model on its head, with the staff noticing problems both at its own and at management levels, and then finding solutions for management to implement. This is fine in theory, but it is impractical.

The most practical model for professional service leadership is this author's orchestral model. Here the traditional triangle is laid on its side. What does the leader of an orchestra do? A conductor is involved in

- Policy making
- Establishing the concert schedule
- Coaching
- Resolving day-to-day issues
- Setting the tempo during performances

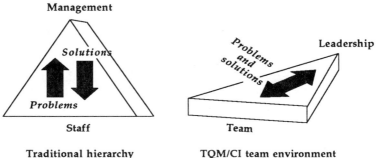

Traditional hierarchy   TQM/CI team environment

Each manager must learn to become an orchestra conductor
and give up being a soloist.

Figure 1.9. The orchestral model.

Conductors are musicians who, while in the limelight during a perfor-mance, make no sound. They manage and facilitate the orchestra, and it is the music that the orchestra plays that the audience wants to hear.

Project managers are technical specialists who, while in the limelight during a project, may perform no technical work. They manage and facilitate the team whom the client has engaged to perform a project. In the same way, principals and senior managers conduct the firm's daily activities, orchestrating sound results through the players.

The parallels between the orchestra and the project team, and the conductor and the team leadership are quite remarkable. The players in the different sections of the orchestra are all in touch, they are all on the same page, and they all play the same piece, in harmony, under the direction of the conductor. The conductor guides the tempo, the entrances and exits of the various instruments, and provides a rhythm based on the score—the scope of work. The leader and the players are a team and together they make music.

Professional Service Relationships

The Multi-Dimensional Network

The ideal professional service environment is one where information easily flows up, down, sideways, and transversely. In fact, this multi-dimensional flow is essential to make information readily available to all team members, including subconsultants, owners, regulatory agencies, and contractors. In the traditional organizational structure, shown at the top of Figure 1.10, information tends to flow vertically. This is akin to the customer-supplier chain, shown at the right. Both of these models are too simplistic to depict the real professional service world.

The illustration at the bottom of Figure 1.10 depicts information flow in all directions, to all interested parties. These are the three dimensions. The fourth dimension is time. Past decisions and historical data and records need to be accessible, and future decisions, visions, and directions need to be shared. The information flow will vary from assignment to assignment, but the information channels must be designed to facilitate efficient communication. This is further illustrated

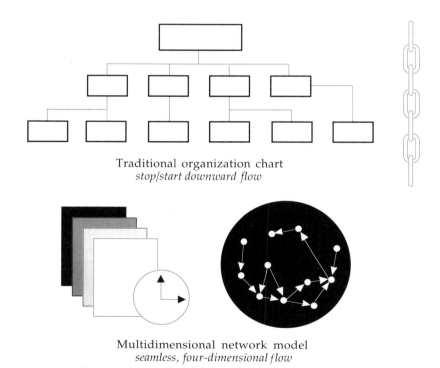

Traditional organization chart
stop/start downward flow

Multidimensional network model
seamless, four-dimensional flow

Figure 1.10. Professional service relationships.

by the circle at the right showing a multidimensional network of inputs received from numerous sources, often simultaneously, and outputs for coordination, review, and feedback all interlinked within a system. This is the real world of professional services. This model leads to the following discussion of information flow.

Clients and Service Providers

Traditional TQM holds that everyone in an organization is an internal customer for some transactions, and a supplier for other transactions. For professional services an adjustment in terminology is required, and the concept must be transplanted into a multidimensional network.

First, the issue of terminology. The term *customer* is not used in most professional services. Here customers are called *clients*. The word *supplier* denotes a vendor. So a more appropriate term to use is *service provider*, shortened to *provider*. In this way the customer-supplier becomes a client-provider relationship. Second, each team member can be an internal client to several providers, just as each team member can be a provider to several clients.

What would happen if everyone in an organization had their own definition of quality? Most people would unhesitatingly answer, "chaos." This is not true, however, in the professional service environment. In fact, it is essential that each person does have his or her own definition of quality. But each definition must be clearly expressed and fit within the corporate quality vision. This vision, endorsed by the executive leadership, becomes the backbone of the quality assurance manual that may itself be continuously improved. This can be accomplished with a very powerful tool, this author's input-process-output (IPO) audit, described in Part III. Examples of client-provider interactions in the A/EC world include the following:

- A computer technician who is a project engineer's client. The project engineer (provider) must provide input to this technician (client) to facilitate efficient production.

- A project architect who is a computer technician's client. The technician (provider) must provide output to the project architect (client) to facilitate the effective use of the documents.

- An accountant who is a project manager's client. The project manager (provider) must provide input to the accountant (client) to facilitate the most efficient way to invoice and collect fees.

- A public agency who is a project manager's client. The project manager (provider) must provide output to the agency (client) to facilitate the smoothest possible permitting process.

- A secretary who is a scientist's client. The scientist (provider) must provide information to the secretary (client) to facilitate the effective production of letters, reports, and documents.

- A subcontractor who is a general contractor's client. The general contractor (provider) must provide input to the subcontractor (client) to facilitate the most efficient way to complete assignments.

- An economist who is a public utility district's client. The utility district (provider) must provide input to the economist (client) to facilitate a realistic rate study.

In summary, garbage in, garbage out, and conversely, quality in and quality out.

The Interaction Between Systems and People

Traditional TQM Perspective

Traditional TQM expresses the viewpoint that quality is far more dependent on systems than on people. A commonly accepted model is the 85-15 breakout, meaning that 85 percent of quality depends on the systems established by management, and only 15 percent of quality depends on the people working within the system. This is not appropriate for professional service firms. The manufacturing sector, from which the ideas of total quality control and the various permutations of TQM originated, produce tangible products. The professional service sector produces intangible ideas. This makes it far more dependent on people to solve client's needs, especially as most of those needs vary from assignment to assignment. This added dimension of custom solutions within a complex web of team interactions means that the people employed by professional service firms are much more responsible for ultimate outcomes than even those in the service sector.

For example, a project manager can review regulations, examine constraints, consider the creative interpretation of technical issues, and prepare a technical assessment. This is the science part of the job. The art part includes listening to clients, communicating ideas, being empathic, delegating without giving the impression of dumping, and coordinating with internal and external peers.

The Professional Service Paradigm

Figure 1.11 shows a more realistic 60-40 breakout. The importance of the system remains critical, but the influence of the people in the system is vital too. Project managers have, and should have, discretion about how they are going to run their projects. But they must not have carte blanche to do anything they want. Their freedom to manage must be contained within the boundaries of an effective system.

For example in the A/EC world, each building project is unique, or a one-off. Even designs developed from prototypes will be constructed upon different terrain, to different building codes, and in conformance with regional constructability variations. So there are no jigs, no tooling, and no assembly lines, and the project managers, engineers, and architects see themselves as problem solvers. With a continuous improvement mind-set they can also learn to become highly skilled problem preventers—an important distinction.

Another reason for the 60-40 split is the greater need for leadership throughout the duration of professional service assignments. In the manufacturing world, the design of a product is conceived, developed, tested, and refined before a full production launch. Once launched, production can go on for decades. In the professional service A/EC world, the design is conceived, developed, and refined through the

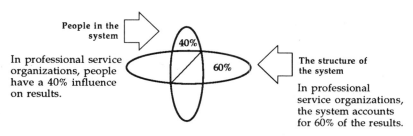

People in the system

In professional service organizations, people have a 40% influence on results.

40%

60%

The structure of the system

In professional service organizations, the system accounts for 60% of the results.

Figure 1.11. TQM/CI systems and people.

duration of the project, and when it is launched, it is time for the next assignment. Code revisions, changed conditions, client changes, regulatory agency changes, and subconsultant and contractor input all may result in normal project-in-progress updating. Indeed, this has led some to express the opinion that TQM can't be applied to professional services. These critics are right! Without adjusting the original manufacturing TQM concept, it doesn't apply very well. That is why the adaptations that this book describes are necessary. So all of these continual changes require people to adapt and interact within the complex web of team relationships involved in the development of each project.

- Why not an 80-20 split? An 80 percent dependency on systems would still imply too much reliance on the system to solve problems. Creative problem solving and innovation may be stifled if the system is too rigid.

- Why not a 50-50 split? This implies too much reliance on people and not enough on structure. Systems are often more amenable to continuous improvement than people.

- Why not a 20-80 split? An 80 percent dependency on people is common in most professional service firms. Having few effective system and process guidelines results in too much reliance on the individuality of people. Some project managers are excellent, some good, and some poor. This leads to inconsistent and inefficient results. Without a consistent, systematic, and effective framework, work is done by the seat-of-the-pants method with everyone interacting and scrambling haphazardly to get the job done and to meet deadlines. The net result is unpredictability in client satisfaction and profitability.

More emphasis on people opens up the possibility that it will be easy to blame people for inefficiencies. A distinction must be made between total power and partial power within a structure, and a 40 percent dependency on people for quality is highly efficient.

Small Firm Gains

The majority of professional service firms are small. There are four convincing reasons for small firms to get and stay involved with TQM/CI.

1. To have a marketing edge on other small firms
2. To remain on the teams of larger, prime consultants who utilize TQM
3. To retain staff members who are interested in improving their work environment through TQM/CI
4. To become more profitable, through greater efficiency, in a tough, low-fee marketplace

Small firms can achieve huge gains for a moderate investment. In addition, small firms will find that they can take bigger bites out of issues and solve their problems more quickly than other firms. This is because they start off with simpler systems, easier communication channels, and frequently with less politics than larger entities.

Commitments

Commitment to Clients

Once enthusiasm for TQM/CI has been generated, it is important to make a commitment—a commitment to the process, a commitment to external clients, and a commitment to internal clients. This will foster the right type of team effort and generate enthusiasm, and enthusiasm is the breeding ground for success.

More entities in the public and private sectors prefer, or even insist, that their professional service providers have a quality system. They may want to know about the guiding philosophy, QA standards used, and successes achieved.

These entities include the U.S. Navy, the U.S. Army Corps of Engineers, many state departments of transportation, state and local governments, school districts, public utilities, chemical and pharmaceutical manufacturers, national laboratories, banks, hospitals, the pulp and paper industry, and manufacturers of all types. The list is growing.

Commitment to Change

Change can be frightening to the unprepared. That is why it is important to acknowledge that the TQM/CI journey is all about change. This change includes bad habits to good habits, overwork and rework to seamless work, and low profits to good profits. Along the way, quality and client loyalty improve.

There are four ways that leaders react to change.

1. They prevent it.

2. They remain neutral to it.

3. They assist it.

4. They drive it.

The third and fourth ways are both important to continuous improvement.

The Profile of Change

The first change does not have to occur at the top. It can be sparked at the top, center, side, or periphery of the corporate mass, and still light up the entire structure. Start by deciding where the change focus will be made. Not everything can be healed at once, but one must start somewhere. Should the strategic direction, project management, operations, or human resources be the first beneficiaries of change?

The Depth of Change

The extent of the change must be assessed. Will change involve only one department, office, or region, or will it be taken deeper to embrace a larger slice of the organization? It is tempting to heal only where it hurts, but this might only alleviate symptoms.

The Rate of Change

Once one slice of the organization has undergone a positive transformation, other related slices should catch the wave of change too. But how quickly will this occur? Change working in unison with change often results in a synergistic transformation, so that the whole is greater than the parts.

Change without milestones can result in failure, because if the end result is not achieved, management may give up, believing that the goal was unattainable, that the people were not trying, or that the vehicle to achieve the goal was inadequate. With milestones, it is obvious that progress is being made, and this spurs further achievements.

Change for the Sake of Change

When change fever supplants improvement fever a dangerous situation can develop. The former changes things because it feels right. The latter changes things because there are data to back up the validity of the change. A species does not evolve because it feels like it; it evolves as part of an adaptation to a changing environment. If the change is sound, the species will thrive. If the species does not change, it becomes extinct. This law of nature applies equally to business.

Commitment to Patience

The commitment to TQM/CI includes a recognition that it may take years to fully implement. While it can get going in the professional service arena much more quickly than in other sectors, there will always be a certain percentage of managers and staff who will be very enthusiastic, some neutral and others who are antipathetic. It takes time for the groundswell of enthusiasm to catch up with the resisters.

Waiting until everyone is excited about TQM/CI means never starting. It's like buying a computer; one could wait forever for the perfect model. It is better to jump in, start computing, and upgrade as part of continuous improvement. So TQM/CI has to start somewhere, and it may take a while before an organization is fully immersed in the process.

Figure 1.12 shows a guideline for the length of time that it might take to implement TQM/CI, depending on the size of the organization.

Total number of staff	Time
1–10	0.5 year
11–25	0.5–1.5 years
26–50	1.5–2.5 years
51–100	2.5–3.5 years
101+	3.5–5.0 years

Figure 1.12. Time to fully implement TQM/CI—size.

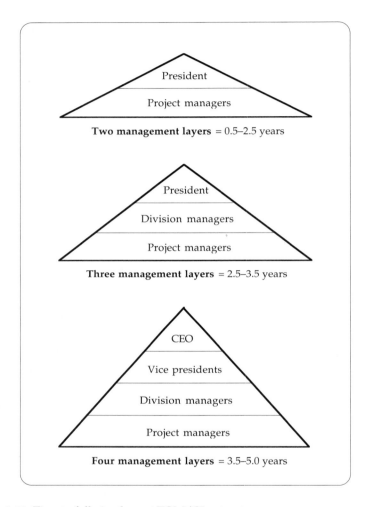

Figure 1.13. Time to fully implement TQM/CI—structure.

Professional service firms tend to have few management layers, and flexible boundaries between the different layers. These conditions are favorable to TQM/CI.

Figure 1.13 looks at implementation from a structural perspective. These time estimates assume that the TQM/CI processes detailed in this book are used. Other systems may take longer.

CHAPTER 2

Five Keys That Unlock TQM/CI

Overview

Many of the ideas described in chapter 1 coalesce into the five key concepts given in this chapter. Most improvements will relate to one or more of these keys. If several readers were to compare ideas on these keys, they could form the nucleus of a task force that initiates TQM/CI within their organization.

The First Key: Fixing Problems Upstream

Consider the following:

- An automobile manufacturer has a major recall because a part is defective.
- A new generation appliance malfunctions.
- An improved food product is rejected by consumers.
- A key part of a do-it-yourself assembly kit is missing.
- The Hubble telescope is impaired by a flawed mirror.

In all these cases, the customer brings the problems to the attention of the manufacturer after the sale, and the impacts can be huge. Figure 2.1 shows the exponential increase in impacts based on the time it takes to identify and correct an error or omission. The potential impacts are listed on the left-hand side of the illustration.

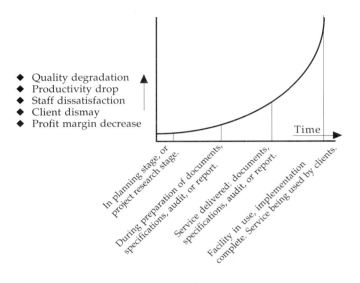

◆ Quality degradation
◆ Productivity drop
◆ Staff dissatisfaction
◆ Client dismay
◆ Profit margin decrease

Time

In planning stage, or project research stage.

During preparation of documents, specifications, audit, or report.

Service delivered: documents, specifications, audit, or report.

Facility in use; implementation complete. Service being used by clients.

Figure 2.1. Upstream versus downstream solutions.

The sooner the problem is identified, the smaller the impact on quality, productivity, morale, client attitude, and profits. Five professional service examples, each with three worsening results, are listed. These are all examples of downstream impacts when errors and omissions are not identified and corrected upstream.

• **An important descriptive table is missing from a report.**

Result a: The consultant realizes the omission after a few days and sheepishly issues a supplement.

Result b: The client requests the missing information.

Result c: The omission is not noticed and the consultant has greater legal exposure than if the omission had been noticed.

• **A specification omits vital information.**

Result a: The omission is not noticed until the equipment has been specified.

Result b: The omission is not noticed until the equipment has been ordered.

Result c: The omission is not noticed until years after the project is complete.

- **A contract omits a clause that covers terms of payment.**

  Result a: Asking the client to add the clause immediately after signing the contract may initiate bad feelings.

  Result b: Later in the project, the client might demand a concession to add the clause.

  Result c: Legal action after the project may be traced back to the missing clause.

- **An important detail is missing in a set of documents.**

  Result a: Coordination is hampered by the omission, causing schedule delays.

  Result b: Incorrect estimates are made leading to future claims.

  Result c: An installed system fails causing a collapse.

- **An important analysis is forgotten.**

  Result a: A detail is rejected by a regulatory agency.

  Result b: A failed test causes added costs and delays.

  Result c: A component fails in service.

Summary of the First Key

Continuous improvement focused on upstream problem solving can effect tremendous gains.

The Second Key: Adding Value and Eliminating Waste

It is surprising that one of the most powerful TQM concepts is emphasized less than improved service, relationships, teamwork, and leadership. Viable continuous improvement implies a dual focus on the elimination of nonvalue-added activities and the refinement of value-added activities (VAA). Examples of nonvalue-added activities that can be eliminated include the following:

- Damage control
- Reanalyzing

- Revisions caused by mistakes and miscommunication
- Excessive approval loops
- Nonproductive and unnecessarily long meetings
- Equipment shutdown caused by lack of maintenance
- Pursuing prospects who will be difficult clients
- Reports that don't get implemented, or even read
- Tracking data that are never used
- Attending seminars and not implementing good ideas
- Searching for lost information

Note: The total elimination of items in this list may never occur, yet the ongoing effort to whittle them down to the bare minimum will pay huge dividends.

Examples of value-added activities that can be refined include the following:

- Scope of work planning
- Kickoff meetings
- Analyzing
- Work load leveling
- Producing documents
- Writing requested reports
- Productive and timely meetings
- Professional development activities
- Pursuing key prospects that will give repeat work
- Information access

TQM do-it-yourselfers often focus on value-added activities, not recognizing that they should start by eliminating what is not right. They expect that by refining the value-added activities somehow everything will be better. This does not always work. The bar at the top of Figure 2.2 depicts a hypothetical process in an organization. Only 20 percent of the activities are value adding, which means that 80 percent of the activities are unnecessary, wasteful, and nonvalue-added. Assume that the TQM do-it-yourselfers refine the way they do their work, perhaps with a faster computer or an improved tracking form, and actually improve efficiency by as much as 10 percent. The overall effectiveness will have improved only a mere 2 percent. This is because the vast reservoir of waste remains undetected and untouched. Far better to start TQM/CI by first eliminating the unnecessary and wasteful tasks. Then the organization can further reap benefits by refining its value-added processes.

The lower half of Figure 2.2 shows the breakout when those wasteful activities have been trimmed back and the value-added activities have been refined. The latter now constitutes 65 percent of the overall effort, and effectiveness, morale, quality, and profitability are all vastly better.

A major cause of waste is the ineffective transfer of information between project team members. When this occurs it can transform value-added activities into nonvalue-added ones, and an effective project into a disaster. Figure 2.3 shows diagrammatically how this occurs. A relay race can be tactically planned, the race superbly run by the athletes, with excellently timed and executed baton handoffs, until the baton is dropped. Then the value chain is lost, and all that went before is wasted.

When the baton is dropped at work, the process must be stopped to pick up the baton. If this occurs upstream the impact might be insignificant compared to finishing the race without even realizing that the baton is lost. This leads to a downstream project repair, and the

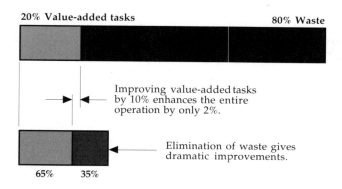

Figure 2.2. Eliminating nonvalue-added activities.

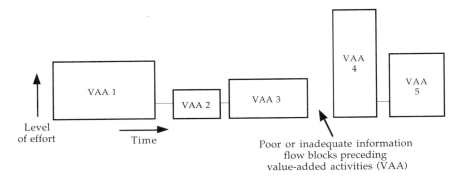

Figure 2.3. Turning value-added activities into waste.

damage control crisis team will need to be mobilized. Staff members must be secure in the knowledge that they will not be penalized if they stop the process to pick up the baton as soon as it drops, in order to save large delays downstream.

Summary of the Second Key

1. Eliminating waste and nonvalue-added activities, often through system breakthroughs, provides a very high return on investment, especially early in the continuous improvement process.

2. Refining value-added activities brings additional returns and can stimulate new breakthroughs.

The Third Key: Quality Reviews

How does quality control (QC) and quality assurance (QA) relate to TQM? Are they to be discarded? QC and QA are familiar terms for most professional service organizations. Some, in error, use the terms interchangeably, but they are quite distinct in their meaning. Readers are referred to the definitions in the appendix for this author's interpretations. The examination of this issue will start with a look at problem solving.

The Problem with Problem Solving

Professional service providers, whether they be accountants, attorneys, financial planners, economists, management consultants, scientists, or the entire A/EC industry, see themselves as problem solvers. This mind-set is damaging as it sets up an expectation that there will be problems to solve. So problems are the fuel that enables these service providers to demonstrate their problem-solving prowess. Unfortunately, the fuel often catches afire, the fire gets out of control, and the problem solver gets burned. An examination of the debris often reveals a problem that did not really need to be solved, or a problem-solving fixation. The following lists examine the difference between the problem solver and the continuous improver.

Problem solvers

- Problem solvers expect that things will go wrong and that the resulting problems will be solved.

- Problem solvers get on with production and then compare their output to the specifications in order to ensure compliance.

- Problem solvers focus on a quick fix. This occurs because problems are seen as interruptions, the budget is about to be impacted, and the schedule must be maintained.

- Problem solvers tend to point fingers. "Who is responsible?" is asked whenever a problem surfaces.

Continuous improvers

- Continuous improvers expect that things will go right and that there will be no problems to solve.

- Continuous improvers study the specification first, then they produce their output. They also compare their output to past results in order to ensure that future specifications are more practical.

- Continuous improvers focus on long-term healing to prevent interruptions, budget overruns, and schedule impacts.

- Continuous improvement cannot occur without teamwork. When problems surface, continuous improvers focus on improving the system.

Problem solvers	**Continuous improvers**
• Problem solving is seen as a cost-cutting tool. Solving problems mitigates client dissatisfaction.	• Continuous improvement is seen as a value-adding process. Eliminating waste and adding value builds client relationships.
• Problem solving focuses on finding cures for daily symptoms.	• Continuous improvement focuses on prevention of symptoms by eliminating root causes.

The way to rely less on problem solving and move toward continuous improvement is via a quality assurance/quality review (QA/QR) system.

Quality Assurance Manual

Quality reviews are based on the QA manual's guidelines, checklists and standards. Some firms may wish to extend the scope of their QA manual to cover all of their work practices. An outline of this broader-scoped manual is provided in the appendix.

1. Strategic planning
2. Operational procedures
3. Project management and document production
4. Marketing and business development procedures
5. Professional development guidelines
6. Partnering

Quality Reviews

When an organization's employees rely on getting the job done through quality control, they become reactive problem solvers, and they may not be able to consistently maintain their quest for excellence. This is because QC in professional service firms is usually a downstream activity. Solving problems is seen as a damage control tool. The result is business as usual with some days great, but most days still frantic.

Figure 2.4 shows how QRs extend the benefits of the QC process by doing more than controlling results. Readers will notice how these benefits tie into the payoffs shown in Figure 1.1.

When QRs are implemented, everyone self-checks their work to comply with the scope and the QA manual section that pertains to that process. This self-check system means that the work product is no longer taken off the production line and controlled, much as a river is controlled by a dam, stopped downstream, and then released in controlled amounts after inspection. In a QR system, the work, like the

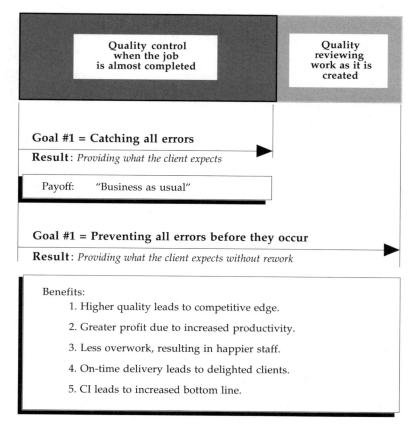

Quality control
when the job
is almost completed

Quality
reviewing
work as it is
created

Goal #1 = Catching all errors

Result: *Providing what the client expects*

Payoff: "Business as usual"

Goal #1 = Preventing all errors before they occur

Result: *Providing what the client expects without rework*

Benefits:
1. Higher quality leads to competitive edge.
2. Greater profit due to increased productivity.
3. Less overwork, resulting in happier staff.
4. On-time delivery leads to delighted clients.
5. CI leads to increased bottom line.

Figure 2.4. The quality review payoff.

river, is simply monitored and self-checked by the producer as it passes along to its destination. This is depicted in Figure 2.5.

Furthermore, the QA manual and its procedures and checklists are subject to continuous improvement. Using the analogy in Figure 2.5, this means that the channel along which the work travels is improved to reduce friction and increase the efficiency of the work flow.

Summary of the Third Key

1. QC is business as usual. Most errors are identified downstream through inspection of completed or nearly completed work. By the time the errors have been corrected, large time, money, image, and morale impacts may have occurred.

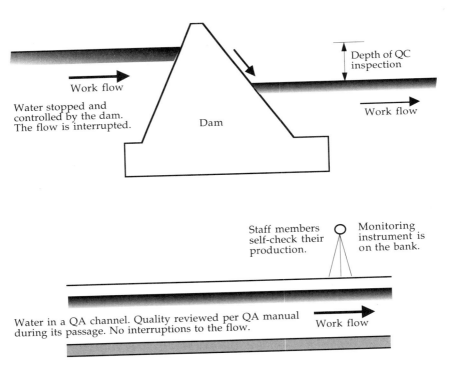

Figure 2.5. Off-line quality control versus quality reviews.

2. Upstream, self-check quality reviews by every staff member can eliminate large chunks of waste. These QRs are conducted in accordance with QA guidelines. The overall benefits in terms of time, money, image, and morale may be enormous.

The Fourth Key: Solving Chronic Problems

Many people love to solve puzzles, and most have strong opinions. The talented individuals found in professional service firms are even more powerfully endowed with these traits. Their true avocation is problem solving, and they will heroically leap over tall buildings into the flames to rescue a burning issue.

Yet after the fires are doused, the underlying causes of the blaze are rarely investigated other than to affix blame. These troubleshooters are often so pleased with their Band-Aid fix that they don't suspect that the underlying causes, lurking deep beneath the surface, are ready to reignite. Sometimes the troubleshooters know that there is something wrong with the system, but have to respond to the next fire alarm leaving no time to deal with anything that is not currently on fire.

This occurs so frequently in professional service firms that it has become a way of life for project managers. They are actually rewarded with bonuses for being such efficient firefighters, while fire prevention officers—the project managers who have devised project crisis prevention techniques—go unnoticed and often unrewarded. Many of the firefighters actually cause their own fires by being undisciplined, inattentive, and poorly organized. Thus, the quite normal sparks that occur on every assignment catch fire, often smoldering for weeks before the alarm signals go off and all hands are called on deck. When it is the same alarm that sounds, month after month, a chronic problem has emerged and the time must be found to identify the cause and defuse the detonator. TQM do-it-yourselfers often focus on symptom healing. This can have devastating effects. For example, a computer-aided design (CAD) department improvement could seriously affect design productivity; or a billing department improvement could adversely impact project managers; or a project management improvement could bottleneck support staff production.

Figure 2.6 shows a symptom tree. Many project managers find themselves eating the bitter fruit on project after project, without

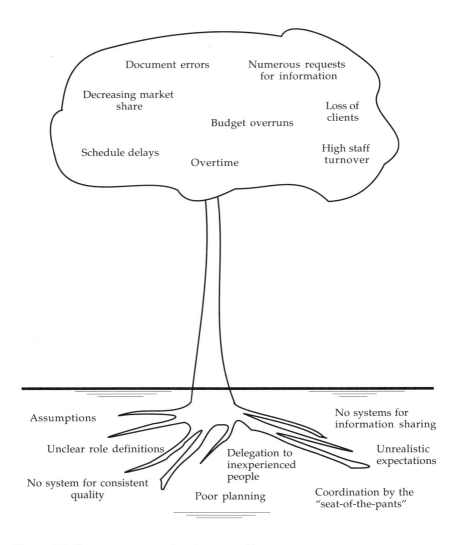

Figure 2.6. Symptoms versus chronic root problems.

realizing that there could be a sweeter way. TQM/CI traces the clues back from the fruit, along the branches, down the trunk, and below the ground to the roots.

There, an examination of the root causes can lead to the break-throughs that eliminate nonvalue-added activities and refine the value-added work processes. The poison fruit, now transforms into documents without errors, diminished requests for information, increasing market share, budget and schedule compliance, gain of clients and greater profit, while staff gain in pride and loyalty. This is the sweet fruit of success.

Summary of the Fourth Key

Responding to symptoms with quick solutions is inefficient, wasteful, and expensive. Focusing on fire prevention and solving chronic problems through root cause identification and elimination has far-reaching benefits. Part II describes a process to effect this change.

The Fifth Key: Recognizing the Cost of Stagnation

The term, *cost of quality* commonly used by TQM practitioners is misleading when applied to professional services. The cost of quality reports dollars, typically expressed as a percentage of sales, that are spent in order to achieve quality. The word *quality*, however, limits the vision when considering the global potential of continuous improvement. The *cost of stagnation* is a term better suited to get the point across. Stagnation is here defined as

- Firefighting and reactive business practices
- Quality control at the conclusion of the project
- Failure to eliminate waste
- Failure to refine value-added activities
- Failure to continuously improve

Prevention Costs

These costs comprise continuous improvement team meetings, training activities, TQM/CI coaching, project partnering meetings, process measurement activities, and the time spent on quality reviews. These costs are productive, beneficial, and necessary.

Quality Control Costs Before Delivery

The following list is merely a sample of the activities that result in the high cost of quality control. These occur when an organization practices inspection, believing that any error will be caught before the work goes out the door. Using inspection to ensure compliance leads to

- Schedule disruption
- Expediting late projects
- Coordinating identified errors and omissions
- Errors leading to nonbillable troubleshooting
- Bottlenecked administrative and support staff
- Missed deadlines
- Overtime
- Overnight mail due to late work
- Frustrated, pressured, harried, and irritated staff
- Annoyed clients

Many of these items cannot be totally eliminated. Perhaps a 10 percent overall reduction in the first year is reasonable, but it is important not to get stuck on the numbers. Perhaps even more dramatic reductions are feasible!

Costs of Changes Made at Delivery of Service

The following list shows the results of errors and omissions resulting from poor planning, communication, and coordination. A project manager who reacts rather than plans would find this list familiar.

- Budget overruns
- Unnecessary meetings and travel
- Getting changes coordinated
- Time and energy spent in trying to find documentation
- Time and energy spent in getting the client to accept changes
- Time and energy spent in pursuing extra fees
- Attempts to get a supplemental contract
- Blaming leading to mistrust

- Mistrust leading to drop in productivity
- Low staff morale leading to high staff turnover
- Write-offs
- Angry clients

When these downstream occurrences appear project after project, the costs of stagnation will take big bites out of the bottom line.

Costs of Changes Made After Service Is Implemented

The following list shows the results of errors and omissions resulting from poor planning, communication, and coordination that were not caught until days, weeks, months, or years after the service was completed.

These are so far downstream that they have skyrocketed to the end of the exponential curve shown in Figure 2.1. Organizations that stagnate, doing nothing about TQM/CI practices, increase the chance that one day they will come face to face with all the items on this list.

- Lost market share and tarnished image
- Crisis management and damage control
- Disaster public relations
- Legal costs
- Lawsuit damages
- Higher insurance rates
- Lost clients
- High stress and susceptibility to illness
- Business failure

These items are no longer nonvalue-added, they are value destructive. Unfortunately, they are not so unusual. It is not easy to calculate the financial impact of the cost of stagnation. Yet companies ignoring the need for positive change may face ruin.

Pre-TQM/CI Scenario

Figure 2.7 puts the whole question of the cost of stagnation into focus. For organizations that have not commenced TQM/CI, the costs of stagnation run from 10 percent to 35 percent or more of billings. While their prevention costs are little or nothing, these companies practice quality control inspection and fall prey to enormous downstream waste.

Scenario When TQM/CI Is Started

Organizations that commence the TQM/CI process find that their prevention costs suddenly go up. Training, getting familiar with the tools, and taking the time to partner and implement something new takes extra time and effort, just as learning to drive demands extra attention

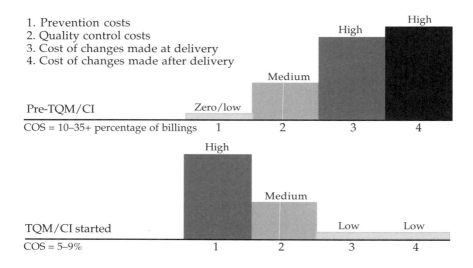

Figure 2.7. The cost of stagnation—COS.

until the skills are in place and are effortlessly employed. The quality control costs of these TQM/CI firms remain the same for a few months, because TQM/CI takes time for the beneficial effects to be felt. With the elimination of wasteful activities, large gains will be made, perhaps even in the first year. This translates into far fewer unexpected costs when the service is delivered, and after the delivery, such as after a project is complete.

Scenario When TQM/CI Is Operational

When the TQM/CI process is firmly embedded in the organization, prevention costs decrease to a maintenance level. Training new staff, partnering, and ongoing continuous improvement, however, will still take time. Quality control now has a low priority, because the modus operandi of stopping the work to check if it is right has been eliminated. The QR process monitors the work as it is produced and then QC simply verifies its excellence. This results in few, if any changes at the delivery of the service. Difficulties will still occur from time to time, but systems will be operating to deal with them. Finally, changes occurring after the service has been completed will have been virtually eliminated.

Administrative and support staff members are often concerned about how their activities tie in to the concept of adding value to a service. While their work may not directly add value to the end product, their work is far from being value neutral. They supplement the organization's services, and add value to internal client-provider relationships.

Actually, anything can be wasteful. Even TQM can be nonvalue added when it gets offtrack and results in improvements that have low practical use, new procedures that add work for little return on investment, manuals that are cosmetic, and measurements that look good, but are not related to continuous improvement.

Summary of the Fifth Key

Cutting down the high costs of stagnation reaches far beyond better quality. Continuous improvement of all activities can make struggling organizations healthy; healthy organizations thrive; and thriving organizations reach their full potential.

PART II

Implementing Professional Service TQM/CI

CHAPTER 3

The Shearer TQM/CI Model

Overview

The implementation of TQM/CI needs more than skilled and dedicated team players. It requires a model as a foundation. The model guides the implementation, which in turn facilitates efficiency and continuous improvement of systems and processes. A number of models can be used to reach the same destination, so management can use this chapter to determine the structure, shape, and direction of the model that will guide its continuous improvement program.

The Malcolm Baldrige Model

The Malcolm Baldrige National Quality Award, sponsored by the U.S. government, and administered by the National Institute of Standards and Technology, provides a model for a TQM/CI program. Organizations, both manufacturing and service, are eligible to apply for the award. The components of the 1994 award are as follows:

1.0 Leadership—95 points

    1.1 Senior Executive Leadership—45

    1.2 Management for Quality—25

    1.3 Public Responsibility and Corporate Citizenship—25

2.0 Information and Analysis—75 points

    2.1 Scope and Management of Quality and Performance Data and Information—15

    2.2 Competitive Comparisons and Benchmarking—20

    2.3 Analyses and Uses of Company-Level Data—40

3.0 Strategic Quality Planning—60 points

    3.1 Strategic Quality and Company Performance Planning Process—35

    3.2 Quality and Performance Plans—25

4.0 Human Resource Development and Management—150 points

    4.1 Human Resource Planning and Management—20

    4.2 Employee Involvement—40

    4.3 Employee Education and Training—40

    4.4 Employee Performance and Recognition—25

    4.5 Employee Well-Being and Satisfaction—25

5.0 Management of Process Quality—140 points

    5.1 Design and Introduction of Quality Products and Services—40

    5.2 Process Management: Product and Service Production and Delivery Processes—35

    5.3 Process Management: Business and Support Service Processes—30

    5.4 Supplier Quality—20

    5.5 Quality Assessment—15

6.0 Quality and Operational Results—180 points

    6.1 Product and Service Quality Results—70

    6.2 Company Operational Results—50

    6.3 Business and Support Service Results—25

    6.4 Supplier Quality Results—35

7.0 Customer Focus and Satisfaction—300 points

    7.1 Customer Expectations: Current and Future—35

Baldrige Model Advantages

Clearly, the Baldrige Award reflects the competitive spirit of the United States. The components not only encourage continuous improvement, but the award requirements are also updated and continuously improved each year. The categories are well thought out and comprehensive. With some adaptation, the Baldrige Award criteria could provide a sound basis for a practical, professional service TQM/CI model.

Baldrige Model Cautions and Disadvantages

1. The idea of assigning a set of points for each category can mislead. For example, the item employee well-being and satisfaction is given far fewer points than senior executive leadership, and the category customer focus and satisfaction gets four times more points than information and analysis. This author believes that this is too prescriptive for a TQM/CI model because the emphasis on various aspects of importance should be custom designed for each organization. Fortunately, tucked away in the Baldrige Award criteria (page 35 in the 1994 version) is the admission that the items "may not be equally applicable or equally important to all businesses, even to businesses of comparable size in the same industry."

2. The score assigned to each category can limit continuous improvement in that category. When organization leaders believe that they have full points for a category, they will turn their focus to getting points in the next category. It almost becomes a sports contest—strategizing how to get the most points to win the prize, with a deadline thrown in to win this year. No wonder that some past winners have slipped after winning. This is not meant to discourage organizations from participating in the award. By promoting

quality, the Baldrige Award provides an enormous service; the only caution is to know the limitations. It might be best for professional service firms to ignore the competitive aspect, use the guidelines as a model, and focus on long-term, global improvement without any limits in any category.

The ISO 9000 Model

The International Organization for Standardization (ISO), founded in 1947, is currently comprised of the national standards organizations of almost 100 countries. ISO guidelines are not European standards, as many believe; they are international standards. Their focus is on promoting the development of standards for many different areas of specialization, and ISO's goal is to foster international trade. The ISO 9000 series, first published in 1987, is based on the British Standard Institution BS 5750. In the United States, the ANSI/ASQC Q9000 series is the exact equivalent of the ISO 9000 series.

For professional services the closest document in the series is ISO 9004-2, *Guidelines for Services.* It is not possible to be registered to ISO 9004-2; it is simply a quality management model for services. This model provides guidance for those who are interested in a quality system, but has little on continuous improvement. Most sections are very brief and simply mention what needs to be done without much detail. But these sections do cover a lot of ground and might stimulate creative quality thinking.

For example, the section on quality system principles gives a description of customer interfaces, management commitment, policy, goals, objectives, and activities. Statements concerning the roles and responsibilities of senior management and personnel, and the need for documented reviews, are given.

Motivation, training, communication, equipment, and software are also mentioned, and the model encourages structure and preventive actions. A quality manual, the need for a quality plan, procedures, quality records, and audits are mentioned. This section also overviews client relations and customer communication issues.

The section on operational elements touches on market research and mentions the importance of documenting obligations for consistency. Brief statements on a service agreement, early service planning needs, image, and honesty in advertising are also given. This section includes an overview of work planning, contingency planning, and the need for accuracy and precision. It mentions good communication, comprehensiveness, and subdividing the process, and it lists work phases and subcontractor selection. It covers the need for a formal review at the end of each phase, discusses specification compliance, and provides a short validation checklist.

Other items in the document include controlling specification changes, supplier quality, image perceptions, measurement of customer satisfaction, internal debriefing and tracking, accountability, early identification of problems, and corrective action. There is a short statement on the need for continual evaluations, and it lists ideas for both short- and long-term continuous improvement.

ISO 9000 Advantages

ISO 9004-2, available through the American Society for Quality Control (ASQC), is clearly a generic guideline for all types of services. With a good deal of work on the part of an organization adapting the document to professional services, it could be an outstanding model. Its focus on documentation of processes in order to maintain consistency is especially well linked to the concept of a QA manual and quality reviewing work. With this book as a guide, ISO 9004-2 could serve as the foundation for a professional service continuous improvement program.

If a professional service firm wants to become registered, however, it will need to use the manufacturing-oriented ISO 9001, 9002, or 9003 standards. Of the three, ISO 9001 is most applicable to A/EC firms. Registration demonstrates that an organization has clear documentation of policies and procedures to facilitate consistent processes. This will give the firm an international marketing advantage.

ISO 9000 Cautions and Disadvantages

1. Just as a building can comply with a code and standards, and still be an inefficient and poorly designed structure, being registered is no guarantee that an organization provides quality outputs.

    a. Nonvalue-added results can be accepted if procedures are thoroughly documented, with corrective actions applied when errors occur.

b. The documentation of processes might well result in bottle-neck and waste elimination, but surveillance and reassessments do not specifically require continuous improvement. The revisions released in 1994 align paragraphs in the different standards and clarify some of the text, but leave much to be desired in the area of continuous improvement.

c. There is no avenue to correct inefficient, downstream activities, and these might not be eliminated, even if they are carefully documented and monitored.

d. A company may use outdated processes, equipment, and methodologies, but if the process, controls, and client feedback are thoroughly documented, registration is still achievable.

2. Documentation of processes and subprocesses must be done by the actual staff involved in those activities. This is the heart of the registration process, and it is extremely valuable for consistency. If management does not keep the big picture in focus, however, the opportunity to link processes into improved systems, and systems into an improved structure, may be missed.

3. While it is not mandatory for assessors to know anything about the type of business they are registering, it is advisable to engage those who have professional service experience. There are also consultants who prepare organizations for the registration audit. Without careful guidance, the process can devolve into a rubber-stamping of firms that meet the letter, but not the spirit of the standards.

4. The registration investment can range from several thousands of dollars for a small organization to hundreds of thousands of dollars for a large organization. The bulk of the costs go into improvement efforts, and should be recoupable, while the balance goes toward document reviews, preassessments, and registration costs and fees. In order to retain registration, an organization must also undergo periodic surveillance and a full re-registration audit every few years. All of these compliance efforts must provide a return on investment to prevent registration from becoming a financial drain.

5. Not all registrars represent the same accreditation body. Registration in one country will not automatically mean that an organization is registered in all other ISO countries, which is a current weakness for a standard that purports to be international. Organizations wishing to do business overseas must ensure that their registrar's accreditation body is recognized in the country in which they plan to operate. These issues are being studied and by the end of the decade, mutual recognition should be well advanced.

Note: The British Standard BS 7850 Part 1: *TQM, Guide to Management Principles* was published in 1992. BS 7850 Part 2: *TQM, Guidelines for Quality Improvement* has a 1994 revision based on ISO 9000. These documents total about 35 pages and are generic to all organization types.

Summarizing the Ideas Behind Baldrige and ISO 9000

The Baldrige Award is a model that is competitive, customer oriented, and global. It covers everything from research to planning to continuous improvement. ISO 9000 is more focused on internal process documentation and consistency. There is no explicit link to satisfy customer needs. Because of these differences, a company using the Baldrige model would probably find ISO 9000 registration easy, while an ISO 9000-accredited firm might struggle with the Baldrige model.

This book directly supports both the Baldrige Award and ISO 9000. The international standard provides the process methodology and tools to achieve the results demanded by the Baldrige Award; and the Baldrige Award focuses on continuous improvement to supplement ISO 9000 compliance needs.

The Shearer TQM/CI Model for Professional Services

A third option is the Shearer TQM/CI model, created specifically for professional services. The outline given has an overriding focus on global continuous improvement. It invites each organization to add detail to each item in accordance with its needs, market position, and direction. The key advantage of the Shearer model is its comprehensive reach and its focus on the professional service environment.

1.0 Direction and Guidance

    1.1 Executive leadership tasks

    1.2 Steering committee tasks

    1.3 Steering committee and executive leadership links

    1.4 Steering committee ground rules and operations

    1.5 The continuous improvement manager

    1.6 Improvement suggestions

2.0 Implementation Structure

    2.1 Process improvement teams and task teams

    2.2 Team leadership

    2.3 Team membership

    2.4 Stakeholder involvement

    2.5 Training

3.0 Implementation Procedures

    3.1 Chronic problem selection

    3.2 Team procedures

    3.3 Problem statement

    3.4 Breakouts

    3.5 Baseline data

    3.6 Root cause analysis

    3.7 Trial solution

    3.8 Data collection and evaluation

    3.9 Standardize improvements

4.0 Implementation Tools

    4.1 Decision-making and organizing tools

    4.2 Breakout tools

    4.3 Diagnosis tools

    4.4 Variation and relationship monitoring tools

    4.5 Measurement procedures and benchmarking

5.0 Continuous Improvement

    5.1 Strategic planning improvement

        5.1.1 Share visions, directions, and objectives

        5.1.2 Improve market and service assessments

        5.1.3 Assess practice and proposal histories

        5.1.4 Improve competitive benchmarking

        5.1.5 Improve risk assessment, budgeting, and milestone goal setting

        5.1.6 Establish an implementation plan

        5.1.7 Track and report continuous improvement

    5.2 Operations improvement

        5.2.1 Productivity tracking

        5.2.2 Management information systems

        5.2.3 Staff planning, hiring, and reduction practices

        5.2.4 Staff communication and administration

        5.2.5 Financial management and structure

        5.2.6 Accounts payable and receivable systems

        5.2.7 Contract administration

        5.2.8 Operational quality reviews

    5.3 Project management improvement

        5.3.1 Work plan management

        5.3.2 Teaming and coordination

        5.3.3 Schedule control

        5.3.4 Budget control

        5.3.5 Documenting, tracking, and reporting

        5.3.6 Standard operating procedure compliance

        5.3.7 Quality reviews

    5.4 Marketing improvement

        5.4.1 Market planning

        5.4.2 Opportunity research

For professional service companies neither planning for ISO registration nor pursuing the Baldrige Award, it is suggested that the Shearer model be used as a guide. The remainder of this chapter will explore sections 1 and 2 of the model, and subsequent chapters will explore the balance of the Shearer model.

1.1 Executive Leadership Tasks

The first task for the executive or senior leadership is to create the steering committee. This includes the following assignments.

1.1.1 Identifying the continuous improvement (CI) manager. This is often a senior manager, but may be an assigned or hired full-time manager. The CI manager's role is reviewed in more detail in Section 1.5.

1.1.2 Identifying the members and chair of the steering committee.

1.1.3 Establishing the committee's function, role, and duties.

1.1.4 Formulating their links and frequency of contact with the steering committee. Large organizations may have a steering committee for each division or regional office. In these cases, each steering committee would report to, and be administrated by a single executive steering committee. Any existing QA managers might train to become TQM/CI managers and be involved in these steering committees. Most organizations, however, need just one steering committee.

1.1.5 Decide how regional offices will handle TQM/CI.

- Will each office have its own teams?

- How will the CI manager coordinate activities?

- How will the steering committee and teams interact?

1.1.6 Decide how team members will be recognized. There are many vehicles to give personal and team recognition besides money. Recognition, awards, and evaluations will be discussed in chapter 5.

1.1.7 Establish a budget for continuous improvement. TQM/CI is not initially free. Although the return on investment can be huge, it costs money to implement a continuous improvement process. The cost of stagnation, Figure 2.7, can help to guide the creation of a budget for the first year. Large organizations may also subdivide their budget for each division. It is important to budget for both continuous improvement activities and result tracking. It may be found that a greater investment results in an even greater return on investment.

1.1.8 Assign time sheet tracking codes for team and continuous improvement activities.

1.1.9 Decide if a consultant will be helpful in guiding the company through the implementation process. This individual should

- Have experience with professional services

- Be experienced with TQM/CI implementation

- Endorse the importance of continuous improvement

- Have a successful consulting track record

- Be a good communicator, coach, and facilitator
- Be willing to commit availability

1.2 Steering Committee Tasks

The steering committee is an essential component of TQM/CI. Without a steering committee, the teams may splash around with no direction, solving problems that management does not believe are important, and deriving solutions that management will not accept. Each organization will select a name for this guidance group. Names encountered by this author include process improvement committee, TQM advisory council, quality advisory board, management advisory board, quality steering council, quality management board, quality implementation board, and simply, the steering committee.

Who sits on the steering committee? Usually senior operations, human resources and financial managers, division managers, and often project managers, and technical and support representatives. A total membership of 3–12 is the norm.

A rotation of 50 percent of the steering committee membership every 6–12 months is recommended. This will allow many more project managers, technicians, and office support staff to have an opportunity to serve with the top leadership on the committee.

The steering committee's tasks include the following:

1. Establishing the parameters and setting the ground rules
2. Administering and monitoring ongoing team activities such as
   a. Administrating training
   b. Establishing teams
   c. Coordinating with team facilitators through a CI manager
   d. Interfacing with the teams at milestones
   e. Publicizing progress and success
   f. Promptly acknowledging suggestions
   g. Administrating a recognition program
   h. Keeping knowledgeable about new TQM ideas, literature, and tapes

    i. Reviewing the CI manager's return on investment tracking reports

    j. Preparing regular reports to executive management

    k. Individually attending improvement team meetings from time to time, and possibly acting as team facilitator

1.3 Steering Committee and Executive Leadership Links

Some large, and most medium-sized and small firms will have executive management represented on the steering committee. In these cases most, if not all of the listed questions and issues may be resolved by the steering committee. Additional steering committee decision issues are reviewed in the next section.

1.4 Steering Committee Ground Rules and Operations

First the steering committee will establish the basic parameters.

1.4.1   Start with the drafting of a TQM/CI vision statement. Some call it a mission statement, and some distinguish between the two. The main purposes of the vision statement are to help focus the management and staff, get people thinking about continuous improvement, and demonstrate a commitment. The vision statement should not be a slogan, just an expression of the direction of TQM/CI. The following component list may help in the formation of the vision statement.

- Client service and satisfaction
- Process improvement
- Staff involvement and teamwork
- Quality assurance
- Ethics and integrity
- Open discussion
- Continuous improvement

The vision statement is an optional activity, so readers are urged not to get bogged down in debate.

1.4.2   Decide on the TQM/CI model. Some organizations select their model at the executive management level. Others allow the steering committee to select the working model, be it Baldrige, ISO, the Shearer, or some other model. This must be a recommendation given with supporting reasons to the executive leadership for its endorsement. The committee uses the model to keep focused and to guide the formation of global QA guidelines.

1.4.3   Select a TQM/CI liaison officer who will represent the committee on a day-to-day basis. In most cases this will be the CI manager.

1.4.4   List potential team facilitators who might wish to volunteer for an improvement team. It is wise to establish a pool of talented people who are interested in TQM/CI.

A typical TQM/CI structure is shown in Figure 3.1. This summarizes many of the steering committee tasks, and also shows the team structure.

The steering committee concludes its start-up activities by establishing the team ground rules.

1.4.5   How will improvement suggestions be obtained?
- Client surveys?
- A suggestion box or staff debriefing meetings?
- Steering committee suggestions?
- Task team recommendations?

1.4.6   Team size and composition?
- Generally 3–12 people
- Composition usually dependent on the team topic

1.4.7   When will teams meet?
- During billable hours?
- On their own time?
- Half-and-half?

Note 1: Task teams often meet solely during work hours, as their process is usually short and they often come to a resolution quite quickly.

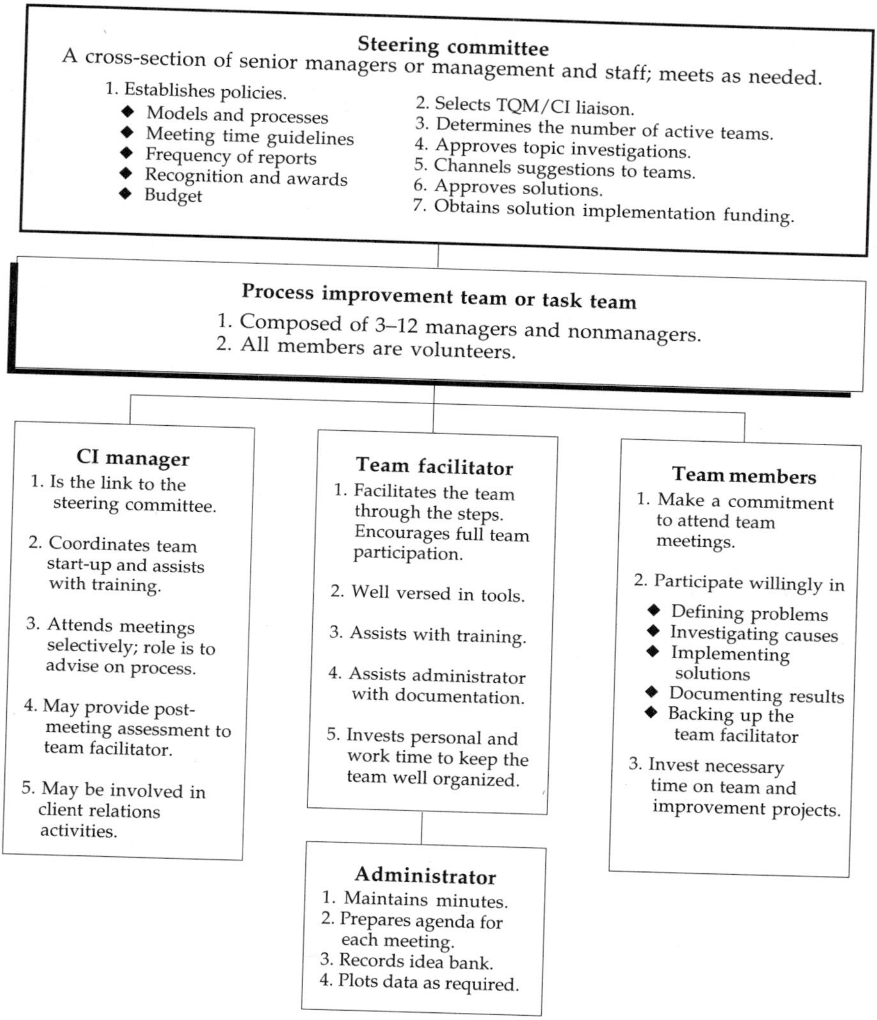

Steering committee

A cross-section of senior managers or management and staff; meets as needed.

1. Establishes policies.
   - ◆ Models and processes
   - ◆ Meeting time guidelines
   - ◆ Frequency of reports
   - ◆ Recognition and awards
   - ◆ Budget

2. Selects TQM/CI liaison.
3. Determines the number of active teams.
4. Approves topic investigations.
5. Channels suggestions to teams.
6. Approves solutions.
7. Obtains solution implementation funding.

Process improvement team or task team

1. Composed of 3–12 managers and nonmanagers.
2. All members are volunteers.

CI manager

1. Is the link to the steering committee.

2. Coordinates team start-up and assists with training.

3. Attends meetings selectively; role is to advise on process.

4. May provide post-meeting assessment to team facilitator.

5. May be involved in client relations activities.

Team facilitator

1. Facilitates the team through the steps. Encourages full team participation.

2. Well versed in tools.

3. Assists with training.

4. Assists administrator with documentation.

5. Invests personal and work time to keep the team well organized.

Team members

1. Make a commitment to attend team meetings.

2. Participate willingly in
   - ◆ Defining problems
   - ◆ Investigating causes
   - ◆ Implementing solutions
   - ◆ Documenting results
   - ◆ Backing up the team facilitator

3. Invest necessary time on team and improvement projects.

Administrator

1. Maintains minutes.
2. Prepares agenda for each meeting.
3. Records idea bank.
4. Plots data as required.

Figure 3.1. TQM/CI organization chart.

Note 2: There are distinct benefits to having the process improvement teams (PITs) meet in the half-and-half format.

- PITs meeting during work hours may contain a few members who attend because they feel like taking a break from their daily routine, who believe that it will look good if they attend, or who enjoy a gripe session on company time.

- PIT meetings that extend into a personal time will be comprised of members who are there because they don't mind giving their own time to the firm, who believe that continuous improvement is important, and who feel an espirit de corps developing within their team.

1.4.8   How often will teams be encouraged to meet?

- Weekly?
- Two or three times a month?

Note: Weekly is recommended as it keeps the energy flowing.

1.4.9   When may team meetings be postponed?

- Team facilitator absent?
- More than 50 percent of team absent?

Note: Both are recommended.

1.4.10 Prepare a tracking form to measure team progress and success. An example is shown in chapter 4.

1.4.11 How will TQM/CI be publicized?

- Install a separate TQM/CI bulletin board?
- Use newsletter or memo announcements?
- What information should be released to clients?
- What, if anything, should be released to the media?
- How does marketing get involved?

Note: The bulletin board is especially recommended.

1.4.12 Finally, decide how frequently the steering committee will meet.

- On an ad hoc basis, on a regular schedule, or both?

1.5 The Continuous Improvement Manager

The steering committee should identify a representative who is capable of looking at the parts being continuously improved and relate them to the big picture. As the day-to-day link between the steering committee and the teams, the CI manager will be an administrator, a coordinator, and a champion. Being excited about TQM/CI and having knowledge of the process are paramount. As mentioned, this person may be a principal or a senior manager, but large firms may hire a CI manager who may even chair the steering committee. The qualifications for this individual are as follows:

- Has the full trust of the executive leadership and the steering committee
- Is well respected by peers and staff
- Thoroughly understands and endorses TQM/CI
- Has the ability to coach successfully
- Is an optimist and is able to absorb resistance
- Knows when to do, and when to delegate
- Is comfortable in being an expeditor
- Is forceful but not demanding in reminding people to carry out their commitments
- Is not put off by paperwork
- Is reliable; can consistently get the job done

This is not an easy position to fill, but it is important to find the person who comes closest to meeting these requirements in order to fulfill the quality mission.

Note: If the CI manager is to be a full-time position, a part of this person's responsibility may include client relations. This would include surveys, visits, and follow-up coordination, debriefing, and benchmarking.

Caution: Do not overpublicize the CI manager's role. This may cause the management and staff to feel that continuous improvement is the sole responsibility of the CI manager, thus leaving them with no sense of ownership in TQM/CI.

1.6 Improvement Suggestions

1.6.1 Benchmarking

The term *benchmark* stems from land surveying and denotes a mark on the earth's surface used as a control point. The term has come to include baseline measurements and even the concept of studying world-class organizations in order to see what they are doing. This is a worthy goal, but not an easy one for professional service organizations to achieve.

Getting specific, useful, comparative information on nonpublicly held companies ranges from being difficult to impossible. Some obtain this information via hearsay or by reading published surveys. The participants in these surveys are rarely a true random sample, so the data need to be interpreted with care.

Aside from that issue, what is a world-class company? Does a Malcolm Baldrige National Quality Award service winner automatically qualify? One might decide that if a firm is listed at, or near the top of one of the numerous annual lists of the top firms, it qualifies as a world-class company. But most lists are based on size and earnings, so being at the top of a list may be a measure of power, but not necessarily of quality.

Even if one could gather valid data on world-class firms, how could that help? Trying to emulate the successes of another firm can be difficult and frustrating. Each practice has its own talented people, whose creativity is almost impossible to duplicate. While their organizational procedures, project management software and marketing approach can be imitated, each firm has its own professional ambiance. Perhaps the best way to use benchmarking in this context is to stimulate ideas and to inspire.

An admirer of genius, say an Einstein or a Bach, could not hope to replicate his creations. But the admirer could look at what they achieved and strive to allow his or her own creativity to flower. The processes of a world-class organization may be excellent, but simply transplanting its ideas to another company might lead to disappointment.

When Dr. Christiaan Barnard performed the first human heart transplant in 1967, it was a breakthrough supported by previous continuous improvement in medical research. Transplanting an organ from one patient to another, however, was not that simple. The body's own immune system tried to reject this foreign protein, causing a decrease in patient survival rates. Immune suppressive drugs were used to help the body accept the new organ, but the patient then became susceptible to infections.

In the same way, companies might react negatively and resist a transplanted idea. Should management be insistent and suppress the resistance, it may find that other systems go out of control as the organization attempts to absorb the transplanted process. Even if there is no resistance to a great transplanted idea, it may not work if the systems required to support the idea are not in place. For this reason external benchmarking is especially dangerous in the early stages of TQM/CI. Better to focus, at this time, on waste elimination.

Benchmarking, however, does have value. The best way for professional service firms to utilize benchmarking is to learn, as best they can, what others do, and then adapt, translate, or adjust their own processes. Even better would be to allow the information gathered to become the catalyst for originality, inspiration, and creativity. An ideal time for this activity is to wait until TQM/CI is fully embedded in the culture.

This author suspects that spending a great deal of time and energy in the pursuit of world-class information may be a symptom of procrastination in starting one's own transformation. The root cause of this procrastination may be a fear of change.

But why must it always be world-class organizations that are investigated? Can not ordinary companies be the source of inspiration? Indeed they can, and one might learn even more from ordinary firms. Confucious was seen by some of his friends walking along a path with tramps and beggars. Aghast, the friends later asked Confucious why he would spend time with such people. He answered that when he spent time with people of high attainment, he learned what to do, and when he spent time with less-successful people, he learned what not to do. So we can learn from the mistakes of others, grateful that we did not fall prey to the same pitfalls.

Perhaps the most valid form of benchmarking for professional service firms is not the comparison to world-class firms, but to oneself. Internal benchmarking avoids the competitive aspects of trying to stay ahead of the pack, and focuses on what can be controlled—better service to one's own clients. What are the organization's current performance measures? How can they be improved? Two examples of simple, yet revealing performance measures are staff turnover and percentage of repeat work. There is, however, a pitfall associated with internal benchmarking. It is not always easy to be objective when assessing one's own operation. Uncritical praise or unsubstantiated criticism are usually politically motivated. Consider having someone from the outside come in to balance the scales and give an objective appraisal. Once this has been done, and once milestone goals based on organizational self-improvement have been set, the organization will be on the sure path to success.

1.6.2 Gathering Usable Data

There are four sources for problem identification.

1. Client surveys
2. Staff suggestions
3. Steering committee
4. Task team

Client Surveys

A lack of complaints may mean that a service is good, but the competition may still be perceived as better. Design the survey to elicit useful answers in the form of symptoms or even potential solutions. Surveys may be conducted by mail, on the telephone, or in person.

Mailed survey steps

1. List all clients served in the past three to five years.
2. Divide them into private and public sectors.
3. Divide them into categories such as market area and building type.
4. Under each category, subdivide clients by size.
5. Categorize each as a past client, a current client, or even a prospective client. One sometimes gets more valuable information from past clients than from current clients. Current clients provide clues about continuous improvement tune-ups needed, and past clients may provide clues about necessary repairs. Any sample used should be randomly selected.

6. Compose the questionnaire.

    a. Keep it simple and short.

    b. Use a ranking system, say 1–5.

    c. Allow space for additional written comments.

    d. Provide a prepaid reply envelope or card.

    e. Make sure that a PIT will be able to use the information.

For example, don't ask vague questions such as, "Rank our communication skills," or "Rank our quality." There will not be any practical value in the answers. Be more specific in order to make sure that the survey will yield useful information. A pilot survey can help to fine-tune questions. Then ask for ranked feedback on items such as technical skills, cost estimates, and schedule compliance. Allow space for written comments.

Caution: These surveys have a limited value when used to benchmark future continuous improvement.

- People have short memories and tend to remember only the very last interaction with the organization, good or bad, and respond to the survey accordingly.

- One can never be sure who completes the survey. Some owners ask their office managers and project secretaries to complete the questionnaire.

There are ways to verify valid continuous improvement feedback from small samples. For example, ask respondents to sign the survey and when it is mailed again the next year, show the respondents how they ranked each question the year before. Ask, "How are we doing—the same, better, or worse?" Request a new ranking and leave space for comments. One can call ahead to inform respondents that the survey is coming and that their personal attention will be valued. This entails more work, but ensures more valuable responses.

In-person survey steps

Steps 1–5 are identical to mailed surveys.

    6. Interviewers could be a CEO, president, or senior manager.

7. Assess where to conduct the interview. If in a plush restaurant, the message may be seduction. The best place might be a meal in an excellent, but not exceptional restaurant. A meal can assist in relationship building.

8. Relationship building and damage control meals don't need any type of survey questionnaire. But if the purpose of the interview is to collect information for a survey, interview responses must be written down. This may not be easy in a restaurant, but preplanning can ease this logistical problem.

Telephone survey steps
Steps 1–5 are identical to mailed surveys.

6. Ask either a professional interviewer or a staff member with excellent telephone skills to make the calls from a quiet room.

7. When a call is made, always start by asking if the interviewee is available for five minutes for the survey, or if a telephone appointment would be preferable.

8. As the interview proceeds, the interviewer should quickly jot down rankings and keywords in order to speed the interview. Immediately after the conversation has ended these keywords should be expanded into sentences on the survey form.

Summary of Surveys
The mailed survey can reach thousands, but it is impersonal and the percentage returned may be small. Nonrespondents can make the conclusions unreliable. The in-person interview is best for special relationship building or rebuilding. The reach is small, so the value of the in-person survey for continuous improvement is very limited. The telephone survey has the benefit of cost effectively obtaining many opinions. It is quick, it can be friendly and it is easy. It provides a fair balance between the impersonal, mailed survey and the slow and expensive in-person survey.

Once the data have been gathered and tabulated, they need to be summarized. The survey result matrix shown in Figure 3.2 summarizes responses and frequencies. In this example, the numbers within the matrix represent the total responses to each question. This matrix

	1 – Poor	2	3 – Acceptable	4	5 – Excellent	Yes	No	Not sure	Comments
Team member response	6	25	32	23	9				
Scope clarification	0	22	28	16	7			27	
Team member coordination	11	57	25	1	6				
Interaction with clients	7	42	31	19	1				a.b.
Public agency coordination	2	23	43	8	2			22	
Project mgr. responsiveness	6	31	29	18	10			6	c.
Clarity of documents	12	32	30	21	5				d.e.
Construction phase service	15	25	45	7	3				
Postproject follow-up	52	11	16	18	1			2	f.
Billing structure	49	34	9	3	0				g.
Strength of market	4	24	26	26	8			12	
Is business improving?						67	18	15	
Any planned projects?						37	63	5	
Will you be a reference?						21	3	13	

Key   a. Several misunderstandings
b. Not enough communication
c. Pat and Chris don't return calls
d. Very comprehensive
e. Sometimes inconsistent
f. Slow response to call backs
g. Not enough detail (many comments)

Figure 3.2. Survey result matrix.

can help to organize information and assist in spotting trends. Matrix formats are limited only by one's imagination, and quality function deployment (QFD) may be used to translate client needs into an action plan outline. The more complex QFD approach will not be explored in this book as the improvement teams might use the raw data. The results shown in the figure may also be illustrated with a bar graph or a Pareto chart.

Staff Suggestions

Staff debriefing

Once or twice a year, gather the staff together. Have a facilitator ask the following:

1. What needs improvement in your work area?
2. Give an example of a recent improvement you have noticed.
3. What is still lacking in this example?
4. What else needs improvement in the company?

The statements should be asked one by one, and the facilitator should allow time for each item to be considered and discussed by small groups. This author suggests that approximately 15 minutes be given per statement. Then the answers may be called out and recorded on a flip chart. If a white board is used, someone present should also be capturing the answers on paper. This process will

- Demonstrate that the staff's opinions are valued.
- Provide suggestion and solution component ideas.

Both at the beginning of the session, and at the conclusion, it must be strongly emphasized that

- The ideas go into an idea bank of suggestions.
- Staff must not expect immediate results because the organization has committed to long-term improvements rather than short-term fixes.
- Staff members may volunteer for task teams and PITs once they have participated in TQM/CI training.

The problems encountered tend to be fairly typical, but it is important for the staff to be heard and express its opinions. Some suggestions may be quite thought provoking.

Suggestion box

A suggestion box is not essential, but if it used, it should be located at a central point, perhaps adjacent to the TQM/CI bulletin board. This will encourage employees to make frequent suggestions. Another idea is to regularly distribute 3" x 5" cards for ideas and ask that these be returned to the CI manager by a certain date.

Suggestions may be anonymous or signed. The majority of suggestions will be in the form of "Why don't we . . . ?" Others will be "fix-this, fix-that" types, essentially a list of symptoms, while some will point directly to chronic problems.

One-on-one interviews

Another format for gathering staff input is for a supervisory manager or the CI manager to interview known staff opinion leaders. Be sure to include gripe opinion leaders too. Sometimes they are a little reluctant because, by being interviewed, they can no longer claim that no one listens to them. This points to the pitfall of game playing. A persuasive gripe opinion leader may know that he or she can gain the sympathy of that particular manager on an issue that has political undertones. These include personal rivalries, empire building, and pet peeves. Game playing includes the groupthink ploy: "The whole department wants . . . ." with the implication that all department members are solidly behind the gripe opinion leader. It is best to listen without commitment, then gather more information and opinions to share with the steering committee. Getting others' opinions can also persuade the gripe opinion leaders to join an improvement team. The structure given in chapter 4 will get these individuals working for positive results.

Self-audit

A form for this useful tool is illustrated in Figure 3.3. This can be circulated to all process stakeholders. In manufacturing organizations trained auditors may carry out audits. In professional service organizations, a 10-minute, stand-up department meeting will explain the form and ask for cooperation. Give a deadline. Those who choose to complete and hand in the audit get to be a part of future solutions. Those who decline lose gripe justification power, because their opinions were requested. There will always be some who are too busy doing the work to participate.

A very valuable and little used self-audit tool is the project debrief. Broken down into its most basic form it asks three questions.

1. What worked?

2. What did not work?

3. How can we improve next time?

	Input observations	
Working well	Needs attention	Recommendations
	Process observations	
Working well	Needs attention	Recommendations
	Output observations	
Working well	Needs attention	Recommendations
What motivates your group?	What demotivates your group?	Recommendations

Name _____   Department _____
Date _____   Due date _____

Figure 3.3. Staff self-audit.

This should be asked of all team members, both internal and external. The project debrief usually yields outstanding information.

Assessing and responding to suggestions

Many organizations measure success by the average number of suggestions per employee. This is not applicable for professional service firms. Overemphasis on how many suggestions are lodged sets up excessive, unrealistic expectations. This can lead to premature TQM/CI failure when the majority of expectations are not met. Staff members must be trained to realize that the symptoms that they notice will be examined to improve systems, and will not be tackled piecemeal. They must know how improvement teams use ideas. This can be illustrated very simply with Figure 3.4, showing that some ideas will be tackled promptly, and others will be held for later consideration. Staff must also be aware that suggestions tackled individually, rather than in the context of structures and systems, can be dangerous.

Suggestions should be acknowledged within 72 hours. For example, send a note such as, "Your suggestion was received and has been placed in our idea bank." The concept of the idea bank will be fully explored in chapter 4. Another way to acknowledge suggestions is by posting them on the TQM/CI bulletin board.

Steering Committee

Steering committees may go through their own brainstorming process to identify issues that they wish to assign to teams. One of the great benefits of this is the leadership's involvement and commitment to the continuous improvement process. This dramatically improves the chance of TQM/CI firmly taking root.

Task Team

A task team might list suggestions or review and categorize the ideas contained in the idea bank. Task team members may also present their own ideas to the group. An example might be a project manager who wants to find a better way to interact with another division, or a secretary who wants a work prioritization system.

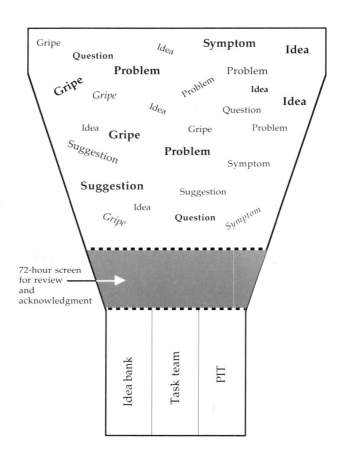

Figure 3.4. Suggestion processing.

Brainstorming is a great way to solicit these concerns. Once suggestions have been gathered, they must be prioritized in order to select a real and chronic problem with a solution that will provide the biggest bang for the buck.

Caution: Everybody wants their pet issue looked at first. Don't get derailed by debate. If this occurs, use one of the decision tools in Part III to work toward consensus.

2.1 Process Improvement Teams and Task Teams

2.1.1 The Crisis Team

The crisis team reacts to emerging firefighting and damage control issues. It is called together in haste to get an out-of-control situation back into a stable state. Firefighters called in to tackle a blaze don't stand around discussing how to improve the layout of the burning warehouse. They are there to put out the fire. Preventing future fires and actually improving the layout of the warehouse is the job of the process improvement team (PIT). The PIT, however, will want a full forensic report from the crisis team after the fire has been put out. A major early goal of TQM/CI would be to eliminate the need for crisis teams.

2.1.2 The Process Improvement Team

This team proactively tackles issues that require investigation. It might be involved in any improvement issue including project management systems, planning, operations and marketing, training, and partnering. While the team is never involved in specific external clients' projects, it may use the feedback from projects and project managers as data for improvements. PITs work to eliminate waste and to refine value-added activities. They may examine structure, systems, and processes, from the macro, right down to the smallest micro level. The focus is on finding out why something is not working, and then finding a better way to make it work. Thus, PITs

- Eliminate waste in structures, systems, and processes.
- Refine structures, systems, and processes.
- Find a better way to use resources.
- Assess why things go wrong.
- Devise better ways to communicate and coordinate.
- Investigate and improve links.

Task teams often assist PITs with data-gathering or implementing solutions.

Typical PIT tasks are as follows:

1. Find a better way to use the firm's communication systems.
2. Assess why field investigations miss data.

3. Improve construction administration.
4. Improve competitiveness.
5. Find better ways to gather data.
6. Find better ways to link staff training to job demands.
7. Improve project management processes.
8. Improve deficiencies in the minor item purchases program.
9. Investigate a better productivity incentive system.
10. Investigate the link between productivity and office layout.
11. Improve information access.
12. Find a better way to utilize office talent.

A PIT flowchart is shown in chapter 4.

2.1.3 The Task Team

A task team often works in parallel with the PITs. Their modi operandi are very similar, but a task team can provide very quick TQM/CI returns. Task teams tackle issues that require investigation or decisions, including project processes, operations, and marketing. Task teams work at the process level, never getting involved in structure and system issues. They generally do not get involved with nonvalue-added problems; they are more involved with value-adding refinements and improvements. Most of their nonproject tasks will be related to continuous improvement, such as

- Developing checklists, forms, standards, and guidelines
- Research and testing
- Policy making and the creation of new programs
- Data gathering

Because task team issues may be resolved in as little as 30 minutes, it is often impractical to have the steering committee notified before every activity. The CI manager, the representative of the steering committee, must, however, be in the information loop, either directly or via a department head or group leader. Why must the steering committee be in the loop? Not to control or direct, but to facilitate and coalesce the team's improvements with others.

Caution: In the introductory stages of TQM/CI, a group lacking full understanding of the differences between a task team and a PIT issue may attempt to force a process improvement through in 30 minutes. This will be spotted by having the steering committee in the loop. The CI manager can then ask the group to form a PIT to rework its issue. But first the CI manager should find the root cause of the TQM/CI misunderstanding that led to this rework. Perhaps the training was unclear, perhaps the team members did not listen or forgot, or perhaps it was a power play.

Note 1: Task teams are very similar to crisis teams in that they respond to expressed needs, but they are not in the crisis mode.

Note 2: Task teams are very similar to PITs in that they follow the processes of the PITs, but they do not delve as deeply into issues.

Typical task team continuous improvement tasks are as follows:

1. Research equipment such as phone systems.

2. Develop a field conditions checklist.

3. Develop a constructability checklist.

4. Benchmark the competition.

5. Gather data for a PIT.

6. Develop a staff training tracking form.

7. Write a new chapter in the project management manual.

8. Develop guidelines to allow minor item purchases with no management permission required.

9. Create a new recognition program.

10. Design a more efficient conference room.

11. Develop library indexing standards.

12. Write job descriptions.

Note 3: Many readers will have already participated in teams solving these kinds of issues. The task team process has the distinction of making problem solving focused, efficient, and coordinated.

Note 4: Readers will find that a line-by-line comparison of this task list with the PIT task list provides immediate clues to the differences between PITs and task teams.

Note 5: A task team flowchart is shown in chapter 4.

Note 6: As a point of interest, this author has noticed that TQM do-it-yourselfers tend to focus only on task team issues while believing that they are practicing full-scale TQM.

2.1.4 Summary of the Distinction Between Task Teams and PITs

Task teams work at the detailed process level, often on value-added refinements and improvements. PITs work at all levels—structural, system, and process. They work on both waste elimination and on value-adding refinements and improvements.

Another way to illustrate the differences between the teams is to consider the ways to defend a country from a missile attack.

Level 1: Antimissile missiles destroy attacking missiles in-flight. This is the crisis team.

Level 2: Destroy the enemy's mounted missiles on the ground. This is the task or crisis team working on crisis intervention.

Level 3: Destroy the missiles before they are mounted for launch. This is the task team working on crisis prevention.

Level 4: Destroy the enemy's missile factories. This is the PIT eliminating nonvalue-added activities.

Level 5: Destroy the raw materials that make missiles. This is the PIT working on continuous improvement.

Level 6: Eliminate the origin of the anger between nations. This is the PIT eliminating the ultimate root cause.

2.2 Team Leadership

2.2.1 Team Facilitator

A team leader can be a volunteer who steps up and announces that he or she wants to facilitate a team. An interested person, however, may wait to be asked by the CI manager: "Robin, I'd like you to consider facilitating the interdepartmental communication task team," or "Kerry, you would be great heading up the computer network PIT." It must be made clear that the person may refuse with no fear of repercussions. So the CI manager should add; "Think about it; it will demand a special effort, so let me know tomorrow." This gives the person the opportunity to think it through, and relieves him or her of the pressure to give the boss a reluctant yes. Conclude the request with something like, "By the way, if you feel that you can't give it your time now, you could just be part of the team." This is the final relaxant. The person can now say no, avoid disappointing the boss, and still feel that he or she is contributing. The team facilitator's characteristics will be similar to those of the CI manager.

- Is very enthusiastic about continuous improvement
- Has perseverance
- Has the full trust of the CI manager
- Is well respected by peers and staff
- Can commit the time needed each month to TQM/CI
- Is knowledgeable about TQM/CI
- Is comfortable in front of a group and able to maintain the structured team process detailed in chapter 4
- Is a team player
- Is comfortable being an expeditor
- Is forceful but not demanding in reminding people to carry out their commitments
- Is not put off by paperwork
- Is reliable—can consistently get the job done

It will be difficult to find anyone who has every quality. Allied to the implementation procedures in the next chapter, these characteristics will lead to success. Facilitators could be senior managers, project managers, or staff members. TQM/CI is for everybody, not just the elite.

Caution 1: A potential facilitator's enthusiasm should not stem from a power or ego trip, or from having great ideas for solutions. The danger is the temptation of a charismatic individual ramrodding those great ideas down the throat of the team. The CI manager can help to keep the team focused and moving through the process if this tendency is noticed.

Caution 2: The term *leader* may imply a dimunition of the role of the team members, while a *facilitator* will elicit information from all participants in a free exchange of ideas, within the bounds of the steps outlined in chapter 4. The team facilitator will, however, wear both a facilitation and a leadership hat. The facilitation hat should be worn when working with the group, even though the characteristics listed are leadership characteristics. But to motivate the group and to keep it on track, the leadership hat may be put on from time to time. For the remainder of this book the term *team facilitator* will be used in reference to leading improvement teams.

2.2.2 Team Administrator

The administrator plays a vital role in the team process. The administrator's characteristics might include the following:

- Is very enthusiastic about continuous improvement
- Is well respected by the team members
- Works especially well with the team facilitator
- Is a team player
- Is not put off by paperwork
- Is reliable; can consistently get the job done
- Keeps accurate, comprehensive, and neat notes

In some cases the team facilitator writes the minutes and the agenda. In other cases the administrator assumes this task, assisted by the team facilitator.

The main role of the administrator is to be an equal team member, while also recording idea bank suggestions as they are expressed, and while sketching out flowcharts, diagrams, and lists as they are developed by the team. These may subsequently be drawn up neatly, or word processed by the support staff for the team to review at or before the next meeting.

The administrator's tasks require thoroughness and extra concentration, and can be a burden for a team member. While most teams work well with an administrator, some teams have a support staff member present to keep notes and to assist the administrator. Still others have two administrators who support each other. Firms may wish to recognize the special efforts of their administrators with a small token such as buying them lunch on the days that the team meets.

Backups for both the team facilitator and the administrator could be identified at the kickoff meeting. The backups will cover for the rare occasions when one of these key players is absent. Often the CI manager will be the backup, and if both the team facilitator and the administrator are absent, the meeting is postponed.

2.3 Team Membership

There is not much point in further training people who would prefer not to become involved in a team because they are unsure, because they lack time or an interest, or because they have issues in their personal lives that need to be resolved before they can commit their energies. That is why the best time to allow future team members to emerge is right after the training sessions. They now know what is expected and have had a chance to think and talk about it. Many will want to get involved.

Insisting that people serve on a team is counterproductive because team members who are not really interested will be disruptive. They may need to devote some personal time, and impatience will readily surface in an unwilling participant.

It is also wise to ask more people than might be needed on a team. Invariably a few people will drop out after one or two meetings. Perhaps they came because they were curious or just wanted to see who else was there. The net result after these dropouts is that a core group of dedicated team members will emerge, participating on a functionally sized team of 3–12 members.

2.4 Stakeholder Involvement

What about the circumstance when everybody wants to be on a team at the same time? This is a judgment call. It is great to have the enthusiasm, but this is usually impractical and costly. Yet if someone is turned down, his or her excitement may turn into apathy. Emphasize that continuous improvement will go on forever and that everyone will soon get to be on a team. Rotating people into the steering committee every 6–12 months also helps. Then start with both PITs and task teams to gain early successes. As noted, task teams usually come up with results quickly, and so people can be rotated into these teams quite frequently. Stakeholders will also be kept informed of team progress through the bulletin board, and they may be involved in taking baseline measurements during the trial solution phase and the final solution implementation. Participation will foster belief in the process and keep enthusiasm going until everyone has an opportunity to serve on, or lead a team.

2.5 Training

2.5.1 Staff Training

The entire staff should be exposed to introductory TQM/CI training, which includes the following:

- What it is
- What it is not
- The benefits to the staff and to the organization
- How it works
- How it will work in the organization

Chapters 1–2 of this book can be used to develop an outline for this presentation. For those staff members who enjoy reading, copies of this book, plus some of the books listed in the appendix, might also be helpful. Encourage the acquisition of TQM knowledge.

The introductory session need not be longer than four to six hours, and might conclude with a staff debriefing brainstorming session to solicit improvement suggestions. This might be led by the CI manager, possibly supported by the consultant.

Many consultants advocate days and even weeks of training. It is this author's experience that this is not necessary in professional service firms where teamwork is the norm. This is especially true when using the structures described in this book.

2.5.2 Follow-Up Workshop

A follow-up workshop covering the implementation procedures in the Shearer model should occur after the initial training. Here staff will have the opportunity to discuss TQM/CI in more detail, have its questions answered, express any concerns about the process, and learn more about the benefits. This session could be led by the consultant, supported by the CI manager.

2.5.3 PIT and Task Team Training

The team members attend a detailed session on the nuts and bolts of the PIT and task team processes. Part II can be used as the basis of this training. Some of the commonly used tools in Part III should also be introduced.

2.5.4 Team Facilitator Training

Team facilitators and the CI manager must have a thorough knowledge of the process and the tools. They should be able to recognize the pitfalls, know which tool is most appropriate in which situation, and know how the tools interact. Facilitation skills will also prove to be a valuable acquisition. The team facilitators and CI manager should be read widely on the subject. A list of recommended books is found in the appendix.

2.5.5 Other Introductory Options

Option 1: As noted, the executive leadership can also be the steering committee. This is especially appropriate for small firms.

Option 2: The steering committee can be the first PIT or task team, with the CI manager as the team facilitator.

Option 3: The first PIT continues its training while solving a real live issue. In other words, the PIT is coached in the process by its consultant while participating in a weekly meeting. In this case, the consultant is the team facilitator. Several weeks later, after the process is complete, the consultant provides follow-up training to describe the tools and techniques that were not part of the first PIT's activities. Subsequent PITs and task teams can be similarly coached, solving real problems, and getting more comfortable with the process.

Option 4: The PIT described in Option 3 is comprised of future team leaders. They learn on the job how to run their own PITs and task teams. When they later facilitate their own teams, the consultant becomes an on-call advisor.

Option 5: The process described in Options 3 and 4 could take place at an intensive three-to-five-day session. Most of the PIT process can be followed, except perhaps the measurement aspects. This can follow directly on the heels of the intensive session.

Caution 1: Avoid a large time lapse between training and the kickoff of TQM/CI. Generally three weeks is the maximum interval to maintain a high level of enthusiasm and credibility.

Caution 2: The sequencing options are given because every organization is different. Trying to beat a specific process to fit a culture may not work. One size does not fit all. The precise content of the training, the ground rules, the interaction between teams and the steering committee, the use of consultants, and the sequence of the activities are all subject to fine-tuning by each organization.

CHAPTER 4

How Process Improvement Teams Work

Overview

The most frequently asked TQM question is "How do we actually implement TQM?" This chapter covers all of the steps required to implement continuous improvement by following the Shearer model.

The beauty of these steps lies in their ability to keep progress flowing, to keep all parties informed and in the loop, and to avoid emotions and the minefield of pitfalls that can destroy teams. The PIT's steps are shown in Figure 4.1 and the task team steps are shown in Figure 4.2. Because the task team process is essentially a truncated version of the PIT, the focus of this chapter will be on the PIT.

The tools that are most applicable are listed at the beginning of each step. These tools will be described in detail in Part III.

Step 1: Chronic Problem Selection

Tools: **Brainstorming**
             Priority voting
             Benefit/LOE analysis
             Force field analysis

Item 1.6.2 in chapter 3 discussed ways to elicit suggestions for improvements. If the problem has already been identified and given to the PIT by the steering committee, then readers may skip this step and go directly to step 2.

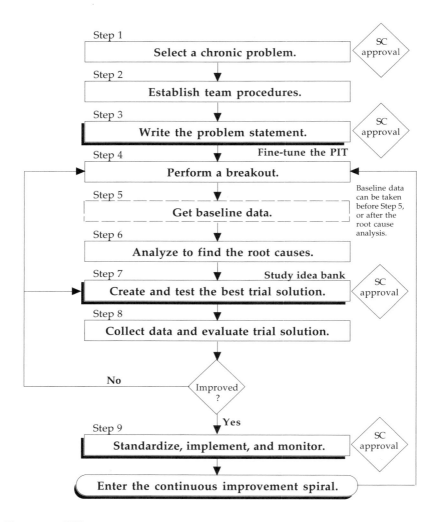

Figure 4.1. PIT steps.

Once a list of issues has been generated and categorized, the following problem selection guide may be useful for choosing an issue.

1. Are these issues all chronic?

2. Which issue needs a solution most urgently?

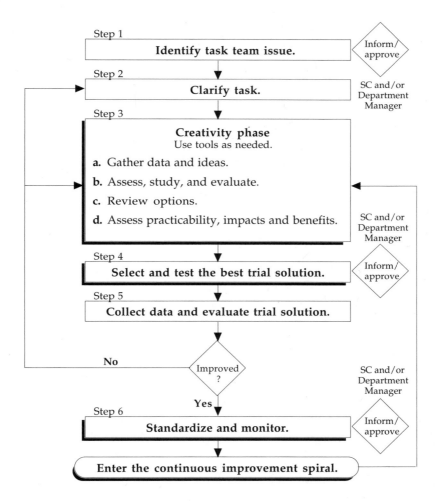

Figure 4.2. Task team steps.

3. What is the likely return on investment (ROI)?

4. Is this a PIT or a task team issue?

5. Is there any other team tackling this problem?

Note 1: If the most urgent issue is really a crisis, give it to a crisis team. Later on a PIT can examine why the fire started.

Note 2: ROI does not have to relate directly to money. It can relate to any one of the payoff benefits shown in Figure 1.1.

When TQM/CI is being introduced, there are five additional considerations.

6. Is there a substantial chance that the team will be successful?

7. Can the PIT issue be resolved within a few months?

8. Can the task team issue be resolved within a few weeks?

9. Will the return on investment tie into a demonstrable financial advantage?

10. Will a successful result in this topic help to convince the doubters about the power of TQM/CI?

Note 3: The final two questions arise because the doubters are wondering, "Does it work?" and "What is all this TQM stuff costing us?"

Tough start-up issues are

- Corporate restructuring problems
- Why the strategic plan is not working
- Barriers to international expansion
- Overhauling the entire management process

Easy start-up issues may be

- Eliminating waste in processes
- Work flow simplification
- Improved time sheet processing
- Improved scheduling and work planning
- Improved project management tracking
- A new master vacation planning process
- A better marketing hit rate
- Developing a proposal tracking form
- Eliminating billing errors
- Improved financial reporting process
- Improved computer scheduling
- Eliminating project stops and starts due to internal delays

It is left up to the reader to separate the task team and PIT issues on this list. The steering committee will be in the loop to approve the choice of a problem *before* it is turned over to a task team or a PIT.

Step 2: Team Procedures

Compose the Process Improvement Team

Process improvement teams may be intradepartmental, interdepartmental, cross-disciplinary, or even interorganizational. It all depends on the issue being solved. If the chronic problem was identified by a task team, as mentioned in step 1, that task team may become the PIT. In addition to possible restructuring, the team may invite guests from time to time to ensure that it gets needed input from different stakeholders.

At first, the 3–12-member PIT will be an all-volunteer group. Later, serving on a PIT once or twice a year will become a normal part of the job and anyone who has not participated in an improvement team will be the odd person out.

PIT Ground Rules and Charter

The first meeting of the PIT provides an opportunity to set up ground rules. Team members, working within the boundaries established by the steering committee, decide the following:

1. Which day of the week they will meet

2. What time of the day is best to meet

3. The length of their meetings

    Naturally there may be debate on these issues and the consensus-building tools described in chapter 6 could be used.

4. It must be understood that meetings will only be rescheduled under special circumstances.

    Why the inflexibility? Invariably, each week some members will be out of town, sick, at other meetings, or working on a deadline. They may make less effort to attend if they know that the meeting will be postponed. On the other hand, if they know that it will proceed without them, they will have more incentive to attend. The only reason to postpone a meeting is if the team facilitator or more than 50 percent of the team is unavailable. If at all possible, and if the steering committee agrees, PITs should meet weekly.

5. It must be agreed that meetings will start promptly and that the meeting will only go overtime if

   a. The majority wants to stay

   b. Those who have other commitments at that time may leave

   c. The energy levels are high

   d. The team is in the midst of a process

   e. Resolution of an issue is close at hand

   f. The steering committee accepts occasional overruns into billable work hours

6. Holding phone calls five minutes before the meeting starts is a good idea.

7. The team facilitator and administrator must ensure that there are sufficient copies of handouts for everyone.

At the end of the first PIT meeting, a representation charter and an interaction charter summarizing the group's agreements should be created and signed by all PIT members. This is a commitment to working together.

A representation charter

- All staff members involved in the work process are PIT stakeholders.
- PIT members represent these stakeholders.
- The PIT will keep stakeholders informed about its progress.
- The PIT will solicit feedback from the stakeholders.

A team interaction charter

- To attend team meetings regularly
- To arrive on time
- To get briefed on meetings missed, before the next meeting starts
- To focus on process improvement, not on fixing people
- To stick to the PIT steps and keep moving toward a solution

- To help the facilitator keep on track
- To be open-minded
- To listen to each other
- To put aside differences and work together

Each team member should get a copy of the signed charter page. A copy may be posted on the bulletin board. Some teams blow it up to poster size and also post it on a wall during each team meeting.

Clarify Team Roles

The group can meet and vote on a team facilitator, but as discussed in chapter 3, it is best if this person is identified before the first meeting. Then the facilitator can ask an individual to volunteer as the administrator before the first meeting, or can lay the assignment on the table at the first meeting. Here too, a premeeting selection is recommended. The reasons for both of these recommendations lie in the quest to eliminate fear in the workplace. The early assignment avoids a pressure cooker situation where no one wants to volunteer in front of the others. Whenever someone is volunteered by a group, it is tough to refuse in front of everyone. This usually leads to a reluctant yes, followed by poor performance. Therefore, no-pressure, one-on-one acceptances are best. While not impossible, it is onerous and inefficient for the team facilitator to also be the administrator.

It may be advisable to have a guide for the first few team cycles. Some large organizations have full-time staff who do nothing but assist improvement teams. Small organizations cannot afford that luxury. There are a few other options.

1. Ask a TQM consultant to fill this role for the first few continuous improvement cycles, and then again upon the request of any team facilitator. This would follow introductory option 3, in Section 2.5.5 of chapter 3.

2. Have an experienced facilitator sit in on a colleague's team.

3. Ask the CI manager to coach.

After one to three years, the need for a guide will fall away because the PIT process will become second nature to the teams.

Two final facilitation tips are the following:

- Facilitators encourage and elicit full team participation.
- As orchestrators, pure facilitators add no voice to the process; however, the professional service PIT and task team facilitator may have a voice equal to, but not greater than other team members.

Agree to Stay with the PIT Process

There are several major pitfalls that await the unwary. Four of these traps are described.

1. **Impatience** People in professional service organizations tend to be action oriented, are ready with quick answers, and are exceptionally time conscious. This combination results in the three desperate *d*'s: dive-in, deal with it, and depart. This is curbed by following the step-by-step PIT process.

2. **Show and tell** "You won't believe what happened on my project," or "I know we want to talk about quality, but I have to first let you know what is going on in my department." The facilitator can give a nonverbal time-out signal; distribute a handout while verbally reviewing it; write the first agenda item on a flip chart and hold up a palm until the storyteller ceases; or just say, " I'm going to have to ask you to hold your story for the end so we can keep on schedule." Regular, on-time starts also establish a we-are-here-to-work ethic.

3. **Politics** "Well, if George is on the team, I'm not going to say much because he always puts me down;" or "Mary has no right to be here so I'm going to cut her off." The interaction charter appeals to professionalism and usually eliminates this problem.

4. **Playing catch-up** Another common pitfall are team members who miss a meeting and expect a full review of what they missed at the start of the next meeting. Worse, they start questioning decisions that were made in their absence. The PIT cannot afford this disruption. If passengers get distracted on a train, they cannot expect the train to back up so that they can see the scenery. The train may never reach its destination if every passenger had this right. Any team member missing a meeting has the responsibility to talk to the facilitator, or other team members, before the next

meeting to find out what transpired and why. If the absentees object to decisions that were taken, they have the consolation that no solutions will be final until implemented and tested on a trial basis.

Note: Any team member who misses a meeting, and then brings up issues already discussed, is asked by the facilitator to phrase those issues as suggestions. These suggestions are, without further discussion, placed into the idea bank, and the meeting then proceeds.

The Golden Rule for Improvement Team Progress

Success lies in staying with the structured step-by-step process. With this golden rule, team members will be less apt to rush into quick solutions, debate incessantly, or allow negative thinking to dominate.

Prepublish an Agenda

The prepublished meeting agenda should not be elaborate. It need only remind members where, when, and what will occur. Bullet formats are best as they are easy to read and compose. Distribute the agenda a day early. Figure 4.3 is an example of an agenda format.

Distribute Minutes

To keep it simple and to minimize paperwork, the form shown in Figure 4.3 also contains the minutes. Detailed notes, such as the reasoning behind decisions, can be written on a second sheet, using headers and bullets to keep it tidy and structured. When lodged in a three-ring binder, the minutes become a summary record of activities and decisions. This format can be used equally well by PITs and task teams. Its use is simplified by completing the top box with all the names just once, and photocopying that page for each meeting. Simply check off who attends each meeting in the small boxes.

Caution: If the ideas, rationale, and steps that led to decisions are not recorded in detail, the team members may struggle the next week to rethink where they were, what was decided, and why. Valuable time can be lost in recreating trains of thought. In addition, if the steering committee asks months later why a particular solution was discarded, the team can produce a documented answer and be taken seriously.

Team agenda and minutes

Problem statement _____

Team facilitator _____ ❏ Administrator _____ ❏

Team members   Date started _____

_____ ❏   _____ ❏
_____ ❏   _____ ❏
_____ ❏   _____ ❏
_____ ❏   _____ ❏
_____ ❏   _____ ❏
              ❏

Team meeting   Date _____

Between meeting tasks   By

_____
_____
_____

Agenda for this meeting

_____
_____
_____

Activities today and reasons for decisions

_____
_____
_____
_____
_____
_____
_____
_____

Tools used_____

Distribution   Steering committee ❏   ❏   ❏

Trial solution ❏   Verified solution ❏

_____
_____
_____

SC approval _____ Trial implement _____ Full implement _____

Figure 4.3. Team agenda and minutes.

Relying on memory is not good enough. As mentioned in chapter 3, the agenda and minutes may be produced by the team facilitator or the administrator, sometimes working in tandem.

Progress Tracking

The simple tracking sheet template shown in Figure 4.4 can be posted on the bulletin board to keep staff appraised of what the teams are doing and how they are progressing. This can also foster partnering in an organization. The headers shown in the figure reflect the PIT process. As shown, the tracking sheet can also depict task team progress. In this case, nonapplicable steps will just be leapfrogged on the sheet.

Conflict Resolution

Teams benefit from give and take. The focus must be on what is good for the office, not on pet opinions and personal agendas. Sticking to the PIT steps will keep the team moving ahead and progressing.

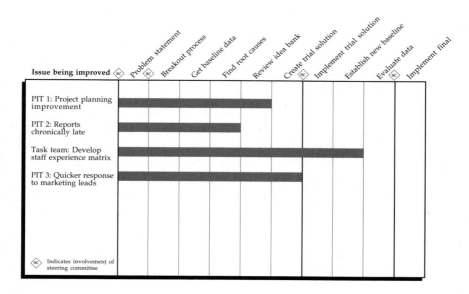

Figure 4.4. Team progress tracking.

Pitfall: If a team is not progressing week after week, call a time-out. The CI manager may sit in for a meeting to help identify the roadblock. The roadblock may be a facilitator who allows discussion to wander away from the steps, or one or more team members who are disruptive. Having the entire team discuss progress, perhaps even using one of the PIT tools to identify the roadblock, will keep this troubleshooting meeting objective and professional.

Step 3: Problem Statement
Tools: Problem statement worksheet
**   Idea bank**

Professional service firm PIT volunteers are generally eager and motivated to seek quick solutions. In many cases a leap of faith toward an obvious solution is an illusion and a continuous improvement cardinal sin.

The problem statement will focus the team, reshape a problem, and provide the framework for the PIT's future work. Without a problem statement the team may

- Open the wrong door.
- Open the easy door rather than the tough door.
- Open the door to the area where the fire is burning, rather than the door to the area where the fire keeps starting. Treating the symptom does little good if the underlying root cause is not identified and cured.

Even if the root cause is identified and cured, the cure might be worse than the original complaint. This can occur when the side effects on the rest of the system, or on other interdependent systems, have not been examined. For example, a production solution may impose very expensive burdens on project management.

The following two techniques will assist in narrowing the focus to a workable problem statement. Chapter 6 shows a problem statement worksheet.

The Forensic Approach

When forensic evidence is prepared for a case in court, it may be factual and based on site observations, records, and photographs. It may also be backed up by laboratory science. Later, opinions will be sought and conclusions will be drawn, but it all starts with the evidence. This is the correct approach for the PIT—seeking and dealing with factual evidence.

The Bull's-Eye Technique

The following dialog shows how a project management problem might be developed into a problem statement.

1. Question: What's our main project management problem?

   Reply: We are late in delivering projects.

2. Question: Is this a historic or a recent symptom?

   Reply: It has worsened a lot in the past two years.

3. Question: In the past two years on all types of projects?

   Reply: It occurs mostly in commercial work.

4. Question: Is it evident in commercial work in all our offices?

   Reply: It is less frequent in Denver.

5. Question: What is the range of the delays in these offices?

   Reply: In the past quarter it varied from a day to three weeks with a median of six days.

This author has named this the bull's-eye technique (BET), since it is a way to probe answers and narrow down broad issues until the target is identified. In the example, the problem statement may now be expressed as "Identify why, in the past two years, we have become late in delivering commercial projects in all offices except Denver. The median in the last three months is six days late." The BET may also be used at other times when probing and issue focusing are important.

Fine-Tune the PIT

The completed problem statement can define the issue to be tackled, such that it may be necessary to fine-tune the PIT membership. For example, someone from accounting should be involved when a project management PIT discusses tracking reports; someone from project management should be involved when a production PIT discusses work process; and someone from word processing should be involved when an operations PIT reviews reports.

These people are not told to participate, they are asked to participate. A key result is buy-in. A superb breakthrough may not be readily accepted if the system opinion leaders reject the PIT ideas. Having the leaders involved promotes a sense of ownership in the solutions.

Once the problem is clarified, the steering committee must be notified in order to give the final go-ahead to proceed. This assures the PIT that it is on the right track.

The Idea Bank

At the end of step 3, the idea bank opens up for business, and it stays open for deposits during steps 4, 5, and 6. This author created the idea bank concept because the management and staff of professional service firms are professional problem solvers, and coming up with solutions is natural for them. Discussing solution ideas during the PIT steps will sidetrack, slow down, or even derail the process. Yet the flow of solution ideas should not be discouraged. PIT members understand that their ideas will be immediately deposited in the idea bank and not discussed, debated, or examined until step 7 when idea bank withdrawals are made.

Step 4: Breakouts
Tools: Structure flowchart
System flowchart
IPO audit
Idea bank

Process breakouts can be performed on three levels. Each takes the problem apart to examine its component pieces. This step should precede any attempt at analysis.

The Golden Rule for Breakouts
In problem solving, depict the way the structure, system, or process currently works, not the way it should work.

Level 1: Structural Level Breakouts

These are the least detailed and most global of breakouts. The structural flowchart examines system linkages and information flow using an organizational tree format. The examination can be carried out on a corporate, divisional, branch, or departmental level. It may also be used as a tool to examine information links with other entities such as contractors, subcontractors, public agencies, architects, engineers, scientists, accountants' offices, lawyers' offices, and clients.

Level 2: System Level Breakouts

The system flowchart depicts the way that processes or steps are linked together to form a system. A small structure, such as a single department, may comprise only a few systems, while a large structure may comprise numerous systems interfaced in a complex network.

Once the work flow is mapped out, teams and stakeholders are often surprised at the complexity of their own systems and the amount of waste and rework identified.

Level 3: Process Level Breakouts

As described in Part I, everyone in a professional service organization has two roles—as a client and as a service provider. Most staff members are multiple clients and providers in numerous processes. It is important to understand each role in terms of input, process, and output. These concepts are keystones to both system and process breakouts.

Input. Those providing inputs are responsible for the quality of their inputs. Using preestablished QA input checklists, they perform a QR self-check of their input before they hand it over. This means that they treat the work processor as a client at the transfer point.

Process. Those involved in doing the work perform a QR self-check for completeness, level of detail, and accuracy of their work. This review will be based on the input requirements, the scope of work, output expectations, and on the preestablished QA checklist for that work process.

Output. Those receiving information are the clients of the work processors. The clients are responsible for verifying that the output is in accordance with a preestablished QA output checklist.

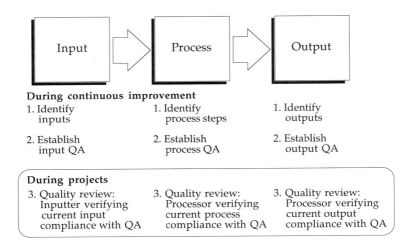

Figure 4.5. The basic building blocks of TQM/CI.

QA guidelines keep standards uniformly high. Self-checking one's own work to verify compliance with the checklists results in a sense of pride and ownership in the process. Any subsequent QC is usually just a formality, verifying the excellence of the work.

Figure 4.5 depicts the input-process-output (IPO) model, the basic building block of TQM/CI. Used in conjunction with the IPO audit tool, this model guides the IPO process breakout and the subsequent creation of QA standards. Once the standards exist, the bottom of Figure 4.5 describes the way that the QRs and the QA standards interlink on actual work projects.

Outputs

For both process breakouts and systems breakouts it is usually best to start with the end product, the output. Outputs might include the following:

- Reports
- Estimates, drawings, calculations, and specifications
- Market research projections
- Workload projections

- Manuals
- Spreadsheets
- Paychecks
- Invoices
- Proposals
- Presentations
- Letters
- Strategic plans
- Image

The following questions may stimulate ideas for the idea bank.

- What do the current outputs look like?
- When are they delivered?
- How are they delivered?
- Who delivers them?
- Are there QA guidelines for the outputs?
- Is the processor currently self-checking outputs, and if so, to what documented standard?

Inputs

Next focus on the inputs, which may include the following:

- Data for reports
- Information regarding drawings, estimates, calculations, and specifications
- Financial data
- Workload information
- Market research data
- Scope of work
- Budget information
- Schedule information
- Project roles and responsibilities

- Client/team information
- Client expectations
- Regulations, specifications, codes, and standard practices

The following questions may stimulate ideas for the idea bank.

- What inputs are required to produce the output?
- When are the inputs given?
- Who gives them to the processor?
- In what form are they given?
- What information should be omitted?
- Are there QA guidelines for the inputs?
- Is the inputter currently self-checking inputs to ensure QA compliance, before giving them to the processor?

Processes

Each process must be repeatable so that the output quality is predictable. The following questions may be asked about the process.

- How does the process start?
- What are the steps and sequences?
- What concludes the process?
- Who is involved?
- What are the governing standards and controls?
- Do these controls help or hinder the process?
- How are clarifications handled?
- Is information readily accessible?
- What are the information gaps?
- What checklists are used?
- What documentation is required?
- What are the variables?
- What bottlenecks are encountered?
- What are the rework loops and how frequently do they occur?

- Are there QA guidelines for the process steps?
- Is the processor currently self-checking the process steps to ensure QA compliance?

Use the IPO audit to perform a process level breakout. This tool, shown in chapter 6, is used to establish these input, process, and output needs and expectations. It can lead to the creation of the QA guidelines and checklists. The staff self-audit form, Figure 3.3, is a simpler version that may also be useful in this context.

Systems Thinking

As Figure 1.10 illustrated linear interactions as a chain and professional service interactions as a network, so must the IPO building blocks, shown in Figure 4.5, be modified away from linear thinking and toward systems thinking. For example, in discussing a revision with a client, the average project manager will ensure that the information is clear and unambiguous, and will then look at the schedule impact, the code impact, and what needs to be done to incorporate the revision. The systems thinker does this too, but the IPO model is adjusted as shown in Figure 4.6 to also consider the impact on work completed, peripheral impacts on subconsultant work, contractors and subcontractors, permits, and scope expectations. Contractual agreements,

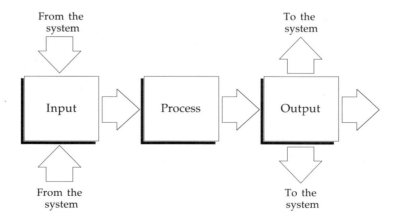

Figure 4.6. TQM/CI systems thinking.

liability, and downstream effects must also be reviewed, as must the impact on staff morale regarding rework and possible overtime. Outputs, too, are rarely linear as they must be transmitted to numerous interested parties. In summary, professional services demand systems thinking both on global and micro levels.

Sequencing

Some PITs commence a cause-and-effect diagram without examining any breakouts. This may cause them to miss information flow and rework clues. Also, the ideas developed, expressed, and stored in the idea bank during the breakouts are very valuable.

Some PITs will establish a baseline measurement before the breakout. This might help in focusing on the problem statement. In this author's experience, in most cases, the breakout reveals new information that may influence the choice of the baseline measurements.

Breakout Summary

It is hard to fix or improve any object or system until it has been taken apart to enable one to examine the components. The purpose of gathering this information is to look at the parts, clarify roles and responsibilities, verify quality standards and controls, examine interfaces, and expose bottlenecks. The breakout can also help to pinpoint where to measure. Ultimately the breakout leads to solutions that will eliminate waste, prevent nonconformance, and add value.

Incidentally, working out the relationships between service providers and internal clients using the IPO audit is an effective example of team building in action. Those linked to each other by processes become part of a value chain that bonds their activities.

Step 5: Baseline Data

Tools: **Check sheet**
Pareto chart
Scatter diagram
Control charts
Idea bank

Many people believe that professional services are hard to measure because the client usually gets a one-off product such as a drawing, a report, an audit, artwork, a plan, a legal defense, or a specification. In reality, there is actually very little that cannot be measured. The product may be a one-off, but the processes used to create that product are the same. This opens up the possibility of being able to measure professional services.

Why Obtain Baseline Data?

Many teams can't be bothered to measure. They rush off to test their theories, convinced that they intuitively know what is currently happening, and positive that they can improve it. They might even be right, but how will they be able to convince the steering committee, and those not yet converted to TQM/CI, that their solution is really better than the current way of doing business? The members of the steering committee may have their own opinions, pet solutions, and political or fiscal reasons to turn an idea down, or they may just want hard evidence.

The only answer is to have a baseline measurement of the current way the process operates, and to test, measure, and compare the proposed solution results to the baseline before going back to the steering committee. With data to demonstrate the magnitude of the improvement, perhaps in terms of time and money saved, the PITs' evidence will be irrefutable. A comparison with baseline data is the way to gain total respect for a solution.

This author recommends that at least two measurements be taken. A physician faced with a set of symptoms may take the patient's temperature and also order a white cell blood count. After medication, each measurement will show a different response, and this will help to demonstrate the extent that the medication effected the cure. One measurement on its own may not be conclusive.

A related concern is the question of measuring the solution versus measuring the symptoms. It is not necessarily the solution itself that has to be measured; the effect that the solution has on the system is the most important issue. While directly measuring the solution could be vital, the disappearance of symptoms along with improved health in related areas informs the team that the process or system is healed.

For example, measuring the number of times that an input improvement was utilized would be a solution measurement, while the effect of the improvement on sick outputs would be a symptom measurement.

This situation might call for both measurements to be taken, although only the output symptom would have a baseline for comparison.

In summary, continuous improvement demands baseline measurements of the current process, followed up by at least one measurement of the improved process. This is called management by facts!

Two Kinds of Baseline Data

Current Occurrence

Process stakeholders are asked to record on a check sheet how frequently something occurs or is experienced over a period of weeks. Staff needs to be reminded, especially in the early stages, to do this consistently. Posters that change frequently, memos with cartoons to bring a smile, and touch-base visits by the team facilitator, administrator, and CI manager can help. It may take someone from the very top levels of management to walk over and ask for cooperation before resisters decide that they do, indeed, have the time to participate.

Historical Data Occurrence

Research is done into past records, projects, or purchases to identify how frequently something occurred in the past. A task team may be assigned to get this information, which is recorded on a check sheet.

Action 1: Identify the Measurement Categories

Start off by identifying the broad umbrella categories of measurement to focus the measurement plan. Examples might be

- Process steps
- Frequencies of occurrence
- Dollars
- Units per time, per person, or per step
- Wasted materials
- Wasted time
- Cycles

A note about wasted time. Time is often more critical than dollars. It's a nonrenewable resource. Dollars can be recaptured, time never.

Action 2: Decide What to Measure

Use one of the umbrella categories and pick a practical item to measure using the following measurement tips and examples.

Measurement tips

- Measure what is important to clients.
- Measure aspects that will guide future decision making.
- Measure process variations, not people variations.
- Measure for strategic information, not to control people.
- Measure to improve, don't measure just to measure.
- Measure to identify the cost of waste and rework.
- Measure to improve what is already working.
- Use random samples—not everything has to be measured.
- Be practical—how precise must the measurements be?

Measurement examples

Estimating measures

- Costs per step or per cycle
- Range of hours to complete a drawing type
- Actual task hours versus estimated hours
- Total throughput time of a process or a project type
- Actual budget versus estimated budget at the end of a phase
- Cost of document production as a percentage of the fee
- Hours per document with a similar scope and complexity
- Range of error in estimating per project type

Rework measures

- Hours resulting from change orders
- Time spent with owner to clarify issues on each phase
- Change orders as a percent of the original contract
- Cost of input errors and omissions (E&O)
- E&O change orders as a percent of the original contract

- Unanticipated changes caused by regulatory agencies
- Number of rework hours related to scope noncompliance
- Cost of nonconformance with specification or scope
- Number of errors per document or revisions per assignment
- Project rework due to client misunderstandings
- Project rework related to subconsultant coordination
- The cost of field changes
- Number of resubmittals per project
- Number of revisions per document type
- Total hours spent per completed CAD document
- Total number of sheets plotted to obtain one completed CAD document
- Quality control hours

Performance indicators

- Schedule conformance per phase
- Number of projects without budget overruns
- Response or mobilization time
- Percent of milestones met
- Percent of work delivered on time
- Rate of change of improvements
- Staff utilization ratio
- Time taken to check submittals
- Staff turnover per quarter
- Unrecovered legal fees per annum
- Work backlog divided by the number of staff
- Annual billings divided by the number of staff

Financial and accounting function measures

- Overtime per month
- Chargeable versus nonchargeable ratio

- Cost overruns and write-offs
- Profit per project (breakout per project type)
- Billing cycle time
- Time taken to resubmit invoices
- Time taken to review and process time sheets
- Administrative rework
- Return on assets
- Profit margin

Marketing measures

- Market gain per year
- Client satisfaction via survey feedback
- Percent of work stemming from repeat clients
- Proposal and presentation win ratios
- Number of business development contacts

Action 3: Establish the Measurement Process

A detailed action plan is required in order to conduct the measurements. Action 2 selected the items to measure, now the PIT addresses the following nine questions.

1. How will it be measured?
2. Which tool will be used?
3. Who will collect the data?
4. Who will interpret the data?
5. How much data will be collected?
6. What level of precision will be required?
7. How frequently will the data be collected?
8. Will data accuracy spot checks be made?
9. For how long will the data be collected?

There is no rule that says that only the members of the PIT may measure. PIT members are not an elite band, independently deciding on the fate of the group. They represent all the process stakeholders. All of the stakeholders may be asked to help with taking measurements, or, as a minimum, kept informed of the baseline measurement process via the TQM/CI bulletin board. Also let teams in other offices know what is to be measured.

Complex issues such as data assurance methodologies, statistical risk assessments, and levels of uncertainty need not be addressed for most professional service situations.

Random Samples

When gathering historical occurrence baseline data, it may be impractical to research all past projects. For organizations that complete hundreds of assignments each year this would border on the impossible. The answer is to obtain a random sample of past projects.

Generally 30 samples give statistically valid answers, but by accepting less certainty, one can work with 20 samples. If one cannot obtain 20, work with whatever is available. In gathering these samples for the baseline, it is important to avoid bias. There are three kinds of bias.

Personal Bias

Suppose a staff member is assigned to research past projects to gather fee estimate overrun information. The normal reaction would be to pick out the familiar jobs—the ones, perhaps, on which this staff member had worked. The further inclination might be to pick out the projects that had a good track record, simply because this researcher is proud of the results.

Documentation Bias

Another common pitfall is to look at a list of past projects with the line of thought, "I need data, so which projects were well documented?" Any correlation between thoroughly documented projects, managed by well-organized project managers, and fee estimate overruns could skew the results.

Client Bias

Certain clients might demand better record keeping than others. Knowing this may lead to the temptation to research only those clients' projects in order to get the baseline data quickly.

Avoiding Bias

Project Type Grouping

It is suggested that readers consider subgrouping their historical data. The data for hospitals may be different for schools, and that of retail outlets may be different from data for airports.

Geographic Grouping

Projects completed in Seattle may have a different set of constraints from projects completed in San Antonio. Projects in Hamburg will certainly be different from those in Hong Kong.

Caution: Do not subgroup by project manager. It is the system that is under investigation not the people. One may note the project managers' names to get data clarification.

Subgroup Sampling

Using a Die

1. List the projects completed over the past two to three years.
2. Restructure the list into subgroups.
3. Draw a line under every sixth project number.
4. Throw a die and pick one file from each group of six.
5. Proceed in this way, until 30 or more samples have been obtained. This may not give truly random samples, but it has the advantage of being relatively bias free, simple, and quick.

Using Random Numbers

1. List the projects completed over the past two to three years.
2. Divide the subgroup into, say, nines.
3. Lay a sheet of paper containing a random orderings of numbers from 1 to 9 on a desk.
4. One person, with eyes closed, half-turns away from the desk and points at the sheet with a pencil, while another person randomly moves the sheet on the desktop. Don't jab—accidents can happen!
5. In this way, pick one file from each group of nine.

6. Proceed until 30 or more numbers have been randomly selected. Random ordering of numbers for different sets of numbers is available from ASQC.

Note: While not as bias fee, if the project numbers are sufficiently randomly jumbled on a sheet of paper, it might be simpler to use this pencil technique directly with the subgroup list of project numbers.

Using a Roulette Wheel

1. Draw a line under every 36th item.

2. Spin the wheel and record the number from 1 to 36.

3. Proceed in this way until 30 or more numbers have been obtained.

Caution: The assumption that data gaps will be similar to already identified data is invalid. Why are the data missing? Did someone forget it? Did someone remove it? Was it a cover up?

Sampling is a vast and specialty subject, and there are more accurate and statistically valid sampling techniques. This author, however, considers that for the degree of accuracy needed in professional service data gathering, the described methods are useful, practical, and reasonable.

Step 6: Root Cause Analysis

Tools: **Brainstorming**
Three-boundary search
Force field analysis
Cause-and-effect diagram
I/O cause-and-effect diagram
Pareto chart
Pareto cause analysis
Idea bank

Step 4 broke up structures, systems, and processes without analyzing them. Step 5 measured activities and past results to establish baselines. Step 6 may occur concurrently with step 5, so if baseline data gathering has not yet been fully completed by a task team or by the stakeholders, don't wait. Move directly to step 6.

In some cases, it may be prudent to get baseline measurements only after the analysis has taken place. This will depend on the judgment of the team facilitator. In any event, by the time step 6 is reached, the problem has usually been broken up into its component parts.

Suppose something was wrong with a car, and the engine was disassembled in order to fix it. There wouldn't be much point in putting it back together again until the parts had been examined, and the items in need of repair, modification, or replacement had been identified. In professional services, nonvalue-added parts taken out can even be thrown away without putting back any replacement! The focus of step 6 is to examine the parts to find the root cause or causes, and to stimulate creative solution ideas that are duly noted and stored in the idea bank.

The story of the patient who visits the physician or chiropractor for a cure, only to find that the side effects of the prescribed cure are worse than the original symptoms, bears repeating. This is because step 6 is the diagnostic step. Deleterious side effects are avoided by having representatives from overlapping processes, departments, or systems join the team for one or two sessions as guests. An attorney may be invited to join an environmental services PIT to share the legal rationale for the processes. A guest contractor may join an architect's PIT, or an architect may sit in on a contractor's team. A public relations specialist may be invited to join a marketing PIT, a developer may sit in on a facilities PIT, a property manager on a developer's team, and an insurance specialist may be a guest on a loss prevention team. The possibilities are many. Doing this gives a holistic approach to the analysis. It also delves into the situation where the root cause of an inefficient system is found buried in the processes of an outside organization. Important byproducts that these guests offer are the opportunity to capture their ideas in the idea bank and to strengthen the partnering bond.

Approach 1: Brainstorming the Breakouts

Examine the step 4 breakouts—the structure flowchart, the system flowchart, or the IPO audit. Brainstorm, using the BET, and dig deep and wide. Leave no stone uncovered in the search for the root cause or causes, especially the causes of the rework loops.

If more than one breakout has been performed, see if they are compatible with each other. Does a gap appear in one and not in another?

Are the redundancies in one duplicated in another? If so, why does this occur? Be fearless. Answers such as "Because that's the way we've always done it around here," are not acceptable. Why is this so? What if it was no longer done that way on every job? What are the written guidelines, if any? Are they compatible with the breakout? Probing in this way may yield important clues to the origin of the problem.

Approach 2: Use Analysis Tools
Instead of brainstorming the breakouts, move right to a specific analysis tool. This might be the three-boundary search, a cause-and-effect diagram, the I/O cause-and-effect diagram, or the Pareto cause analysis.

Approach 3: The Blockbuster
For a thorough analysis, search the breakouts for compatibility and consistency per approach 1, then explore the three boundaries, followed by a force field analysis, to identify the influences that support or promote the problem on the one hand, and mitigate or prevent the problem on the other hand. Using the energy flowing out of these brainstorming interactions, plug in one of the remaining three power tools listed in approach 2. If nothing else uncovers the root cause, this blockbuster combination should crack it open.

Step 7: Trial Solution
Tools: **Symptom overlap matrix brainstorming**
     Idea bank assessment
     Force field analysis
     Priority voting or comparison matrix

Golden Rules for Solutions
   1. *Prevent rather than cure.*
      Seek the solution that is the highest upstream.

   2. *Be driven by systems thinking.*
      A system or structural cure may heal process pains.

   3. *Focus first on waste reduction, then on refining value-added activities.*

Note 1: If a step or action is redundant, is hindering information flow, is hampering coordination, or is not adding value to the process, cut it out.

Note 2: While elegant solutions are often best, still distrust the obvious and avoid jumping to conclusions.

Using the Idea Bank

Because the idea bank has been in operation since step 4, there is usually a wealth of solution ideas from which to choose. The problem is often one of managing these ideas rather than soliciting new ideas.

Most professional service trial solutions will be comprised of a composite of several ideas that form the trial solution components (TSC). Only rarely will there be a single, magic-bullet cure.

These TSCs are created by grouping and coalescing, and perhaps weighting, evaluating, and then prioritizing the proposed idea bank solutions. All or some of the following tools can assist in moulding these ideas into TSCs.

1. The system overlap matrix facilitates the grouping, coalescing, and verification of symptom healing.

2. Brainstorming facilitates weighting.

3. The idea bank assessment evaluates the ideas.

4. Priority voting or the comparison matrix narrows down the choices.

The surviving TSCs are then packaged as the best trial solution, to be field tested for a reality check.

The Trial Solution Check

In the search for a trial solution, seek more than workable answers; seek the best pragmatic solution. Also be alert for the breakthroughs discussed in chapter 5. Reassembling and relinking the pieces might help to confirm the strengths, expose the weaknesses, or find the fatal flaw of the proposed solution.

- Does simplification make sense?

- What is still missing?

- Will the bottlenecks open up?
- Which inputs are still nonvalue-added?
- Are there still input conflicts or redundancies?
- Which outputs are nonvalue-added?
- Are there still output conflicts or redundancies?
- Do any gaps remain?

Proposed solutions should not overlap or adversely impact other processes, and the revised flow diagrams may spot these flaws. With these tests passed, the new structure flow or system flow could be drawn to illustrate the improvement. The trial solution may also require new QA checklists or documentation.

PIT Close-Out

Prior to the submission of ideas to the steering committee, the PIT concludes their final session with a close-out checklist.

1. Are all of the original symptoms addressed by the trial solution components?
2. How, and by whom, shall the solutions be presented to the steering committee?
3. Should the presentation detail implementation recommendations?
4. Should a PIT skeleton crew continue to meet during the trial solution period?
5. Who will measure the effects of the trial solution?
6. How frequently will measurements be taken?
7. Who will record these measurements and report on progress?
8. Who will receive these measurements and interim progress reports?
9. When should the full PIT reconvene to assess trial solution results?
10. How can the PIT process be improved?

The checklist concludes with two recognition questions.

1. Who should be commended to the steering committee for exceptional support to the PIT members?
2. How can TQM/CI be further publicized?

Getting Approval for the Trial Solution

When the best trial solution has been identified, the steering committee gets back into the loop to approve a trial solution test. Because the committee originally gave its blessing to the problem statement, and because it has received copies of all the meeting minutes and has been kept up-to-date by the CI manager, its approval often needs little debate.

Trial Solution Test

The trial solution will need a plan to test it in the workplace. This plan should include the following:

- Knowledge of the setup costs.
- Where it will be implemented?
- Who will get it moving?
- Who will install it?
- Who will monitor it?
- Who will measure the effects?
- The length of the test drive.

Step 8: Data Collection and Evaluation
Tools: **Check sheet**
Pareto chart
Run chart
Control charts
Scatter diagram

This step reveals how well the trial solution lives up to its expectations. Because progress has been publicized using the team progress tracking chart, shown in Figure 4.4, the stakeholders already know about the PIT's progress. They may have taken measurements and now get involved by again taking measurements while the trial solution is being tested. Utilize the same measurement protocols used in the baseline study. Try a brief, stand-up meeting to announce the start and end dates of the trial and to answer any logistics questions.

Pitfall 1: Don't get into a debate over why a particular solution was chosen. If anyone asks, make the breakouts and all the other data available. These doubters are usually the ones who originally decided that they had no time to participate. Chapter 5 will discuss these resisters.

Pitfall 2: If the baseline measurement was of the occurrence type, such as "how frequently did this occur," make sure that the stakeholders testing the trial solution are the same individuals that were involved in the baseline measurement. Otherwise the data will be invalid because different people have different occurrence baselines, and the comparison will be inconsistent.

The team facilitator and administrator will again need to remind stakeholders to measure. This is particularly important when the measurement starts. Review the reminder ideas discussed in step 5. The team administrator gathers the stakeholders' check sheets and processes them. Again, some stakeholders will agree to help, and then forget or be "too busy" to fill in the check sheet. The team facilitator and administrator must decide if they have sufficient data to proceed.

Note: It can be very instructive to identify all those who decline to participate. Looking for common attributes could reveal a lot about how TQM/CI is perceived, prior negative experiences, perceptions of empowerment at certain staff levels, and morale among certain groups. Search for causes and work toward improvements.

Evaluating the Improvement

Most evaluation questions must be answered with data.

- Have outputs reached a higher standard of quality?
- Have inputs become simpler or easier to use?
- Have productivity and work flow improved?
- Is the staff pleased with the solution?
- Are external clients delighted?
- Are there positive signs on the bottom line?
- What specific measurements support these conclusions?

If the trial solution improves the situation, eliminates waste, refines the process, and simplifies the work, the data will almost always be positive. But there is another question to be asked. Did the trial solution adversely impact any other process or system? For example, if the solution saved project management $2000 per month, but caused the production department to lose $3000 per month, an investigation is warranted. Perhaps the PIT lacked production department representation, or perhaps an aspect of their operations was not fully considered. If the reason for the malfunction of the solution is clear, adjust the solution, discuss it with the steering committee and retest. Otherwise go back to step 4 to search for more clues.

Sometimes the trial will reveal new information. Hidden issues may emerge. This information could be overt, such as the exposure of a bottleneck that everyone knew was there, but no one recognized as a bottleneck; or the information could be covert, that is, hidden in the data. Neither of these situations is an occasion for despair. This is just another step in the right direction, a positive sign indicating that the continuous improvement spiral is being entered.

Step 9: Standardize Improvements

Tools: **Brainstorming**
Force field analysis
Benefit/LOE analysis

Getting Final Approval

Before the trial solution can become a standard operating procedure, the steering committee must approve the trial solution results. If a formal presentation is requested, include a summary of the steps that the PIT followed, the tools used, the measurement results, and the benefits and savings involved. Because the steering committee has been in the communication loop all along, this formal presentation is usually only requested when the issue is wide ranging and when the board of directors or the executive leadership wants the full story before the steering committee is granted permission to go ahead. This situation can be dangerous and should be avoided. If the solutions are rejected, TQM/CI is on a slippery slope. The antidote is found upstream at the source of TQM/CI. If the ground rules in the Shearer model were followed, this top group will be in the information loop, having at least one of its members represented on the steering committee. In any event, salvation in this situation is usually found by the comparison between the baseline data and the data gathered after the trial solution was implemented. It is hard to argue against a solidly constructed body of evidence. Hard, but not impossible.

When emotion overrides logic, anyone can refute anything. When the executive leadership or president is dictatorial, or when the ultimate authorities are not interested, the whole effort can fall apart. Readers are referred back to Figure 1.6 to recall that TQM/CI cannot work in management by decree, nor management by chaos environments.

Developing a Step-by-Step Implementation Plan

Trying to implement a permanent change without a plan can be hazardous to the health of the solution. The PIT or task team could devise this implementation plan, and then have the steering committee approve it. Or the steering committee might take care of implementation planning.

Many business ventures have failed, not for the lack of ideas, but because those great ideas gathered dust on a top shelf—useless without an implementation plan. The plan must answer questions similar to the trial solution implementation in step 7, but it will also need to cover the following:

- Who will spearhead the plan?
- Who else will be involved, and what are their roles?
- Who will announce the new procedure?
- What are the steps involved in implementation?
- Will a schedule be required with implementation milestones?
- Is training involved?
- Is a new manual or revision involved?
- Are there new hires or transfers involved?
- How will the change be monitored?

An assessment should also be made regarding the probabilities of success. A force field analysis could assess the following:

- What will decrease the probability of a successful implementation? How can this be prevented?

- What will increase the probability of a successful implementation? How can this be encouraged?

If the solution requires a change in the way the work is done, communicated, or coordinated, the standard operating procedure must be clarified and published. Sequencing changes might be assisted by the benefit/LOE analysis. Changes may include the following:

- Quality assurance check sheets and guidelines
- New or revised project management methods
- New or revised project management reports
- New or revised accounting practices
- New or revised marketing protocols
- New or revised operations manual
- New or revised job descriptions
- New or revised work flowcharts

These documents have multiple uses. For example, flowcharts can be used to

- Help sell the solution within the organization.
- Promote further interest in the TQM/CI process.
- Launch new ideas and suggestions for improvement.
- Assist project managers who estimate projects by reminding them of the steps and processes that they need to take into consideration.
- Assist outside providers and suppliers understand their clients' processes.
- Coach new employees in the way the work needs to be performed.
- Show clients how the process works, including a clarification of the importance of their role in the process.

Monitoring the Improvement

Monitoring leads to the continuous improvement spiral—cycling through the PIT process to further enhance value-added activities. Monitoring encourages staff to keep thinking about how to do an even better job, and to channel its suggestions to the CI manager. After the

PIT or task team has disbanded, the team facilitator remains to monitor results and coordinate with the CI manager. Ongoing monitoring might be best achieved with statistical process control as statistical monitoring will facilitate the continuous improvement search for

- Large deviations beyond specification
- Unusual, nonrandom distribution patterns
- Data trends

Monitoring is also a way to prevent resisters from slipping back into their old way of doing things. It can help management to see if the staff is implementing the new procedures and is promoting continuous improvement thinking.

Summary of the PIT Process

Figure 4.7 summarizes the PIT process. It shows how ideas are narrowed down, screened, filtered, and then coalesced into the best trial solution.

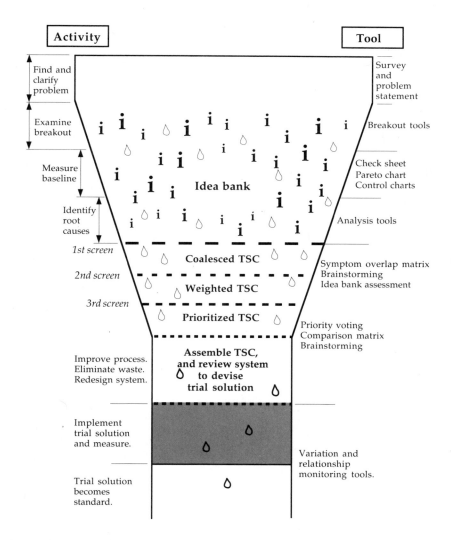

Figure 4.7. PIT process flow.

CHAPTER 5

Implementation Tips

Overview

Implementing TQM/CI is rarely easy. The keys to dealing with difficulties are pragmatism and patience. It will take time for all the pieces to fall into place. Sometimes one must be kind and understanding, and at other times one must be tough. This is nothing new for experienced managers. If it is acceptable to seek out those who do well in order to recognize their achievements, is it not also reasonable to identify resisters in order to eradicate their sabotage? This chapter takes an honest look at these difficulties and opportunities, and provides pragmatic tips for meeting them head-on.

Dealing with Apathy, Resistance, and Sabotage

Apathy

There is almost always at least one individual in each organization who is apathetic toward TQM/CI. When apathy is tackled head-on, it may lead to resistance. When resistance is tackled head-on, it may lead to sabotage. An upstream approach is best. Tackle apathy, but not necessarily head-on. This may include

- Peer pressure
- Public recognition of team participants
- Awards to team participants

Change is painful, but perhaps *not* changing might be even more painful. Readers will recall the cost of stagnation as proof of that statement. Personal change is no less painful, and often no less essential. Most people merely apathetic or neutral to TQM/CI eventually convert into believers, but it may take a while until they see that continuous improvement is just not going to go away.

Resistance and Sabotage

Being an active resister is more serious than being apathetic toward TQM/CI. There are those who resist because they fight structure and thrive in crisis situations. This energizes and stimulates them, and makes them feel heroic. If these people cannot change their ways, they do not belong in a professional service firm. A career change to fire-fighting, police work, or mountain rescue is advised.

There are those who resist because they are afraid that continuous improvement will lead to them working harder, that it will result in efficiencies and job cuts, or that it may highlight their past failures. Layoffs are always possible with or without TQM. Surely resisters to continuous improvement will be the first to go!

Then there is the project manager who says, "I am not going to change because my way is the best." Suppose the PIT's data prove that the resister is wrong. Now the resister's reputation is publicly at stake. A logical resistance may turn into an emotional resistance, which may lead to sabotage. Instead of comparing data to prove who was right, just get on with the continuous improvement process. The harder that resisters are challenged, the tougher they become; change must never degenerate into a personal issue about who is right. With more people adapting to continuous improvement thinking, the river of change flowing around these resisters silently undermines their temporary position. One day, with nothing being said, they may just release their grip on their cherished ways and swim along with those moving with change.

There are also those resisters, often managers holding key positions, who try to roadblock progress in their department. The antidote is to commence TQM/CI in another division or branch and allow the results to speak for themselves. If the resisters still hold their ground, given the evidence of TQM/CI success, ask them to permit measurement of their processes. Perhaps they really have some good ideas that could be shared. Or perhaps not! Resistance generally collapses when baseline measurements are taken. Not many will fight to demonstrate that nothing can be improved when they know they will be fighting measurements. If they refuse to change in spite of data supporting change, they are considered saboteurs and may need to be moved to another assignment, perhaps with another firm. Managers who will not buy in, might have to be bought out. Twenty-first century firms can't afford to have dictatorial, closed-minded, nonteam player and project managers. TQM/CI is just too important to allow a handful of people to prevent it from flourishing.

In the early stages, TQM/CI is as fragile as a great redwood tree that starts off as a small, vulnerable seed. The antidote to this early vulnerability is to collect baseline data as soon as possible. And the baseline data must be translated into dollars. Faced with clear-cut evidence demonstrating the cost of stagnation, renegades find that they have no ammunition to fire and are powerless to stop the movement toward continuous improvement. In fact, measurement is a very powerful resistance breaker. Resistance is almost always based on opinion. Measurement can crush the barrier of opinion and break through to management by facts.

Sharing recognition for improvements is another reason for resisters to let go of their fixed ways. Resisters are not stakeholders in the new process, so their share in the recognition is in direct proportion to their involvement; it is zero.

Some organizations mandate that all project drawings and reports must be accompanied by a self-checked project quality review sheet. Staff is given the authority to refuse any work that is not accompanied by this completed checklist. So resisters learn that if they don't follow the mandated QA guidelines that are reflected in the checklist, their work remains untouched, and their projects will not be processed. This, coupled with management by system and process measurement, is the final clincher that can crumble resistance within an hour and awaken resisters to improved cooperation, communication, and continuous improvement.

Performance Reviews

The topic of the performance evaluation sends chills up and down the spines of many drive-out-fear practitioners. Professional service firms are populated by highly degreed, creative talents who bend to nobody's will but their own. Implementing one new process or a thousand makes no difference to them. Driving out fear is a very admirable concept, but eliminating performance reviews is not the answer in this environment.

This author does not advocate these reviews as a punitive evaluation, rather as a coaching tool. Instead of annual reviews, the concept of short but frequent one-on-one discussions with a manager to applaud what is working, to look at what is not working, and to plan how to overcome obstacles is preferred. There are no rankings in this coaching meeting; simply mentoring, positive objectives, and written commitments. Coaches don't coach their team once a year, so why would anyone in a management by partnership culture not coach frequently? Ongoing coaching mirrors the quality review concept shown in Figure 2.5 and avoids the dam of a once-a-year quality control performance evaluation. These reviews make it clear to the resisters that whole-hearted participation in continuous improvement is the key to team and personal success. Supplementing these mentoring sessions could be an annual review, perhaps involving peers.

Measurement of performance works. It is not a measure of subjective matters, nor a ranking of people. Rather it is a measurement of items done or not done, and the extent of success. These can include timely invoicing, marketing contacts, PIT attendance, participation in training, and many other nonjudgmental items. These are factual, unemotional, specific, and indisputable performance measures. When they are based on preagreed personal goals tied directly to team and system improvement goals, reviews work especially well.

These reviews tie into the way that improvement teams are evaluated; by process, participation and progress, not by their results. If both teams and team members achieve these three p's, the results follow by themselves.

Turning Failure into Success

A last word for those who resist because they don't believe change can succeed.

- Success is good—it's the path of today's winners.
- Failure is good—it's the path of tomorrow's winners.

The lessons learned in failure are the stepping-stones to tomorrow's success.

Recognition

Why should people change? What might motivate them to adjust their previously acceptable work methods? Recognition for continuous improvement efforts can be one of the motivators.

Selecting Those to Recognize

How are selections for recognition awards made? Generally, PITs will nominate themselves because they are proud of their accomplishments. If the organization wants to develop a means to find the most worthy teams, the following ideas may be used.

- Recognize the PITs that met most consistently, or whose members showed consistent attendance.
- Recognize the PITs and task teams that had the greatest impact on the company.
- Recognize the stakeholders who were not team members, yet contributed greatly to the success of the teams. Team members often nominate these individuals.
- Recognize all PITs and task teams that completed all of the improvement steps, regardless of the outcomes.

Recognition strictly on the basis of specific results should be avoided. This is because when improvement team meetings are well attended, and the steps rigorously followed, results naturally follow.

Awards

Ideas for awards include the following:

- Pins
- Certificates or plaques
- Trophies
- TQM windbreakers, baseball caps, T-shirts
- Decals for hard hats

- Golf balls, TQM mugs
- Team dinners
- Recognition in print
- Trips to conferences
- Days off work

Some manufacturing companies have implemented successful reward systems including bonuses tied to improvements. Profit sharing based on a percentage of savings resulting from an improvement might be a great motivator, or it might not!

1. Rewards, especially monetary rewards, transmit the message that an incentive is required in order to do the job right.

2. Rewards are totally inappropriate for long-term continuous improvement. When the rewards run out, continuous improvement will flag. Continuous improvement should be done because it needs to be done, not because of a monetary gain.

3. Professionals work best on continuous improvement when they are self-motivated to do the best job possible.

4. Awards are much more appropriate than rewards. They tie into professional pride, self-esteem, and a striving for personal excellence.

Ask teams what, besides money, they would like for a reward. Most professionals will decline anything extravagant.

Who gets these awards—the team facilitator, the entire team, or the entire department involved in measuring and implementing a change? Will award winners be selected by their peers? Should recognition be divided up by divisions, disciplines, offices, or regions? A task team might be set up to answer these questions. At this point it is useful to remember that people never complain because they are getting too much recognition.

Award Presentations

How an award is presented is more important than its cost. Consider a hypothetical quality award. It consists of a six-inch, solid gold cube. Its intrinsic value would be considerable. Suppose it was awarded by being mailed at the fourth class bulk mail rate, wrapped up in old newspapers contained in a tattered grocery store cardboard box. Suppose further that the unsigned note that accompanied it was dashed off quickly on the back of a used envelope, and contained several spelling and grammatical errors. No publicity came with the award, no write-ups, and no announcements. How much emotional value would be attributed to the award? Not much.

Suppose again that the award was merely a crisp dollar bill attached to a cardboard certificate contained in a simple $8 wooden frame. This award, however, is presented by the president of the United States before the entire assembled United Nations and the presidents of the top 10 industrial nations. Each head of state signed the certificate and congratulated the winner. The event would be shown on television in countries around the world. It would make the headlines in the daily business press, and would be featured and highlighted in international journals. That simple $9 award would be treasured far more highly by the recipient than the solid gold block delivered in the mail.

The message is simple. It is not the value of the award, it is the way that it is presented and the appreciation expressed in front of others that really counts.

The Pitfalls of Rewards for Suggestions

Staff suggestions that point to a future improvement, but that cannot be immediately implemented go into the idea bank. The recognition in such a situation is the follow-up, signed note from a manager recognizing that this person cares about future improvements.

Suggestions pointing out an area for immediate savings may warrant an award to the individual or the group making the suggestion, but this leads to a major pitfall that many companies have experienced. Will the idea be resisted for political reasons? Will all of the division managers be prepared to follow a secretary's suggestion, even if it is a breakthrough? Will a division manager with improvement ideas listen to a rival division manager's suggestions? Will a reward to a stakeholder be resented by other stakeholders who have to implement someone else's idea? In a management by partnership environment these issues would be completely irrelevant. In other management cultures they might be stumbling blocks, but there are further concerns regarding immediate suggestion implementation. This is why the steering committee is so valuable as a clearinghouse for suggestions. Suggestions can originate anywhere, but it is the steering committee that orchestrates TQM/CI and coordinates a structured and pragmatic process.

Some organizations, especially in the manufacturing industries, have rewarded people for the volume of suggestions, and actually measure the success of their quality program by the average number of suggestions per employee. This may not be appropriate in the professional service environment. Continuous improvement should not be a contest for the greatest number of ideas, and this author would discourage this practice and encourage the appeal to professional pride and peer recognition.

Publicity

It is important to promote continuous improvement to get people interested in future improvements. Some ideas for publicizing progress and success are as follows:

- TQM/CI bulletin board
- Progress bar graph as shown in Figure 4.4
- Company newsletter
- Client's newsletter
- Announcements to stockholders
- Marketing materials
- Articles in the media
- TQM/CI open house celebration

Continuous Improvement Realities

Change is the uncomfortable aspect of continuous improvement. Those who see the bottle as half-empty will fear change just as those who see the bottle as half-full tend to face change with a fearless optimism. Both are in error. It is best to face the future with a positive, but realistic outlook.

Examining what could go wrong is healthy, as it leads to a game plan to overcome potential obstacles. At the same time, the ability to look at what could go right gives managers the motivation, vision, and commitment to drive toward terrain difficult to reach. The managers who do best with continuous improvement are able to study and evaluate all sides of a situation, and make decisions based on sound judgment.

The Impermanency of Solutions

Nothing on this planet lasts forever. Everything has a shelf life. Improvements are not immune from this phenomenon, and every solution is permanent until a better solution is found. This can be readily accepted by adapting a continuous improvement mentality, monitoring improved processes, and verifying proposed changes with the steering committee.

Visualize a car being driven along a straight desert freeway. Without changing speed, the driver gently releases the steering wheel. The car may proceed along a straight path for one or two miles, but quite soon it will begin to stray. In the same way, over time, solutions degrade due to tiny imperfections and environmental changes. Usually all that is required is fine-tuning to stay on the roadway, but one must remain vigilant to correct the corporate vehicle before it strays too far off course.

The Law of Diminishing Returns

Professional service management is subject to the law of diminishing returns, and the spiral of improvement needs to be tempered with reality. Perhaps there are other chronic problems that need more urgent attention before current improvements are further refined. Realism must reign. Consider the following TQM/CI fairy tale.

Once upon a time, the king of a far off land had magic powers to create exquisite jewels. Every year, to celebrate his birthday, he would travel to a different corner of his kingdom to wave his wand over 18 trees. Instantly, each tree's sweet fruit would change into jewels such as rubies, diamonds, sapphires, and emeralds. The people would then excitedly rush to pull off the jewels. Now the trees were very difficult to climb, and only the most agile could lift themselves up near the tops of the trees to get more of the sparkling pendants. But out of the multitude, there were always some who managed to climb high up on the trees, and they happily gathered more wealth.

Something strange happened when each jewel was plucked. A new jewel instantly took took its place, but many of the successive jewels were not only smaller, but also much harder to pull off the tree than the first ones. Also, the jewels that were not plucked became fruit after the second day's sunset.

When night fell at the end of the first day, the people lay down on the soft warm grass, quite exhausted. They happily fell asleep.

The next morning, most went home, glad that they could use their jewels to buy a new farm or to spend at the local fairs. Others decided to try to remove more jewels from the trees. By now the jewels that were easy to reach were quite small and very hard to pluck. But there were also many large ones left high up in the trees. These athletic and determined souls climbed and struggled to gather more wealth. They found that by working in unison they were able to capture and share some wonderful prizes from the treetops.

Near the end of the second day, almost all had gone home, as there was very little to gain by working so hard. But a handful of people, wanted more, and strained extraordinarily hard to remove the remaining jewels. One fell off a tree and broke a wrist; another hobbled off with an injured leg; while a third got wedged between two tree limbs and could not be freed at all. Many others were cut and scratched. Their energetic exertions caused many large jewels that they had earlier plucked to fall out of their pockets and become lost in the tall grass. But the majority of people in the kingdom were overjoyed by their gains and lived happily ever after.

The story is interpreted as follows: The large jewels that were easy to reach and pluck were the TQM/CI breakthroughs, usually resulting from the elimination of waste and unnecessary rework. This waste can be eliminated quite soon after the introduction of TQM/CI. After each breakthrough occurred, there was the opportunity to refine and continuously improve the breakthrough process. This was the small jewel that replaced the large, plucked jewel. After many jewels were plucked, it got harder and harder to remove their smaller replacement gems. This illustrates the law of diminishing returns in continuous improvement. The effort to refine a process must continue only as long as the return on investment (ROI) is greater than the level of effort (LOE).

Some of the jewels were really huge, but hard to reach. Some breakthroughs are very important, but take long and are hard to accomplish.

One must evaluate all possible gains in the light of the effort needed to accomplish those gains. During the morning and mid-afternoon of the second day, those groups that cooperated were well rewarded for their efforts. Most major breakthroughs can only occur when teams and stakeholders are ready to work together.

The group at the end of the second day put in far more effort than was necessary. They forgot about the law of diminishing returns, and in their stubborn persistence, they actually lost some of their early gains. They also lost their focus, and their morale. They were the source of amusement for their wiser companions.

Breakthroughs

The most frequent early breakthroughs involve the elimination of waste. The sudden realization that a whole task does not have to be done any more, or that two tasks can be combined into one, can be thrilling.

Figure 5.1 depicts how breakthroughs and continuous improvement feed upon each other. After the elimination of waste, the value-added processes are refined. This may, in turn, set the stage for new breakthroughs originating from the ideas stimulated by the refinement. Further breakthroughs may follow. The succeeding breakthroughs are often smaller in magnitude, but in contrast to the fairy tale, sometimes a series of small breakthroughs can lead to yet another major advance. This is the stage of innovation and creative system change. Breakthrough examples include the following:

- Better ways to log in projects
- Elimination of invoicing steps
- Formation of a new division to provide a marketable service
- Widespread use of self-checking quality reviews
- Eliminating bottlenecks in word processing
- A new way to enhance client/consultant communication
- A new partnering process
- Simplifying reporting
- Shaving 50 percent of time off a step
- Streamlining payroll procedures

Avoid the temptation of thinking of a breakthrough and then just impulsively implementing it. Inspirational breakthroughs often have disastrous results. There may be no uniform buy-in; the idea may negatively impact other areas; and there may not even be any solid evidence that the breakthrough will be beneficial. Any of the breakthroughs listed, implemented on a whim, could lead to bigger problems than those that they were meant to solve.

A focus on documentation may stifle creativity, and the impulsive implementation of creative ideas may stifle logic. The ideal is to allow the creativity to emerge, then carefully consider the implications using documentation as an implementation tool. The PIT process is a systematic way to unleash creativity, reach a threshold, and then break through to a new level.

Impatience

Patients who are given antibiotics are always urged by physicians to complete the course of medication, even though the patients may start

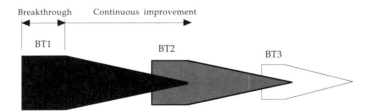

High-volume breakthroughs (BT) often come early in the TQM process. Continuous improvement refines the breakthrough.

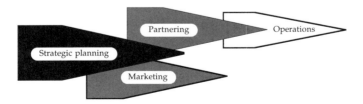

Breakthroughs in one area often lead to breakthroughs in other areas.

Figure 5.1. Breakthroughs.

to feel better after one or two doses. This is because the body is still fighting the infection, and if the medication is stopped too soon, a relapse may result.

Some organizations start to drive out waste, and then relax their guard and drop their TQM program. This is followed by a corporate relapse, the reemergence of symptoms, a drop in morale, and the media proclaiming that TQM does not work. Continuous improvement is akin to preventive medicine—monitoring and evaluating the health of the corporation. The cost of stagnation shows that the cost of continuous improvement wellness is minute compared to the cost of repairing recurring problems, and the staff's loss of confidence in management—classic cost of stagnation symptoms.

Roadblocks and Root Causes

A sign encountered on a highway such as DETOUR AHEAD or ROAD CLOSED is not the true obstacle or cause of the detour. It is just a symptom. The true roadblock is the water line repair caused by corrosion, the new gas main installation required by neighborhood growth, or the pothole repair caused by last winter's weather. When new roadblocks are encountered on the continuous improvement journey, always seek out the root cause. Is the roadblock actually a symptom of something deeper or more extensive? Some roadblocks need to be demolished, some pushed to the side of the road, while others need to be slowly dissolved. Occasionally, tackling surrounding issues weakens the big roadblock, making it easier to eliminate. The first step is to carefully examine the roadblock and any data associated with it.

- What exactly is the obstacle?
- Can its size be measured?
- How did it get there?
- How long has it been entrenched?
- Who wants it maintained, and why?
- Who wants it eliminated, and why?
- What is the most efficient way to remove it?
- What would it cost to remove it?
- How long will the removal take?

- What is the cost of not removing it?
- Who would benefit from its removal?
  —Clients
  —The organization as a whole
  —Top management
  —Project managers
  —Technical, field, or support staff
- What is the worst case scenario if it is not removed?
- What is the best case scenario if it is removed?

Encountering a roadblock is always positive. It is a signpost to future improvements.

The Dissolution of the Steering Committee

Most organizations that are serious about TQM/CI will engage a qualified consultant as a guide through the training, the introduction, and the start-up. Then the consultant can gradually withdraw so that the steering committee and the CI manager can take over the reins. This should not occur until TQM has taken firm root and can fully sustain itself. The consultant will still be available for questions, but will be needed less.

In the same way, the steering committee is an internal consultant that guides and administrates TQM/CI. In several years, after continuous improvement thinking is infused into the firm, the complexion of the steering committee may change. One of the following may occur.

- The executive leadership becomes the steering committee.
- The steering committee decreases in size.
- The CI manager assumes all steering committee tasks.

These potential adjustments are not mandatory. The total abandonment of the steering committee and all controls is not recommended. The steering committee may retain its original size, perhaps with different members rotating in periodically. Readers will recall the car on the desert freeway analogy. Someone must remain at the wheel.

A Summary of Continuous Improvement

Always seeking to do better must be a passion, but not an uncontrollable passion. If processes are refined, then there must be a return on investment. In moving from waste elimination breakthroughs to refining value-added activities, be pragmatic about the return on investment (ROI) , the level of effort (LOE), and the point of no return. The formulae are simple.

When ROI > LOE = proceed with continuous improvement.

When ROI = LOE = stop unless there are intangible benefits.

When ROI < LOE = look for another issue to tackle.

Bear in mind that the return does not always have to be monetary. For example, reduced stress is a wonderful and worthy return.

Overimproving one area, while ignoring symptoms in other areas leads to refined and balanced processes struggling to work efficiently within a rough and imbalanced system. Continuous improvement must always be looked at from a global perspective.

PART III

Implementation Tools

CHAPTER 6

Decision-Making, Organizing, and Diagnosis Tools

Overview

The PIT guide in chapter 4 listed tools under each step. This chapter describes the basic tools. Once the reader is familiar with the tools, ways to apply them interactively will become apparent. There are three common pitfalls in using the tools.

1. Overemphasis on tools is like focusing on the lathe, rather than on the beautiful objects that it can fashion. For an expert craftsperson, the tool ceases to be separate and becomes an integrated part of the process. The tools should serve the process and not control it.

2. Insufficient use of the tools leads to inefficiencies, debate, and opinion. Without the ability to verify results, continuous improvement becomes a guessing game. The tools keep the process efficient and on track, and offer proof of improvement.

3. Finally, not having enough tools to choose from is like giving an artist a limited palette. A wonderful picture may still result, but it may not quite depict reality. Continuous improvement is all about depicting reality and management by facts. So the picture must be painted realistically, and not impressionistically, or worse, surrealistically!

Tool Summary

Decision-Making and Organizing Tools and Their Purposes

- Check sheets to gather data
- Brainstorming to solicit and discuss ideas
- Priority voting to build consensus
- Comparison matrix to focus and select
- Benefit/LOE analysis to focus and select
- Symptom overlap matrix to organize and focus
- Problem statement to clarify issues and symptoms
- Idea bank assessment to collect and assess ideas

Breakout Tools and Their Purposes

- Structure flowchart to link structures and systems
- System flowchart to link systems and processes
- IPO audit—process flow to link process transactions

Diagnosis Tools and Their Purposes

- Three-boundary search to identify problem boundaries
- Force field analysis to assess influences
- Cause-and-effect diagram for multipurpose cause analysis
- I/O cause-and-effect diagram for detail cause analysis
- Pareto charts for frequency distribution
- Pareto cause analysis for data-based cause analysis

Variation and Relationship Monitoring Tools and Their Purposes

- Run charts for time-data plot
- c charts (sample constant) to plot errors per item
- u charts (sample varies) to plot errors per item

- p charts (sample varies) to plot items with errors
- X-bar and R charts to monitor events continuously
- X and moving range charts to monitor individual samples
- Scatter diagram to plot cause and effect

Check Sheet

What It Is

In order to describe the check sheet, it is important to start with the distinction between a checklist and a check sheet. The checklist contains a predetermined list of items to review or follow. It is a guide and reminder, often part of a QA manual. The checklist ensures consistency, regularity, and thoroughness. By crossing or checking off items, the checklist performs the additional, valuable function of being a verification tool when team members transfer work tasks from one to another. The checklist is an important part of the self-check quality review process.

The check sheet is a log that acts as a data-gathering tool. It gathers data for baseline measurements, trial solution verifications, and process monitoring. The check sheet is a tool that serves other tools. For example, if root causes uncovered in a cause-and-effect diagram must be quantified in a Pareto chart or control chart, the check sheet will be used to gather the measurements.

How It Works

- The two kinds of baseline data, described in step 5 of chapter 4, are frequencies of current occurrence and historical data occurrence. The check sheet will be custom designed to suit the data format, the tool being used, and the level of detail required.

- It is important to make the check sheet as simple to use as possible. Otherwise stakeholders will complain that they have no time to use it. A well-designed sheet allows a stakeholder to spend no more than three to five seconds recording what happened. A check mark, pen stroke, or letter of the alphabet is all that should be required for each entry.

- It is also important to plan the location of the check sheet. A well-designed sheet that becomes the lining of an in basket, is buried in a pile of memos, or is placed somewhere in a TQM/CI folder will not be used.

Problem	Day 1	Day 2	Day 3	Day 4	Day 5
Jam..................	I	I I	I	I I I	I I
Overheat.........	I I I I	I I I	⊥⊥⊢⊢	I	⊢⊢⊓ I I
Power fail......		I	I		I
Feeder tear......	I I	I I I	I I	I I I I	I I

Copy machine malfunction

	Project A	Project B	Project C	Project D
January	b.e.d.d.c.. d.d.d.c.c.f.	b.b.b.c.b.c. d.c.a.b.b.e. b.c.e.c.	a.b.c.d.d.c. a.c.e.c.b.	b.c.c.c.b.e.f. e.c.c.b.f.
February	c.c.e.a.f.e.c. b.a.e.	c.c.e.d.a.d. a.	c.b.b.a.d.	d.e.e.b.a.
March	b.b.a.d.	b.b.c.f.a.d.e. e.d.	c.b.b.e.d.b. b.d.a.f.e.e. e.d.d.a.e.	d.c.f.a.c.d.b. b.
April	c.e.a.c.e.d.	d.d.e.a.a.b. f.b.a.b.b.	c.e.e.d.	c.d.c.f.a.b.d. d.
May	b.c.f.	c.d.e.d.e.a. a.d.	c.d.d.a.a.	c.d.b.e.d.e.d. e.a.
June	a.d.e.b.b.	a.e.d.c.	f.a.c.d.b.d.e.b . d.a.c.b.c.	d.c.b.d.a.f.

Communication problems

a. Not available for more than 24 hours
b. Information received late
c. Change not communicated
d. Meeting starts late
e. No show at meeting
f. Document not received or lost

Figure 6.1. Check sheet examples.

- The example shown at the top of Figure 6.1 is a simple check sheet that records the frequency of copy machine events. In this example, the check sheet might be located above the copy machine.

- The example shown at the bottom of Figure 6.1 is a more complex version that records the frequency and details of events. This check sheet might be pinned to the wall above a project manager's desk. Using colored paper and lettering may serve to remind stakeholders to check off events.

- In the first few days, daily reminder notices from the team facilitator or administrator to the measurement participants ease them into the habit of recording events. After the first week, reminders can decrease in frequency, but should be kept lighthearted. A cartoon, perhaps with a custom caption, copied onto the reminder gets attention and avoids the perception that check sheets are a burden.

- Chapter 7 uses check sheets for statistical process control data gathering.

Brainstorming

What It Is

Brainstorming is a nonanalytical idea-gathering process used to

- Identify problems.
- Collect improvement ideas.
- Set a direction.
- Clarify inputs, outputs, and activities.
- Identify root causes.
- Suggest creative solutions.
- Identify pros and cons.

How It Works

Ground Rules

1. Ensure that the topic being examined is concise, unambiguous, and clear to all participants.

2. Write the topic on a flip chart to keep team participants focused during brainstorming.

3. Select a scribe to write down all the ideas as they are presented.

4. The quantity of ideas is the goal; quality will follow in the clarification phase.

5. All ideas are acceptable, even if they seem silly or inappropriate.

6. Building on someone else's idea is very acceptable.

7. Avoid positive or negative verbal comments and nonverbal reactions.

8. No evaluation or discussion of the ideas should occur until the brainstorming is completed.

9. Set a time limit.

10. If the flow of ideas slows, one or more of the following techniques may be used to stimulate creativity.

    a. Remain silent for a few minutes.

    b. Change seats or locations, or take a break.

    c. Use a picture or a drawing of a random object. For example, how does a teapot relate to a new branch office? Without energy, nothing will happen. A full pot takes longer to boil so patience is important in this venture. If the pot is put on the wrong plate nothing will happen, so the office location is important. These kinds of mental images can stimulate new ideas.

Method 1

Random expression of ideas, recorded as conceived. This method is acceptable if everyone participates.

Method 2

1. Each participant offers one idea in turn. This method gets the quieter participants involved.

2. Participants jot down additional ideas in between turns.

3. They may pass if they don't have an idea.

Clarification Phase

After the ideas have been collected, start the clarification phase.

- Explore the recorded ideas.

- Probe for the reasons behind the ideas.

- Try to identify the root of suggestions: emotion or logic? Emotional ideas are not necessarily bad.

- Reword ideas to clarify them.

- Group and merge ideas.

Priority Voting

What It Is

Priority voting rapidly reduces a large number of items down to two to six choices. This tool helps build consensus and to eliminate any tendency for one individual to push for acceptance of a pet issue.

How It Works

First Round of Voting

1. Each person votes for as many items on the list as he or she wishes.

2. Total the votes for each item.

3. Circle all items that acquired 30 percent or more of the votes of the team. For example, if 10 team members are participating, circle and retain all items that captured three or more votes.

Second Round of Voting

4. Count the circled items from the first vote.

5. Each person may now vote for no more than 50 percent of the circled items. For example, if 18 items survived the first round, each participant may now vote for a maximum of 9 items.

6. As before, circle all items that acquired 30 percent or more of the votes.

Third and Subsequent Rounds of Voting

7. Continue the process until the list is down to two to six items. Never vote down to one item as this would eliminate the opportunity to discuss the reasons behind the choices. Not everyone sees things the same way or at the same speed.

8. Decide on a further course of action. This may include the use of a tool such as the comparison matrix or force field analysis to further narrow the choices before making a final decision.

Comparison Matrix

What It Is

Faced with a multitude of choices, the comparison matrix helps to arrive at a single choice. The decision is obtained by means of one-on-one comparisons amongst all of the choices.

How It Works

An example will illustrate the process. The features and benefits of six different software programs have been studied, and it is time for a decision.

Step 1. Label the items randomly as A, B, C, D, E, and F.

Step 2. Create a triangle matrix of squares, as shown in Figure 6.2.

- A, B, C, D, E are assigned to the vertical axis. Omit the last item F.

- List the items in reverse order across the horizontal axis, leaving out the first item A.

Step 3. Study each square, choosing between the intersecting choices. Figure 6.3 shows the completed matrix. A choice has been made between every combination.

Step 4. Prepare a ranking table, as illustrated in Figure 6.4. This shows the frequency of choices.

Step 5. In the second column of the ranking table, record the total number of times that each item appears in the matrix.

Step 6. In the third column, note the final ranking. Although not used in the figure, weighted scores, or other tools such as the force field analysis or benefit/LOE analysis may be used to obtain the final rankings.

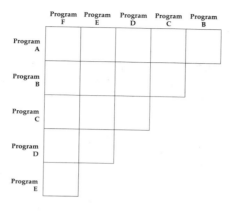

Figure 6.2. Comparison matrix.

	Program F	Program E	Program D	Program C	Program B
Program A	F	E	D	C	A
Program B	F	E	B	C	
Program C	F	C	D		
Program D	D	D			
Program E	F				

Figure 6.3. Completed comparison matrix.

Alternative	Selection frequency	Final ranking
Program A	1	5
Program B	1	6
Program C	3	3
Program D	4	1
Program E	2	4
Program F	4	2

Figure 6.4. Ranking table.

Benefit/LOE Analysis

What It Is

This tool prioritizes a list of improvement ideas or choices. It ranks them according to the potential benefit and the level of effort (LOE) required to implement and maintain the improvement change or choice.

How It Works

Figure 6.5 shows the basis of the process.

Step 1. Rank the benefits from 1–3. Examples of benefits are

- Time savings
- Cost savings
- Safety improvements
- The number of people who will benefit
- The effect on morale

Note: The benefit ranking is based upon the assumption that the idea or change will work. The actual viability of the idea will be proved or disproved by measurement.

Step 2. Rank the level of effort from 1–3. Examples of levels of effort are

- Complexity of investigation
- The time to implement
- The effort to measure
- Resource needs
- Accessibility
- The number of people involved

There are two components.

1. LOE to implement
2. LOE to use and maintain

Note: Cost forms part of this deliberation, but the decision should not be made on cost alone. There are many other intangibles that may be important. The cost consideration should also include the cost to implement and the cost to use and maintain.

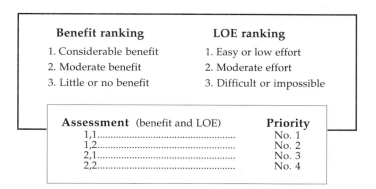

Figure 6.5. Benefit/level of effort (LOE) assessment.

Step 3. Perform the assessment. The ranking assessment is shown at the bottom of Figure 6.5. The decision to rank a 1, 2 ahead of a 2, 1 is based on this author's prescription that a high benefit plus moderate effort outranks moderate benefit plus easy effort.

Problem Statement Tool

What It Is

Ideas for improvement are sometimes expressed as a vague collection of symptoms and concerns. Without a clear direction the improvement team may get bogged down, lose its focus, or even head off into uncharted territory, never to return. By establishing the parameters and boundaries of the problem, the problem statement tool heads off any vagueness that might ambush a thorough investigation. Figure 6.6 shows a problem statement worksheet.

How To Do It

Step 1. Each team member individually writes down the issue as he or she perceives it. This is shown at the top of the figure as a preliminary problem statement. When written, these statements are shared among team members.

Step 2. Each team member individually writes down a list of symptoms that connect to the preliminary problem statements. Guidelines to develop these symptoms are shown in Figure 6.6.

- What
- Who
- When
- Where
- How

Team members should record only the symptoms that they have personally observed, or those they are certain have occurred. Symptoms that might occur, conclusions that might be drawn, and opinions are not counted as symptoms.

Notice that the question why is not asked in the problem statement worksheet because this question will be addressed by specific investigation tools. In most cases there will be no need to deviate from the questions in the worksheet, however, nonapplicable questions may be omitted, or minor modifications may be made to suit the issue being examined.

Step 3. Share and record each team member's list of symptoms.

Step 4. Brainstorm and agree upon the final problem statement as shown at the bottom of the figure. One approach is to derive the final problem statement from the list of symptoms. Another approach is to create a statement of purpose, followed by a bulleted list of symptoms to be healed. A third approach is to use the symptom overlap matrix to develop the problem statement.

Problem Statement Guidelines

1. Symptoms are often found in gaps, obstacles, bottlenecks, rework, misunderstandings, and deviations.

2. Any existing numerical data might be included in the statement.

3. Avoid statements that contain a phrase such as *lack of.* These statements imply a solution.

4. Avoid stating problems or symptoms as questions. The implication is that if the question is answered, the issue will be solved.

Problem statement

Step 1.   Write a preliminary problem statement. ⎯⎯⎯⎯⎯⎯⎯⎯⎯⎯

⎯⎯

⎯⎯

⎯⎯

Step 2.   Brainstorm and record the answers to the following questions.
Some questions may not apply.

What are the symptoms? (List them)

What
   ◆ Procedures are involved?
   ◆ Are the inputs and outputs?
   ◆ Processes are involved?
   ◆ Equipment/supplies are involved?
   ◆ Are the short term impacts?
   ◆ Are the long term impacts?
Who are the
   ◆ Affected stakeholders?
   ◆ Affected clients?
   ◆ Involved consultants?
   ◆ Involved contractors?
When
   ◆ Do the symptoms appear?
      ◆ During which interactions?
      ◆ During which transactions?
      ◆ During which phase?
Where
   ◆ Do the symptoms appear?
How
   ◆ Much is it costing us?
   ◆ Widespread is it?
   ◆ Much has it increased?

Step 3.   If necessary, restate the problem. ⎯⎯⎯⎯⎯⎯⎯⎯⎯⎯⎯⎯

⎯⎯

⎯⎯

⎯⎯

Figure 6.6. Problem statement worksheet.

5. Avoid hinting at solutions. Stick to what is wrong, not why it is wrong.

6. Avoid opinions. Words like *attitude, morale,* and *poor* are too vague and judgmental. Stick to observable facts as would an examining physician. The diagnosis will come later.

Examples of Incorrect and Correct Problem Statements

Presumptious. "Lack of a central tracking system causes duplication in equipment purchase."

Factual. "Duplication occurs in equipment purchases."

Vague and judgmental. "There is a bad attitude to overtime, and schedules are still behind."

Factual. "The Green Division spent \$102,345 on overtime last year; find ways to cut costs and still meet schedules."

Vague and judgmental. "Most people have a poor attitude about filing."

Factual. "During the third quarter, the support staff in the West Wing spent 23 percent of its time tracking down lost files. Improve this situation." The problem can be more simply stated, "Files in the West Wing are being lost. Improve this situation."

Symptom Overlap Matrix

What It Is

This author found that by linking symptoms to umbrella categories, one can better manage the wealth of ideas that arise. This led to the creation of the symptom overlap matrix tool to

- Evaluate symptoms when creating a problem statement.
- Find umbrella causes for a cause-and-effect diagram.
- Verify trial solutions.

Four cases are discussed.

How It Works

Step 1. List the issues, symptoms, and problems that have been noticed or collected. The following is an example of the symptoms that may be collected.

1. Documents are mailed out before being reviewed.
2. Design errors are showing up in the field.
3. Shop drawing reviews are late.
4. Staff talents are not properly used.

5. Field changes are not adequately documented.

6. Departments don't share marketing information.

7. There are insufficient guidelines in the project management manual.

8. More cellular phones are needed.

9. It is difficult to access library information.

10. Field observations are not distributed.

11. Schedule change information is not shared.

12. Material lists are incomplete.

13. Tasks are not clearly defined.

14. Proposal hit rate has dropped.

15. Owners are not being asked the right questions.

16. Support staff is overloaded.

17. Equipment is being lost in the field.

18. A work task tracking system is needed.

Step 2. Number the list from top to bottom, regardless of the content of each item. In the list shown, the issues are quite random, and the numbering is not related to importance. The numbers simply identify the items on the list.

Step 3. Brainstorm and list the umbrella categories that apply. Common umbrella categories include the following:

- Documenting, tracking, and reporting
- Budget issues
- Workload leveling
- Leadership
- Facilities and equipment
- Contracts
- Human resource issues
- Schedule impact
- Risk and liability management procedures
- Team relationships and morale

The 18 random symptoms and concerns have been associated with these umbrella categories, as shown in Figure 6.7.

Note: The assignment under various umbrella categories is subjective, and relies on the perceptions of the PIT.

Symptoms	DTR	Bud	WLL	Lead	F/E	Cont	HR	Sch	RM	Rel
1. Documents mailed out before review.	✓		✓			✓		✓	✓	
2. Design errors show up in field.									✓	
3. Shop drawing reviews late.							✓	✓		
4. Staff talents not properly utilized			✓	✓			✓			✓
5. Field changes not adequately documented.	✓	✓				✓			✓	
6. Departments don't share marketing information.				✓			✓			✓
7. PM manual lacks section on estimating.	✓	✓				✓			✓	
8. More cellular phones needed.	✓	✓			✓			✓		
9. Difficult to access library information.	✓				✓					
10. Field observations not distributed.	✓								✓	
11. Don't inform each other about schedule changes.	✓	✓				✓	✓	✓	✓	✓
12. Material lists are incomplete.	✓								✓	
13. Tasks are not clearly defined.	✓	✓	✓	✓		✓	✓	✓	✓	✓
14. Proposal hit rate has dropped.		✓		✓						
15. Not asking owners the right questions.				✓		✓			✓	✓
16. Support staff overloaded.			✓	✓			✓	✓	✓	✓
17. Equipment being lost in the field.		✓			✓					
18. Need work task tracking.	✓	✓	✓	✓	✓		✓	✓	✓	

DTR = Documenting, tracking, reporting
Bud = Budget impact
WLL = Work load leveling
Lead = Leadership
F/E = Facilities/Equipment

Cont = Contracts
HR = Human resources
Sch = Schedule impact
RM = Risk and liability management
Rel = Team relationships, morale

Figure 6.7. Symptom overlap matrix.

Case 1. Writing a Problem Statement—Use Prioritization

1. Decide which symptoms need to be healed most urgently.

2. Notice the umbrellas that cover those symptoms.

Assuming that matrix item 11 is most critical, a problem statement might be written as follows: "Consistently poor schedule change information sharing in Departments B and D affects documenting, tracking, and reporting (DTR), budget, supplemental contracts, HR staff planning, liability, and team morale."

Case 2. Writing a Problem Statement—Use Frequency

1. Notice which symptoms light up the most umbrella categories.

2. Write a problem statement and start probing for a trial solution under those umbrellas.

Item 13 lit up the most categories, the most prolific in the matrix. A problem statement might be written as follows: "Clients have complained about misunderstandings. This affects every activity in every department."

Case 3. Find Umbrella Categories for a Cause-and-Effect Diagram

1. Find the symptoms most closely linked to the effect.

2. Notice the umbrellas linked to the symptoms.

3. Use those umbrellas for the cause-and-effect diagram.

Using the matrix and item 1 as an example, the umbrellas that would be listed along the spine of the cause-and-effect diagram would be DTR, workload, contracts, schedule, and risk management.

Case 4. Trial Solution Verification

1. Identify the umbrella most closely linked to the trial solution.

2. Verify that the symptoms under that umbrella are healed by the proposed solution.

Using the matrix and the contracts umbrella as an example, any contract system improvement must heal items 1, 5, 7, 11, 13, and 15 in order to be an all-embracing improvement. If that organization also heals human resources, items 4, 6, 11, 13, 16, and 18 should also improve.

Idea Bank Assessment

What It Is

It is impractical to ask talented problem solvers to hold their suggestions for weeks until a trial solution is formulated. Ideas are collected and stored in the idea bank throughout the PIT process. When the trial solution is being created, the ideas are assessed by using the worksheet shown in Figure 6.8.

How It Works

Step 1. Collect ideas. Collect solution ideas as described in chapter 4. During each PIT meeting, these ideas are sequentially numbered and added to a running idea bank list.

Step 2. Sort ideas. Immediately prior to the PIT trial solution step, the team facilitator may study the idea bank and arrange the ideas under umbrella categories. Some or all of the umbrellas listed in the symptom overlap matrix, or any other categories, may be used.

This rearrangement may be performed by the entire team, but it is often more efficient and practical for the facilitator to do it before the trial solution meeting. Nothing is omitted in this step; it is just that the ideas are rearranged into a logical format, and duplicate ideas become obvious.

Once the ideas have been grouped, they should be word processed and tabbed to form a narrow column. The left-hand side column in Figure 6.8 shows where they can be printed or even pasted and photocopied.

Step 3. Implement ideas. The PIT reviews the reformatted list, one category at a time, and discusses how each solution idea might be applied or implemented. This is noted as succinctly as possible in the central column of the worksheet.

Idea Bank Assessment					
Ideas and suggested solutions	How applied How implemented	ILOE	MLOE	VA/B	Who

ILOE = Implement level of effort	MLOE = Maintain level of effort	VA/B = Value added/benefit
1. Easy to implement 2. Moderate effort 3. Difficult or impossible	1. Easy to maintain 2. Moderate effort 3. Difficult or impossible	1. High 2. Moderate 3. Low value/low benefit

Figure 6.8. Idea bank assessment worksheet.

Step 4. Rank ideas. Now the PIT is ready to rank idea viability based on implementation and maintenance levels of effort versus the value-added benefit. This follows the benefit/LOE tool format.

Caution: If possible, try to complete the ranking within one PIT work session. This keeps a uniform, mental baseline. If the ranking process extends over more than one PIT work session, try to keep the composition of the group at the next meeting the same as at the first ranking session. The variation from a uniform baseline and the comparative ranking of ideas is sometimes more revealing than the actual numerical value assigned to any specific idea.

Step 5. Select trial solution ideas. At this point the PIT is ready to combine the best, most viable, and practical ideas into a trial solution, or a series of improvements that comprise a trial solution.

Structure Flowchart

What It Is

The structure flowchart provides a visual check of the systems that link together to form a structure. It helps to spot gaps and redundancies, and may point the PIT toward the root cause. The problem statement may be used to guide the structure flow.

How It Works

The structure flowchart in Figure 6.9 shows an invoicing system.

Step 1. Chart and link all involved systems and key participants.

Step 2. List system responsibilities and the tasks of these individuals.

Step 3. Look for gaps, inconsistencies, and duplication of effort. Brainstorm for root causes and also use the bull's-eye technique to probe deep into reasons behind the reasons.

Note 1: When problem solving, the rule is to chart the current structural flow, not the theoretical flow.

Note 2: If several system flowcharts are diagrammed, it is useful to map them out structurally to see how they are linked. Efficient systems may interface inefficiently and the structure flow may spot these inefficiencies.

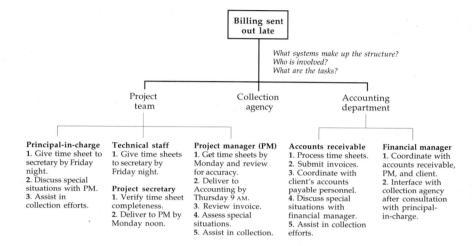

Figure 6.9. Structure flowchart.

Questions that May Lead to Idea Bank Suggestions

- Is information being handed off to the right people?
- Do they get it too late?
- Is there a trend of missed communication?
- How do these systems contribute?
- Are people involved who need not be involved?
- Are people not involved who should be involved?
- Where are the bottlenecks occurring?
- Have these bottlenecks always been there?
- Do some departments not experience these bottlenecks?

System Flowchart

What It Is

This is one of the most popular and useful tools in the toolbox. The system flowchart maps out sequential processes and shows how they are interlinked.

How It Works

Figure 6.10 depicts a purchase order system flowchart.

Step 1. Clearly label the system. It is important for all PIT members to know precisely what they are diagraming. Stakeholders looking at the completed chart on a TQM/CI bulletin board will instantly see its purpose.

Step 2. Each process in the system has an input and an output. It is best to start by listing all the outputs.

- What are the end products that come out of this system?

- What information results from this system?

- What does this system create?

Note: In the illustrated case, the brand evaluation and actual purchase fall outside the bounds of this system. In order to purchase the equipment, the input would be the purchase order, which is the output created by the system illustrated in Figure 6.10.

Step 3. List all the inputs that eventually lead to the outputs. These include guidelines and information sources.

- What scope of information is required to do the work?

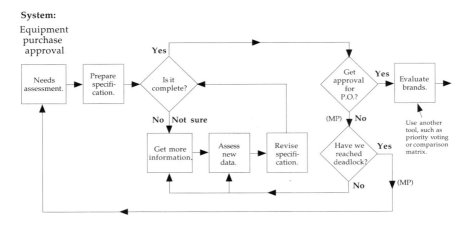

Figure 6.10. System flowchart.

- What document, disk, or information is required?
- What codes and standards govern the work?
- What contractual, financial, and schedule data are needed?

In the illustrated case, the initial input is the needs assessment. In more complex systems there will be multiple inputs.

Step 4. Commence the flowchart, making sure that all the input and output links to processes are clear and comprehensive. Ask the following questions.

- What is done with these inputs?
- What is the first step in the process?
- How do these inputs link to the next activity?

As the system flowchart is created, check off the list of inputs and outputs to ensure that they are all linked into the system. If there are any left over, study how and where they fit into the system.

Note 1: When problem solving, the rule is to chart the current system flow, not the way it should theoretically flow.

Note 2: In all cases, it is important to ascertain where a system starts and ends, and to keep the map plotted within these boundaries.

Step 5. Identify process gaps, redundancies, inefficiencies, and nonvalue-added activities. The three lower blocks in Figure 6.10 represent considerable waste.

Note: It is very useful to create a list of reasons for every nonvalue-added loop. "Why does this loop occur?" These reasons will prove to be a handy supplement in the analysis phase. A cause-and-effect analysis for each of these loops could probe for the root causes of these reasons.

Step 6. When a trial solution has been identified, a new or revised system flow should be diagramed. Verify that any special case exceptions or variations can be absorbed or incorporated into the new or revised system. Also verify that the symptoms shown in the problem statement or the system overlap matrix are healed by the improved flow.

Guidelines

- Drawing the chart neatly and uniformly helps to prevent errors and omissions in complex diagrams. Consistency also helps. For example, draw all yes and no decisions vertically, and draw time flowing horizontally from left to right. Revision and rework loops may double back to the left.

- Complex processes may be multitiered with references to detailed microprocess steps drawn above, below, or on a separate sheet. Most boxes that comprise the system flowchart represent individual processes. Each could be examined in detail with an I/O cause-and-effect analysis, which gives a microscopic analysis of input and output links. This analysis might point to the need for an IPO audit.

- Decision points are shown as diamonds. Data measurement points (MP) may be identified. In the example, the frequency that purchase orders are denied each month, or the number of times that deadlock is reached in a year, might be MPs.

- If an organization has several ways of doing the same thing, a parallel chart may be drawn to show variations.

- Once the current system flow has been charted, it may be distributed to the stakeholders for feedback.

Questions that May Lead to Idea Bank Suggestions

- Are all of the inputs used consistently?

- Which processes are important, but were not diagrammed because they are usually not done?

- How many steps are redundant?

- How many steps are nonvalue-added loops?

- What if a particular step was no longer done?

- What could be combined to make the system simpler?

- Are all of the processes required on all of the projects?

- What holds up the work?

The IPO Audit—A Process Flowchart

The basic building block of continuous improvement is the input-process-output (IPO) model. If outputs are going to meet or beat client expectations, excellence in the inputs and processes must be achieved. A tool to accomplish this excellence is the IPO audit, which exposes and eliminates bottlenecks, miscommunication, and information gaps, and reduces the chance of bad data.

What It Is

This author created the IPO audit to clarify the procedures and interactions between service providers and clients. A project management system, for example, could be broken out and improved.

Visualize a railroad. The trains are projects, and the track is the project management system. During the train's journey there is no time to improve the track. Track and signal system improvements are done during quiet periods, so when the trains eventually come down the line, they will run smoothly and reach their destinations on time.

In the same way, the audit is not designed to be used when a project team is getting on with the work. But between projects, the audit can improve the processes within the project management system. The improved system will have standard operating procedures to be used once projects are on track and under way. The audit may also be used as a tool to plan specific assignments, and it may be useful to start documenting processes for ISO 9000 compliance.

How It Works

Step 1. The system being audited is identified. For example, the following systems may be examined.

- Proposal writing
- Paycheck preparation
- Document production
- Foundation construction
- Report preparation

The various processes that comprise the system may be shown on a system flowchart, or simply listed in sequence. For example, proposal writing links project research with proposal production. Paycheck processing links time sheets with check distribution.

Select a process to audit. Then start with outputs in the audit worksheet shown in Figure 6.11.

Step 2. The process owners, those stakeholders whose work includes the process being audited, meet with the output receivers to identify the outputs. These are listed in the bottom left box of the worksheet. These two groups then discuss ways to improve outputs in terms of clarity, conformance, conciseness, and precision. Meeting or beating the client's expectations is the goal. This information is recorded in the bottom middle box. Finally, output QA guidelines are revised or created. These guidelines, based on the suggestions for better outputs, are recorded in the bottom right box. They guide future output interactions. This may be in the form of a checklist.

Step 3. The inputters meet with the process owners to identify the inputs. These are listed in the top left box of Figure 6.11. These groups then discuss ways to improve inputs to meet output needs and make them easier to process. Any ideas for interactive efficiency are shared. This information is recorded in the top middle box of the worksheet.

Finally, input QA guidelines, based on the improvement ideas, are revised or created. These guidelines, recorded in the top right box, will govern future input content and interactions. These, too, may be created and used in the form of a checklist.

Step 4. The process owners now get together to list the process steps, or the procedures they go through to do the work. These are listed in the middle left box of Figure 6.11. The process owners discuss ways to do the job more effectively, given quality inputs and expecting quality outputs. Their ideas are recorded in the middle box.

Finally, process QA guidelines are revised or created based on desired input and output formats. These guidelines, recorded in the middle right box, will govern future process activities. Again, checklists might be the simplest format for these QA guidelines.

Note 1: The ideas in the left-hand boxes can be obtained during group or during one-on-one meetings. If they are one-on-one, the stakeholder

Process ——————————————— Department ————————————
This process links ————————————— with ——————————————

Input	Input provider — Name———————————— Processor is a client — Name ————————————	
1.	Processor suggestions for more effective inputs	QA input guidelines/checklist
2.		
3.		
4.		
5.		
6.		
7.		
8.		
9.		
10.		

Process Steps	Process owners' suggestions identify the best way to do the work.	QA process guidelines/checklist
1.		
2.		
3.		
4.		
5.		
6.		
7.		
8.		
9.		
10.		

Output	Processor is now a provider — Name ———————— Output receiver(s) are clients — Names ————————	
1.	Output receiver(s)' suggestions for more efficient outputs	QA output guidelines/checklist
2.		
3.		
4.		
5.		
6.		
7.		
8.		
9.		
10.		

Figure 6.11. IPO audit worksheet.

representatives who meet take the audit in draft form back to the stakeholders for more input. Bulletin board posting of the draft audit might also be useful.

Note 2: Readers should not be too concerned with getting the audit 100 percent accurate the first time. Complete the audit and create the QA guideline checklists. Get them out and used. The best refinements will come in use. This will also result in continuous improvement thinking.

Note 3: Some readers may now be dismayed by the thought of all these checklists and paperwork. Yet it is the system that most often needs the greatest improvement boost. Checklists are a great way to get this happening, and get it happening consistently. A final thought on this topic. This author would ask these readers if they would feel comfortable flying with pilots who did not go through their preflight checklists before every single flight. They cannot afford to make a mistake. Can you?

The Five Benefits of the IPO Audit

1. The information regarding inputs, processes, and outputs—together with the suggestions for improvements—are a wonderful source of ideas for a PIT.

2. The meetings and discussions needed to complete the IPO audit are valuable team-building occasions.

3. A commitment may be asked of everyone in the organization to meet with their input and output counterparts within the next six months to complete an IPO audit. As mentioned, they can do this one-on-one or in small groups. These interactions may need to be coordinated by a task team, but this effort will get TQM/CI off to a flying start.

   A triangular matrix, adapted from the comparison matrix format shown in Figure 6.2 to show the interactions between each staff member, will ensure that all interaction combinations are covered. This can be posted on the TQM/CI bulletin board.

4. The IPO audit can be a great coaching tool when used in conjunction with performance reviews. One-on-one reviews might be supplemented with groups of two to three people who look at their results and commit to improve via QA guidelines.

5. Finally, the IPO audit facilitates one of the most useful activities, the previously discussed quality review (QR). The IPO audit leads to QA guidelines written up as checklists, which stakeholders subsequently use to self-check their own work before passing the baton in actual project situations. This is illustrated in its simplest form between three stakeholders, named Boniface, Concordia, and Fiducia, in Figure 6.12. In this illustration, the IPO audit has already been done, the QA guideline checklists have been created, and these individuals are shown working on a project.

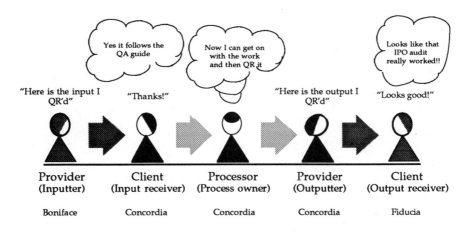

Figure 6.12. IPO flow between stakeholders.

Three-Boundary Search

What It Is

The three-boundary search is an analysis tool. It explores the parameters of problems. Forensic experts and medical diagnosticians use this tool every day.

When to Use It

When it appears that a problem is not found everywhere, is not uniformly large, and does not always occur, the problem has boundaries. An investigation of the limits of those boundaries may point to the source of the problem. This implies establishing the boundaries and then looking beyond them to gather clues associated with the boundaries. The three boundaries are location, size, and time.

How It Works

Step 1. Probe to identify the location of the boundaries. The best method is to ask the team questions. Sample questions include the following:

- Does the problem appear in every department?
    - Where would one go to find it in that department?
    - Is it equally serious in every department?
    - Has it always been that way?
- Does the problem appear in every project?
    - At the same phase or step?
    - In every type of project?
    - On every size project?
    - For every client?
    - With every project manager?
    - To the same extent or depth in each project?
    - Has it always been that way?
- Does the problem appear in every output?
    - The same or different parts of the output?

—Does every piece of equipment produce it?

—Is it tied to the phase of the output?

—Is it the same for all formats of input?

—Is it as large in every output?

—Has it always been that way?

Step 2. Search for clues in the answers. Buried deep within the information might be the one clue that points directly to the root cause.

- If the problem does not occur in every department, on every project, or during every transaction, find out why it occurs in some places and not in others. Here may lie clues to the problem's source.

- If the size, extent, or seriousness vary, identify what mitigates the problem on some projects, in some departments, or during some transactions. This will reveal more clues.

- If the problem has not always occurred, try to establish when things started to go wrong. What event occurred contemporaneously with the first appearance of the problem that might point to a cause? Was a new manager hired? Did a manager change an operational process? Was a new market opened? Did someone resign? Who got promoted? Was a new telephone system installed? Was a new software program launched? Was there a merger or acquisition? Was a branch opened or closed? Did a time crunch lead to a change in task allocation? Were new job descriptions issued? So many changes occur in a professional practice, that any one, or any combination of changes may lead to the emergence of a problem.

- If the problem appears everywhere with the same size, extent, or seriousness, and it has always been that way, there is something wrong with the entire system or structure.

Note: The three-boundary search may be used to identify the precise baseline measurements required. It tells the teams where to start looking and what comparisons to make. Boundary comparisons can also help to break down the resistance of TQM/CI doubters.

Force Field Analysis

What It Is

This tool is useful in assessing and dealing with the forces that affect issues. It will be described in its simplest format.

How It Works

Step 1. Identify the issue to be analyzed or the idea to be studied.

Step 2. List the current positive forces that help or strengthen the current process. As an option, these may be weighted in importance or ranked in strength.

Step 3. List the current negative forces that hinder or weaken the current process. As an option, these too may be weighted in importance or ranked in strength.

Step 4. If weights or rankings are used, note where the median of these forces lies. Does this indicate that the net force is positive or negative?

Step 5. Consider how the current, positive, helping forces might be assisted or improved.

Step 6. Consider how the current, negative, hindering forces might be mitigated, restrained, or eliminated.

Caution: When this is the only tool used by a PIT, there is a great temptation to jump to the conclusion that all one has to do is assist the helpful and cut out the unhelpful forces, and the problem will be solved. This can be dangerous as it does not directly explore root causes. Because of this, this author finds the best use of the force field analysis is with task teams. Nevertheless it may be productively used by a PIT to

- Narrow priority voting choices.
- Obtain the final comparison matrix rankings.
- Supplement the benefit/LOE analysis tool.
- Identify actions needed to overcome barriers and implement needs.
- Assess rankings for the idea bank.

Cause-and-Effect Diagram

When the leaves of a weed are trimmed to ground level, the weed will probably continue to grow rapidly. These symptoms will reappear until the roots are removed. Readers may refer to the symptom tree in Figure 2.6. Negative root cause seeds result in negative effects and nonvalue-added activities. Positive root cause seeds result in positive effects. The laws of cause and effect were explored 3000 years ago in India, so the concept is not new. Japanese TQM master Kaoru Ishikawa used this ancient concept to create the cause-and-effect diagram.

What It Is

1. The cause-and-effect diagram probes hierarchal causes until the root cause is uncovered.

2. It exposes flaws in structures, systems, and processes.

3. It prevents snap judgments and subjective decision making.

How It Works

Step 1. Draw the basic spine and fin shape as shown in Figure 6.13. This may be done on a large board. If the available board is small, or if a flip chart is used, tackle the diagram one fin at a time.

Step 2. Identify the effect. This may be a symptom tied to the problem statement, a phrase that captures the combined effect of several symptoms, a component of the problem statement, or even the problem statement itself. In any event, team members should be guided by the problem statement to make sure that they are following the right path in deciding which effect to study.

Step 3. Decide on the umbrella causes. These are basic headings that guide the direction of the investigation. In the manufacturing world, categories such as costs, machines, methods, and materials may be used. The system overlap matrix may assist in identifying these categories. Umbrella cause categories for professional services may include the following:

- Time
- Financial factors
- Subconsultant factors
- Management factors
- Construction factors
- Legal factors

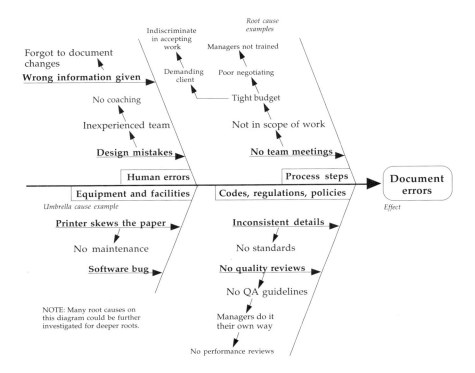

Figure 6.13. Cause-and-effect diagram.

- Human resources
- Equipment and facilities
- Codes and regulations
- Client factors
- Process steps
- Standards and methods

Umbrella causes are traditionally drawn at the ends of the diagonal fins. A more practical location, preferred by this author, is to place these causes along the spine of the diagram. This allows the root cause search to flow unimpeded, away from the spine. This is shown in Figure 6.13.

Step 4a. Use the effect. The team facilitator picks an umbrella cause and asks the team to identify how that cause contributes to the effect under review. This results in subcauses, as shown in Figure 6.13 above the horizontal arrows. A question might be phrased as follows: "How do equipment and facilities contribute to document errors?" The first response in the figure is "The printer skews the paper." This is followed up with the question "Why?" The answer is "There are no maintenance procedures." The facilitator should continue to ask why.

Sometimes one must be innovative in phrasing questions. Try to elicit answers that lead to deeper probing. It is a pitfall to ask questions such as, "How can we prevent . . . ?" Asking for a solution prematurely ends the probing. If solution ideas are mentioned, record them in the idea bank and keep probing.

Step 4b. Use the symptoms. Examine the symptom list associated with the Problem Statement. Taking them one at a time, the facilitator asks the team to identify the umbrella closest to the symptom. Then the team is asked how that umbrella contributes to that particular symptom. The facilitator should continue asking why.

Step 5. For both steps 4a and 4b, the subcauses are probed and further causes identified. Although not fully explored in Figure 6.13, numerous causes could flow from each subcause. For example, the reasons that checklists are not used could include the following: the staff is not trained to use them; current checklists are inadequate; no one verifies their use; or the checklists are too complex. Each of these reasons could lead to even deeper causes and should be further probed. This is done by the team facilitator asking PIT members why these causes occur.

Asking why is an important probing methodology. This follows Ishikawa's dictum and ties into the bull's-eye technique described in step 3 of chapter 4. When the root causes have been uncovered, move to explore the next umbrella cause or the next symptom.

Step 6. When all the umbrella causes and symptoms have been deeply probed, the most influential root causes might be circled and ranked. Some root causes are tough to deal with. For example, the root cause of frequent regulatory agency rule changes may be beyond the control of the team. Antidotes for the circled root causes may be recorded in the idea bank and later combined to form trial solution components.

Step 7. In an archeological search, clues identify where to dig. If one digs in the right spot, artifacts will be found. The next step is to establish the nature, extent, and details of the discovery. So when root causes have been uncovered and identified, the team should document the

- Specific location of the problem
- Frequency and trend of the occurrence

- Date the problem started
- Magnitude and extent of the root cause

This will create a root cause profile, yielding clues regarding their mitigation or elimination. The three-boundary search provides an effective way to establish this profile.

Note 1: Diagrams can get complex. It is important to keep the hierarchial levels organized otherwise information can be lost in the transcription to a paper record. Using different-colored pens is one of the best methods. For example all subcauses might be red, and the next level green. Or different shaped bullets, such as asterisks, circles, boxes, and diamonds next to levels of causes can keep everything in a hierarchial structure. Different-colored arrows can add an extra layer of differentiation. Another excellent method, one that can also be combined with colored pens, is to label the causes with letters of the alphabet to coincide with their hierarchial level.

Note 2: Once an umbrella category has been fully explored, the different levels of causes might be word processed using a hierarchial outline. Figure 6.14 is an example showing the different cause levels extracted from Figure 6.13.

After word processing, these lists can be reduced on a copy machine and pasted onto a cause-and-effect outline. The completed diagram may be posted on the TQM/CI bulletin board.

CAUSE LEVEL A:	**PROCESS STEPS**
CAUSE LEVEL B:	NO TEAM MEETINGS
Cause Level C:	**Not in Scope of Work**
Cause Level D:	Tight budget
Cause Level E:	• Poor negotiating
Cause Level F:	—Managers not trained
Cause Level E:	• Demanding client
Cause Level F:	—Indiscriminate in accepting work

Figure 6.14. Different cause levels drawn from cause-and-effect diagram.

Note 3: Numerous solution ideas and suggestions usually surface during the probing process. Record these in the idea bank.

Note 4: Magnitude and frequency measurements of the root causes may be useful in prioritizing trial solution components.

I/O Cause-and-Effect Diagram

What It Is

This tool complements the standard cause-and-effect diagram. It examines input and output linkages and spotlights process flaws.

When to Use It

This author created this tool specifically to examine work overlaps and redundancies, to clarify misunderstandings, and to expose bottlenecks and information gaps. It works especially well in conjunction with the IPO audit.

The I/O cause-and-effect diagram can also be used to modify and fine-tune a trial solution that did not live up to expectations. The following clues may indicate the need for the I/O cause-and-effect diagram.

- High quality inputs result in poor quality outputs.
- Outputs are excellent, but the process is inefficient.
- Input-process-output responsibilities are unclear.
- Processors and inputters disagree over standards.
- Processors and output receivers disagree over standards.
- There is duplication of effort.
- Outputs are being rejected.
- An IPO audit reveals a bottleneck.
- An IPO audit results in deadlock.

How It Works

Step 1. List the process inputs in Figure 6.15. Inputs might include the following:

- A request for a proposal
- Scope of work

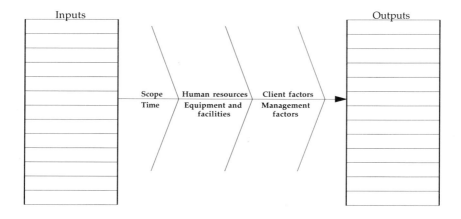

Figure 6.15. I/O cause-and-effect diagram.

- Project research
- A code update
- A CAD specification
- Team member roles
- A specification revision
- A site analysis
- Public agency input
- A zoning code

Step 2. List the process outputs. These might include the following:

- Proposal
- Conceptual plan
- Preliminary cost estimate
- Work plan
- Owner sign off
- Scope breakout
- Cost model
- Outline specification

- Budget reconciliation
- Punch list

The cause-and-effect spine can be moved up or down between the input and output blocks.

Step 3. Start the cause-and-effect diagram by pointing the spine at the outputs to be investigated. The effect will be the output next to the spine arrowhead. The umbrella categories will relate to the associated inputs, linkages, and processes. In many cases, several inputs are required to obtain just one output. Before starting the analysis, check for missing inputs. Another option would be to reverse the arrow and examine a problem input, using a similar methodology.

Step 4. Proceed with the standard cause-and-effect methodology, asking why, identifying all subcauses and root causes, and looking for trial solution components.

Note: Most outputs are created to meet the scope of work and satisfy internal and external clients. As part of continuous improvement, the team may also consider ways to get output that will delight the client.

Pareto Chart

Vilfredo Pareto (1848–1923) noticed that the majority of crimes were committed by only a few criminals. He also showed that most private wealth was held by just a few individuals. This led him to establish his theory of logarithmic distribution.

What It Is

Based on Pareto's observations, approximately 80 percent of problems result from only 20 percent of the causes. This means that the vital few causes account for the majority of problems, and the trivial many causes result in the remaining problems.

As cautioned earlier, continuous improvement can reach a point of diminishing returns. When continuous improvement is allied to a Pareto mentality the consistent search for the vital few will facilitate continuous improvement efficiency. Thus,

- Dramatic results may be quickly obtained.
- Time is not wasted on the trivial.

The Pareto chart is a useful team tool, allowing different team members and process owners to look into different data sets such as occurrence, cost, or location, to yield different perspectives. In addition, the Pareto chart facilitates quick comprehension of the problem intensities for all the stakeholders.

How It Works

Step 1. Use an appropriate tool, such as a cause-and-effect diagram, to search for problem causes.

Step 2. Use a check sheet to gather data on the frequency with which the different causes occur. The check sheet at the top of Figure 6.16 deals with the reason for billing delays. The causes listed as a–e have been monitored, and the frequency of occurrence summarized.

Step 3. Draw the Pareto chart as shown at the bottom of Figure 6.16. The frequency of causes a–e have been converted into percentages and rearranged sequentially as bars with the most frequent to the left and the least frequent to the right. The cumulative percentages are plotted above the bars.

Benefits

The Pareto chart gives a simple graphic translation of data, and can also clarify the problem statement. In the example shown, an original problem statement of "Billing is frequently late," may now be modified to state, "78 percent of late billing can be attributed to late, incomplete, or incorrect time sheets."

Another example might display occurrence baseline data of the reasons for any loops in a system flowchart. Both of these scenarios open the door to a focused analysis.

Caution: Symptom frequency of occurrence does not necessarily correlate to symptom significance. A less frequently occurring symptom may be the most deadly. Assume, for example, that "Reports have errors" is the problem statement. It is shown that 72 percent of the symptoms are "Pages that photocopy with a minor blemish," while only 9 percent of the symptoms are "Chapters missing." The latter, even though less frequent, is far more significant. Good judgment must always be in evidence.

Month	a	b	c	d	e
January	6	1	4	9	2
February	7	0	0	7	1
March	5	1	3	4	0
April	11	0	5	6	0
May	4	0	2	9	3
June	5	0	1	12	1
	38	2	15	47	7

KEY   Total = 109 late invoices
a. Incorrect or incomplete time sheets
b. Lost time sheets
c. Delay in time sheet approval
d. Time sheets not handed in on time
e. Delay in invoice preparation

Check sheet for Pareto chart

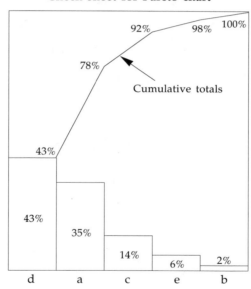

Figure 6.16. Pareto chart.

Pareto Cause Analysis

What It Is

The Pareto cause analysis utilizes cascading Pareto charts to probe deep into the frequencies of the causes. This tool enables the vital few to be exposed by peeling back subcauses, layer by layer, until one finds the frequency of occurrence of the root causes. It relates directly to the cause-and-effect family of tools, by taking their results and illustrating the relative impact of the various root causes.

How It Works

Steps 1–3. Perform a standard Pareto chart analysis. This frequency plot will be the baseline Pareto. The example shown in Figure 6.17 explores the origins of budget overruns. Data have been gathered from a random set of projects, and the frequencies have been plotted to create a baseline Pareto.

Step 4. Identify the most frequent cause, the tallest bar, and treat it as a topic for a data search and Layer II Pareto chart. In Figure 6.17, the most frequent baseline source occurs in the construction phase. An investigation is now launched to ascertain the source of budget overruns in the construction phase. This results in a frequency of occurrence Layer II Pareto.

Simultaneously, the second most frequent source from the baseline, the design phase, may be investigated. This results in another Layer II Pareto.

Step 5. Identify the most frequent cause of each Layer II Pareto, and run a further data search and subsequent Layer III Pareto chart. In Figure 6.17, the owner and the contractor are found to be the most frequent cause of the Layer II construction phase investigation. Investigations are launched to ascertain the specific source of budget overruns in each of these two areas. This results in the "Reasons for C" and "Reasons for D," Layer III Pareto charts.

In addition, a probe of design changes, the most frequent occurrence of the "Reasons for B" Layer II Pareto chart, will result in the "Reasons for E" Layer III Pareto. Although not shown in Figure 6.17, the noncompliance cause in the Layer II Pareto could also be investigated.

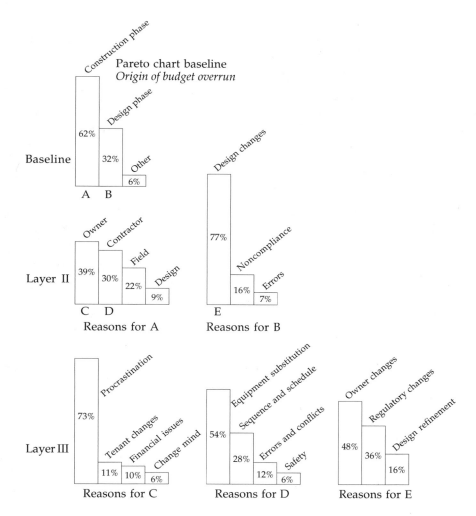

Figure 6.17. Pareto cause analysis.

Step 6. At the discretion of the team, guided by its facilitator, a fourth round of investigations may be launched. Using the example shown in Figure 6.17, the causes of procrastination on the part of the owner, the causes of equipment substitutions on the part of the contractor, and the causes of owner changes leading to design changes in the design phase, could result in Layer IV Pareto charts. Occasionally, it might even be deemed necessary to extend the investigation into Layer V Pareto charts.

The decision to dig deeper, or to choose to follow one path of investigation rather than another, is governed by a review of the problem statement on the one hand, and by the search for a practical trial solution on the other hand. This means that there would be little point in probing the reasons for causes that are totally beyond the control of the PIT. These include regulatory issues, legislative and banking causes, and public opinion.

Variation and Relationship Monitoring Tools

Overview

Statistics facilitate the drawing of realistic conclusions from a small sample of data. The term *statistical process control* (SPC) may conjure up thoughts of complexity and high-powered analysis. The goal of this chapter is twofold.

1. To demonstrate that SPC can be understood by everybody. The level of analytical detail required for professional service use is such that the tools, once clearly explained, become allies rather than strangers. For situations more complex than those presented here, it may be advisable to obtain a book on SPC, attend a course, or consult with a professional statistician.

2. To provide examples that relate directly to professional services. Tools to observe and monitor variability should be available for use by everyone in an organization. When SPC is owned by only a few insiders, the rest of the staff may feel antagonistic. Once the mystery is taken out of SPC, however, the staff may see the value in being able to statistically monitor its own processes.

Having said that, it is important not to blow SPC out of proportion. These tools are there to be used when, and only when, they are most appropriate. The guide in chapter 4 noted when these tools might be utilized, and not every situation will require their use. Many continuous improvement efforts, however, can benefit from the judicious use of SPC.

Variation

One of the great wonders of the world is the almost infinite variation that can be observed in nature. In the commercial and industrial world, infinite variation is equally evident in

- People
- Procedures
- Environments
- Policies

This leads to five statements about professional service variation.

1. No two projects are exactly alike.
2. Variation often occurs in predictable patterns.
3. Measurements may be used to determine the extent of variation.
4. Measurements, observation and subsequent adjustments can change unpredictable variations into predictable variations.
5. Variations, when in statistical control, are predictable and stable.

Common Cause Variation

- Common cause variation (CCV) reflects normal, random statistical variation. It is also known as chance cause or statistical noise.
- CCV is inherent and always present in systems or processes, so its occurrence is not unusual or unexpected.
- CCV is displayed in charts as minor, random, statistical departures from the process center, occurring within statistical limits.
- The only way to influence statistical noise is by improving or changing the system. The variation will still occur, but it will be at a more acceptable level.
- Even though CCV reflects a stable process, most processes are still subject to refinement and continuous improvement.

The following may be common cause variations.

- Variation in
  - —Project manager experience and abilities
  - —Time to produce a specification
  - —Time to produce a CAD document
  - —Time to produce a proposal
  - —Time sheet completion and accuracy
  - —Staff meeting duration
  - —Client payment cycles
- Accidents on a construction site
- Flooding, but within a 50-year return
- Response variations to a questionnaire
- Frequency of change orders

A subway train scheduled for daily arrival at a station at 6:05 P.M. may actually have a series of arrivals, over a six-day period, as follows: 6:03:58, 6:05:07, 6:04:29, 6:04:43, 6:05:21, and 6:04:19. These slight variations are CCVs, and are caused by tiny, random occurrences. If on the seventh day, the train arrives at 6:29:04, something external to the normal system has occurred to result in this large variation. This large variation may not be a CCV. Perhaps the power failed or there was a mechanical problem. These special causes may link back to improper maintenance procedures, or neglect tied to a human root cause. If the driver was ill, a backup plan might have been established for unexpected absences.

Special Cause Variation

- Special cause variation (SCV) is a sign that a system or process may be unstable and unpredictable. It is also known as assignable cause or statistical signal. If the subway train arrived at 6:29:04, the probability would be high that this late arrival was an SCV.
- SCV is detrimental and may result in chaos.
- SCV shows up in charts as data points plotted far from the centerline, or as nonrandom patterns.

- SCV may be traceable to an identifiable cause or something unusual, such as an external influence that is not inherent in normal, random variability. These external influences are often linked to human actions or inactions, such as in the subway train example.
- The sources of special causes must be eliminated, or at least mitigated.

The following incidents are examples of special cause variation.

- Unpredictable client changes
- Unpredictable field conditions such as an archeological find or chemical waste of unknown origin
- Public opinion that arises against a development
- Legislative and regulatory rule changes
- The effect of landmark court decisions
- Key staff absences due to accidents or illness
- Strikes
- Human error, misunderstandings, or unpredictability with sub-causes ranging from stress burnout to substance abuse
- Emotional decisions

These potential SCVs are particularly hard to predict or eliminate. In many cases, designing a system that will deal with, and mitigate the impacts, is the right approach.

Data and Chart Types

In order to select the most appropriate SPC chart for any given application, it is important to be able to clearly distinguish among various data types. These include count, attribute, and variable data.

Count Data

Count data are obtained after an event has occurred. Items or instances are counted, but the total number of items, instances, and nonconformances that could have occurred is potentially infinite. Therefore, only actual occurrences are countable. Because of the unlimited potential for occurrences, boundaries are usually established, such as counting over a limited time, over a fixed area, or within a selected sample.

General Examples
- The number of defects in a product
- The number of flaws in a paint job
- The number of tears in a piece of material

Professional Service Examples
- The average number of days late for receivables
- The number of errors in a document
- Requests for information received in July
- The number of construction defects in a floor slab

Useful Charts
- c chart—occurrences or events per sample (sample constant)
- u chart—occurrences or events per sample (sample varies)

Attribute Data

Attribute data are obtained after an event has occurred. Items in a finite group are counted, so occurrences and nonoccurrences, conformances and nonconformances are all equally countable. This means that in each case the total population or subpopulation can be counted, as can the instances of unacceptability.

General Examples
- The number of staff absent out of the entire staff
- The number of assembly kits found with defective parts
- The number of shipments with broken items

Professional Service Examples
- The number of
  - —Tables with errors in a report
  - —Invoices with errors mailed in July
  - —Permit applications refused in 1994

—Proposals won in the third quarter

—Columns requiring rework

—Staff who worked overtime in August

• Clients with past due accounts in February

Useful Chart

• *p* chart—fraction of items or samples found defective or unacceptable (sample size may vary)

Variable Data

Variable data are measured during a process or event. Data is usually obtained with an instrument.

General Examples

• The height of a tide

• The temperature of a liquid

• Inches of rainfall

• The weight of an individual

Professional Service Examples

• Volume of water flowing past a point

• Time taken to revise a document

• Time taken to photocopy 30 reports

• Air flow in a duct per second

• Deflection in a structural beam under load

• Width of a crack in concrete

• Number of days late at each milestone

• Hours spent on troubleshooting each day

• Percent budget overrun per project at month end

• Write-offs as dollars per month

• Utilization rate as hours per employee

- Monthly overhead as dollars or multiplier
- Number of hours spent on rework each week
- Number of overtime hours worked each month

Useful Charts
- Run chart—plot of occurrences over time.
- X-bar and *R* chart—two charts tracking samples.
- X and moving range chart—two charts tracking individual items.

How to Differentiate Between Count or Attribute and Variable Data

While not an absolute test, the following may be used as a guide to identify data type. Ask, does half of this unit make sense? For example, can there be half a defect, half a client, half a proposal, half an error, half a request, half a staff member, or half an invoice. If half does not make sense, the data are count or attribute data. If splitting the unit does make sense, such as half a dollar, half an inch, or half an hour, the data are often variable data.

Run Chart

What It Is

A run chart plots how data vary over a period of time. It can demonstrate process instability. A run chart is not a control chart because control limits are not established.

The advantages of run charts include the following:

- They are easy to plot.
- They are easy to interpret.
- They can be used in many circumstances.
- No calculations are required.
- When testing a new process, they are easy to read, they indicate possible instability, and they point to the need for improvements.
- No assumptions need to be made about the distribution of the population from which the sample was drawn.

The disadvantages of run charts include the following:

- Observations must be completed before the chart can be interpreted.
- The presence of SCVs may be suspected, but the charts provide no way to pinpoint the variations.
- They cannot track changes due to small process adjustments.
- They are not sensitive to large spikes or outliers.

How to Do It

A run is a sequence of connected data points plotted over time. There are various kinds of runs, and they help to notice instability. Although 10 or fewer points can be plotted, try for at least 20–30 points.

Step 1. Obtain data, using a check sheet if necessary.

Step 2. Label the run chart axes, and plot the data as shown at the top of Figure 7.1. By convention, the vertical axis shows data measured, and the horizontal axis plots time.

Step 3. Calculate and draw the median. The median is the centerline of the plotted data. It is obtained as follows:

1. Count how many numbers have been plotted = n.
2. Sequence the numbers in ascending order.
   a. If n is odd, the median is the middle number. Example: 4, 7, 11, 16, 17, 23, 34, 35, 39; median is 17.
   b. If n is even, the median is the average of the two mid-values. Example: 6, 9, 14, 18, 22, 27, 36, 38; median is $(18 + 22)/2 = 20$

Step 4. Identify the sequences of data points that do not cross the median. Each such group of points is known as a run, as shown at the bottom of Figure 7.1.

Step 5. Count the runs. The figure has 23 data points and 14 runs.

Step 6. Do the first stability check. Use the statistical test sheet in Figure 7.2 to establish if the runs are stable. It will be noticed that for 23 data points, the lower bound is 8 runs, and the upper bound is 16 runs. So any run chart with 23 data points that has between 8 and 16

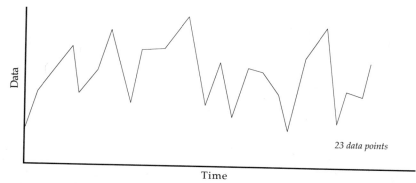

Completed run chart

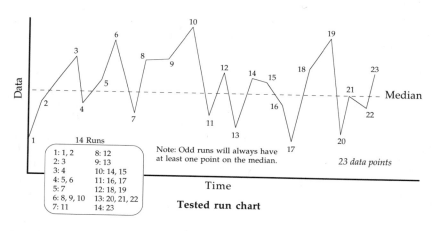

Figure 7.1. Run charts.

runs meets the statistical criteria for stability. Thus, the plot in Figure 7.1 is statistically sound. If the test sheet indicated too many or too few runs, statistical randomness would be absent, and the process would be regarded as unstable. Figure 7.3 shows two examples exhibiting instability.

Step 7. Do the second stability check. Apply the run pattern tests, shown in Figure 7.4, to search for unusual patterns within the plotted

Number of data points	Lower run limit	Upper run limit	Number of data points	Lower run limit	Upper run limit
10	3	8	34	12	23
11	3	9	35	13	23
12	3	10	36	13	24
13	4	10	37	14	24
14	4	11	38	14	25
15	4	12	39	14	26
16	5	12	40	15	26
17	5	13	41	16	26
18	6	13	42	16	27
19	6	14	43	17	27
20	6	15	44	17	28
21	7	15	45	17	29
22	7	16	46	17	30
23	8	16	47	18	30
24	8	17	48	18	31
25	9	17	49	19	31
26	9	18	50	19	32
27	9	19	60	24	37
28	10	19	70	28	43
29	10	20	80	33	48
30	11	20	90	37	54
31	11	21	100	42	59
32	11	22	110	46	65
33	12	22	120	51	70

System is stable between upper and lower limits.

System is stable between upper and lower limits.

This chart tests the number of runs above and below the median.

Source: Adapted from "Tables for testing randomness of groupings in a sequence of alternatives," *The Annals of Mathematical Statistics*, Vol. 14, No. 1, 1943. Published with permission.

Figure 7.2. Statistical test sheet.

data. If any are identified, this would also indicate an unstable process. In general, search for any sequence showing unusual events such as outliers, repetitive patterns, sudden shifts, or jumps in the location of groups of data. Talk to the process owners, and perhaps use one of the analysis tools to search for causes.

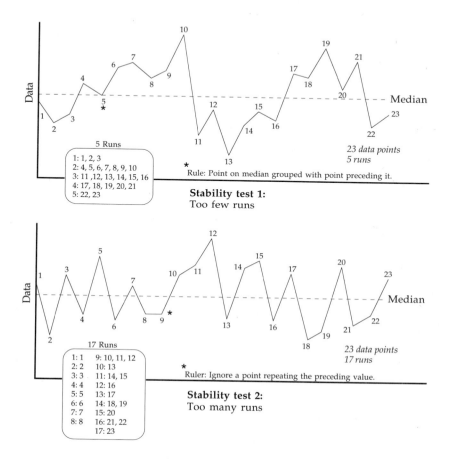

Figure 7.3. Statistical test sheet examples.

Improvement guidelines

- If the run chart exhibits stability, the goal is to continuously improve the system or process to reduce variation.
- If the run chart exhibits instability, the goal is to identify the negative and detrimental root causes, possibly through an analysis tool, and mitigate or permanently eliminate these causes.

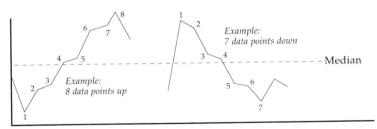

Stability test 3:
Six or more sequential points, all up or all down.

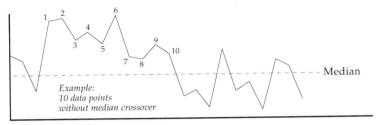

Stability test 4:
Nine or more sequential points on same side of the median.

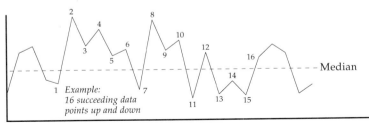

Stability test 5:
Fourteen or more points, alternating up and down.

Source: Reproduced with the permission of AT&T, ©1956. All rights reserved.

Figure 7.4. Run pattern test examples.

Histogram

What It Is

Although an experienced statistician can use the histogram as a valuable quality tool, it is presented here because of the close relationship between the histogram and control charts. Unlike Pareto charts, which result from a rearrangement of data into a frequency of occurrence layout, the histogram shows a raw distribution of frequency of occurrences grouped into cells.

An Example

Suppose a department wanted to improve its meeting process. The staff members decide to continue to meet while they collect data on what causes their meetings to be efficient or inefficient. Suppose, too, that they time their meetings to establish a baseline.

A check sheet for recording the length of their meetings is shown at the top of Figure 7.5. This can be rotated 90 degrees and drawn as a histogram, as shown at the bottom of Figure 7.5. Readers will notice the profile of the tally is approximately bell shaped. This is known as the normal probability curve, which indicates a statistically normal distribution.

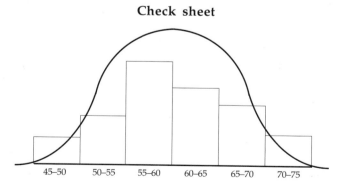

Minutes	Tally	Total
45–50	ЖНΙ Ι	6
50–55	ЖНΙ ЖНТ Ι	11
55–60	ЖНΙ ЖНΙ ΙЖТ Ι ЖТ ΙΙΙ	23
60–65	ЖНΙ ΙЖТ ΙЖТ ΙΙ	17
65–70	ЖНΙ ΙЖТ ΙΙΙΙ	14
70–75	ЖНΙ ΙΙ	7
		78

Check sheet

Figure 7.5. One-hour meeting histogram and bell-shaped curve.

Scenario 1

It might be considered unacceptable by management to finish department meetings too early. This may indicate that not enough time was given for important discussions. It may also be unacceptable to finish the meetings too late. This may indicate poor use of time. Thus, management decides to set a lower specification limit at 50 minutes, and an upper specification limit at 70 minutes. This is illustrated in Figure 7.6.

The figure shows that with these specification limits, meetings less than 50 minutes long, or more than 70 minutes long, produce waste. The dartboard shown in Figure 7.6 is used as an analogy. Darts that don't even hit the board, scoring no points, are outside the specification limits and are considered to be waste.

Scenario 2

In an effort to be more predictable, management decides that meetings ending before 55 minutes are unacceptable because they don't give enough time to air views. Similarly, meetings that exceed 65 minutes just take too long. In practice, this may just increase waste because it forces the members of a concluded meeting to just sit around, waiting for 55 minutes, and it forces important discussions to be cut off at 65 minutes. Figure 7.7 shows this arbitrary improvement, which fails to recognize that it is the meeting process that must change, not just an

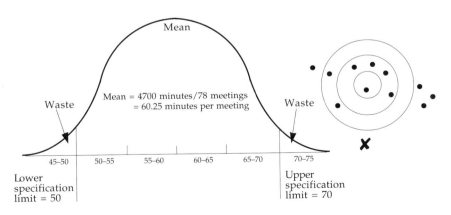

Figure 7.6. Meeting histogram—wide limits.

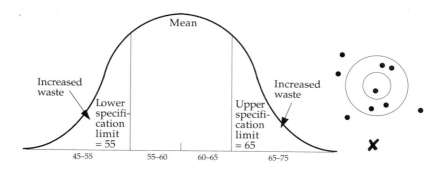

Figure 7.7. Meeting histogram—narrow limits.

artificial adjustment to meeting length. In the dartboard analogy, the throwing system is the same but the dartboard has become smaller, leading to more waste.

Scenario 3

A third attempt at improvement is shown in Figure 7.8. Now management decides that empowerment is the answer. The staff goes back to the first scenario's limits but discussions and decision making are encouraged.

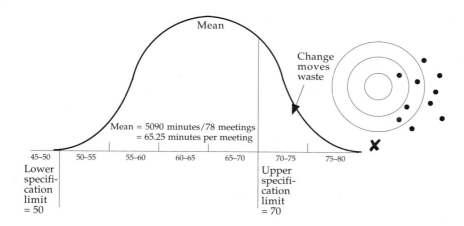

Figure 7.8. Meeting histogram—shifted limits.

After measurement, it might be found that the mean has shifted to the right. With this new emphasis on discussion, meeting participants find it hard to shut down at 70 minutes, and so the waste continues as before. The only difference is the shift in the location of the waste. In the dartboard analogy, the throwing system is the same and the dartboard has not moved, but the aiming point—and therefore the waste—has shifted to the right.

Scenario 4

Finally, management realizes that it needs to change the system. A pre-published agenda, leading to prepared participants, coupled with fair and evenhanded leadership, plus focused discussions and decision making will produce effective meetings. While there is still variation in meeting times, most meetings now end between 57 and 63 minutes. This is shown in Figure 7.9.

The darts are now hitting the center of the dartboard with a very narrow spread. This is because a new throwing technique has dramatically improved results and eliminated waste.

Timing meetings has little inherent value because the time a meeting takes is just a symptom of efficiency or inefficiency. The timing provides a clue, but the root causes must still be found and healed.

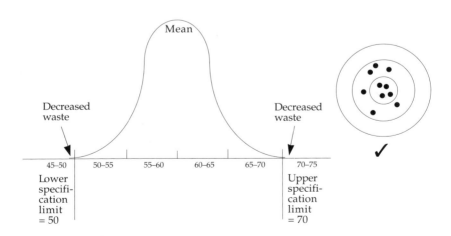

Figure 7.9. Meeting histogram—improved process.

The Histogram and Control Charts

The histogram displays data points in rectangular columns, each one cell wide, that vary in height according to the frequency of occurrence. A normal random distribution can be fitted with a bell-shaped, normal probability curve as shown at the top of Figure 7.10.

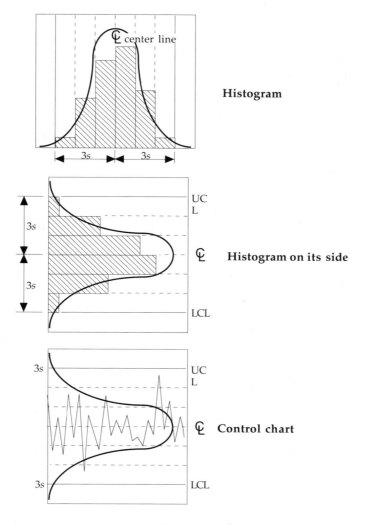

Figure 7.10. Development of the control chart.

When control charts are used for practical purposes, the convention is to divide the normal probability curve into six parts, each equaling one sample standard deviation. Three standard deviations, denoted 3s, occur on each side of the centerline. If a process falls within the 6s range, it is deemed to have an acceptable dispersion. The closer the spread falls to the central or target value, the more efficient the process, and the less rework and waste is present.

By rotating the histogram 90 degrees, a control chart starts to take shape as shown in the middle chart of Figure 7.10. By replacing the frequency columns with the same data plotted and connected along a time scale, statistical control limits can be established, and the patterns of events over a period of time can be displayed. This is the control chart, shown at the bottom of Figure 7.10.

Control Chart Basics

What It Is

Control charts were developed in 1924 by Walter A. Shewhart to provide a visual display of the measured variation in any given product or process. Control charts illustrate how an activity varies, and establish control limits that predict the limits of variability of future operations. This variability will be maintained until an outside influence brings about a change for the better or the worse. The root causes of the SCV, positive or negative, may be identified using other tools.

Four Control Chart Benefits

1. Control. By tracking a process, variation can be monitored and kept within predictable limits.

2. Alertness. By establishing control boundaries, it is easy to spot when a process moves beyond the predictable limits.

3. Clarification. The plotted data may highlight the need for process improvement to any who doubt the need for change.

4. Proof. By demonstrating process changes, the control chart provides proof that the process is getting better or worse.

Control charts take time and cost money. The benefit to be gained by tracking a process must exceed the cost of the control chart. Control charts should not be done just because they are fun, new, or esoteric.

Review of Terminology

Control Limits

As shown in Figure 7.11 the upper control limit (UCL) and the lower control limit (LCL) are each located three standard deviations from the process centerline. Each process has its own inherent control limits. When a process is stable, 99.73 percent of the data points will fall within the $6s$ control limit range.

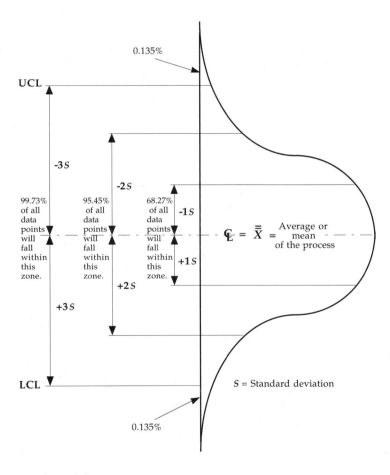

Figure 7.11. Control chart parameters.

Common Cause Variation

When a process is stable, the variability of data points will be statistically random. These data points will fall between the upper and lower control limits.

Special Cause Variation

When a process is unstable, the variability of data points will be abnormal. These data points will either exhibit nonrandom patterns or will fall beyond the UCL or LCL. An out-of-bound data point is a statistical outlier, rooted in an identifiable external influence. This is why SCVs are also known as assignable causes.

Specification Limits

These limits are boundaries, often prescribed by a client, a public agency, or a policy, or by management. Specification limits are arbitrary, and can be changed at any time, as was shown in Figures 7.6, 7.7, 7.8, and 7.9.

Process Capability

If the process is stable and specification limits are established, the process capability can be calculated. This demonstrates if the process has the inherent capability to meet the arbitrary specification limits. This more advanced technique is covered in most SPC texts.

Relationship Between Specification Limits and Control Limits

1. A process can be stable even though some data points fall beyond the specification limits. For example, a company may find that its age of receivable system is stable, but with ages that are unacceptable to management. The company may establish an arbitrary specification limit that is lower than the UCL.

2. A process can be unstable while still meeting specifications. For example, the age of receivable system might have some data points that fall beyond the UCL. Management might decide that this is acceptable, and establish an arbitrary specification limit that is higher than the UCL.

How Control Charts Are Used

Case 1: Common Causes of Variation

The chart at the top of Figure 7.12 shows a stable process with all data points falling between the upper and lower control limits. If the procedures that resulted in this data plot are not changed, and external influences do not occur, future data will continue to be predictable and fall within the control limits. This means that firefighting is over.

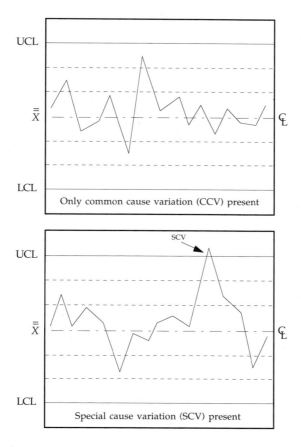

Figure 7.12. Special and common causes.

Opportunities for Improvement

1. The centerline is the mean about which the process occurs. If the process is improved, the centerline would be lowered to reflect the improved level of effectiveness.

2. If the standard operating procedure could be improved, the range variation between the data points might decrease. This would be reflected in a smaller data point amplitude, as is shown at the right-hand side of the top chart in Figure 7.12. When this occurs as the result of an improvement, the UCL and LCL should be recalculated.

Caution: If the points start to exhibit decreased amplitude, but the process has not changed, do not arbitrarily recalculate the limits until the origin of the improvement is known.

3. Sometimes data point patterns exhibit unusual effects. The system might still be in control, yet a trend may be suspected. This might be investigated for clues to further improve the system.

4. Business managers often make key decisions based on very recent events, such as last quarter's results. The control chart forces one to have a longer-range perspective and, therefore, affords better decision making.

Case 2: Special Causes of Variation—Control Limit Tests

The chart at the bottom of Figure 7.12 shows an unstable process, with one or more data points falling outside the upper or lower control limits. If the procedures and external influences that resulted in this situation are not changed, future performance will be unpredictable. This means that the fire brigade, or crisis team, must be ready for action at any time.

Note: If the out-of-control data point was caused by a known, eradicable cause, the process might still be stable and predictable. In this case the reason for the out-of-control point should be noted on the chart. One might then recalculate the limits, disregarding the special cause data point. This decision is a judgment call.

Case 3: Special Causes of Variation—Zone Pattern Tests

The six standard deviation zones shown in Figure 7.11 apply to normal distributions. Some control charts only approximate normal distributions, but may still utilize the zone pattern tests shown in Figure 7.13. These tests, like the run stability tests in Figure 7.4, draw attention to nonrandom pattern special cause variation.

Step 1: Divide the distance between the UCL and LCL into six equal zones.

Step 2: Search for nonrandomness.

Note: The boundary dividing the Zones C may not exactly coincide with the chart's mean value. If they are far apart, it might be best to ignore the zone tests, calculate the median, and apply the run chart stability tests 1 through 5 shown in Figures 7.3 and 7.4.

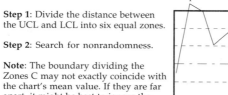
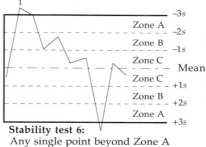

Stability test 6:
Any single point beyond Zone A

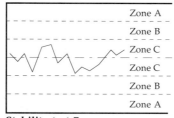

Stability test 7:
A sequence of 15 or more points that never leave the C Zones.

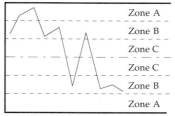

Stability test 8:
Eight points in a row on both sides of the median, with none in Zones C.

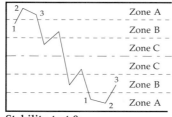

Stability test 9:
Two out of three consecutive points in either Zone A.

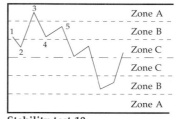

Stability test 10:
Four out of five consecutive points in Zones A or B.

Figure 7.13. Zone-pattern stability tests.

Improvement Steps

1. Search for the root cause of the out-of-control point.

2. Eliminate the root cause.

3. Initiate an improvement that will eliminate the root cause in the future.

4. Make the improvement a standard operating procedure.

Cautions in Interpreting Control Charts

Control charts should be quality reviewed. Sometimes an apparent process problem is really just a reflection of a faulty control chart.

1. If the process is struggling but the control chart does not reveal an unstable situation, perhaps the wrong variable is being tracked. Replot the data using another variable.

2. If the control limits have been calculated using too few data points, premature conclusions may be drawn about the process. If possible, wait until a minimum of 20 points have been obtained before calculating the limits. Thirty or more data points are recommended.

3. It is important that the subgroup be homogeneous. This will ensure that the variation that occurs is statistically meaningful. Nonhomogenous subgroups, such as different types of revisions (for example, regulatory changes versus errors and omissions changes), or data taken from two different client types—such as airports and schools—may exhibit false out-of-control characteristics.

4. If X-bar and R control chart measurements are taken with uncalibrated instruments, or by using different scales or units of measurement, the control chart may exhibit strange behavior.

5. Data observation errors, data-recording errors, control limit calculation errors, and data-plotting errors can all contribute to erroneous charts. An inappropriate choice of control chart scales for the data range may not show amplitude variations clearly.

c Chart

What It Is

By counting all the errors, nonconformances, or occurrences per *constant sample* or subgroup, the *c* chart can demonstrate that a process is either stable or unstable. The *c* chart works with count data.

When the c Chart Is Used

Three conditions must be met in order to draw a *c* chart.

1. All the actual errors, nonconformances, or occurrences in a sample must be identifiable and countable. The sample size *n* is constant at each observation.

2. The possibilities or potential for errors, nonconformances, or occurrences must be infinite. Readers are referred back to the count data section of this chapter.

3. Because the counts must be complete before the *c* chart can be constructed, all the data must be gathered before the chart is commenced. This means that the *c* chart always looks back at how a process performed over a given period of time.

Equations

n = sample size, which is constant.

c = the number of errors, nonconformances, or occurrences that have been observed for each sample. Samples include activities, processes, and documents.

c-bar = the sum of the errors from all the samples, divided by the number of samples observed (not the sample size).

s = the square root of c-bar.

UCL = c-bar + 3s

LCL = c-bar – 3s

These equations are displayed in Figure 7.14.

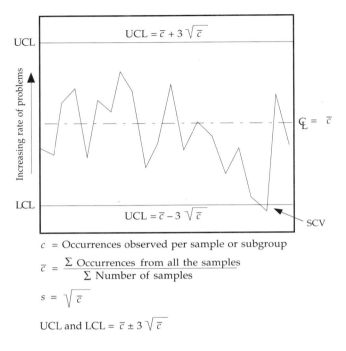

c = Occurrences observed per sample or subgroup

$$\bar{c} = \frac{\Sigma \ \text{Occurrences from all the samples}}{\Sigma \ \text{Number of samples}}$$

$$s = \sqrt{\bar{c}}$$

UCL and LCL = $\bar{c} \pm 3 \sqrt{\bar{c}}$

Figure 7.14. c chart.

How It Works

Step 1. Sample size = n.

Step 2. Count the errors, nonconformances, or occurrences = c.

Step 3. Calculate the c-bar mean.

Step 4. Calculate the upper and lower control limits.

Step 5. Plot the c values, c-bar, and limits on the chart.

Step 6. Search for special causes. Any point above the UCL or below the LCL would be a SCV. The c chart gives a Poisson distribution rather than a normal distribution, but the zone pattern tests may be applied to search for nonrandom patterns.

c *Chart Examples*

The five examples shown in Figure 7.15 illustrate when to use the *c* chart. Each example shows a truncated version of the full data set as a minimum of 20 points are required, and 30 or more are recommended. Each of these examples must fulfill the three conditions for *c* charts.

Average days late for receivables

Samples	Average days late	
January receivables	35	n = constant = 1 month
February receivables	47	
March receivables	55	

Number of clients served per year

Samples	Total clients	
1991	174	n = constant = 1 year
1992	116	
1993	211	

Errors in documents

Samples	Errors in documents	
Week 1	31 typos	n = constant = 1 week
Week 2	23 typos	
Week 3	11 typos	

Information requests per month

Samples	Information requests	
January	12	n = constant = 1 month
February	45	
March	22	
April	17	

Hours spent on rework per week

Samples	Rework hours	
Week 1	34	n = constant = 1 week
Week 2	51	
Week 3	29	
Week 4	47	

Figure 7.15. *c* chart topics.

Worked Example

The first example in Figure 7.15 will be expanded into a case history, starting with the c chart check sheet shown in Figure 7.16, and concluding with the actual c chart in Figure 7.17. It can be observed that the accounts receivable system exhibits several SCVs making it unstable and unpredictable. It should be reviewed by a PIT.

Average days late of all receivables.

	Samples	Occurrences = c	Comments
	MONTHS	Days late	
1	January 1992	35	
2	February 1992	47	
3	March 1992	55	
4	April 1992	69	
5	May 1992	22	*Visit 3 slow payers and get checks.*
6	June 1992	33	
7	July 1992	43	
8	August 1992	59	
9	September 1992	65	
10	October 1992	53	
11	November 1992	51	
12	December 1992	25	*Client's year-end debt reduction?*
13	January 1993	32	
14	February 1993	37	
15	March 1993	45	
16	April 1993	49	
17	May 1993	47	
18	June 1993	51	
19	July 1993	39	
20	August 1993	43	
21	September 1993	49	
22	October 1993	48	
23	November 1993	50	
24	December 1993	32	*Client's year-end debt reduction?*
25	January 1994	41	
26	February 1994	37	
27	March 1994	38	
28	April 1994	63	*Statement age not printed on bill.*
29	May 1994	67	*Statement age not printed on bill.*
30	June 1994	53	*Statement age not printed on bill.*
	Σ	1378	Total

$$\bar{c} = \frac{\Sigma \text{ Occurrences from all the samples}}{\Sigma \text{ Number of samples}} = 45.9 \quad \text{UCL} = \bar{c} + 3\sqrt{\bar{c}} = 66.23$$

$$s = \sqrt{\bar{c}} = 6.78 \quad \text{LCL} = \bar{c} - 3\sqrt{\bar{c}} = 25.57$$

Figure 7.16. c chart check sheet.

PIT: **Billing**												Tracking: *Average days late of all receivables*																
Sample: Months	January	February	March	April	May	June	July	August	September	October	November	December	January	February	March	April	May	June	July	August	September	October	November	December	January	February	March	April	May	June
c	35	47	55	69	22	33	43	59	65	53	51	25	32	37	45	49	47	51	39	43	49	48	50	32	41	37	38	63	67	53

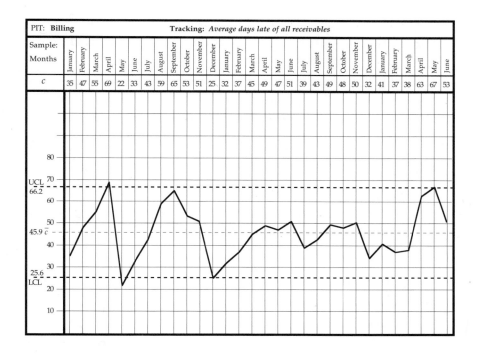

Figure 7.17. *c* chart example.

u Chart

What It Is

By counting all the errors, nonconformances, or occurrences per *variable sample* or subgroup, the *u* chart can demonstrate that a process is either stable or unstable. The *u* chart works with count data.

When the **u** *Chart Is Used*

Three conditions must be met in order to draw a *u* chart.

1. The number of errors, nonconformances, or occurrences in a sample must be identifiable and countable. The sample size *n* can vary at each observation.

2. The possibilities or potential for errors, nonconformances, or occurrences must be infinite. Readers are referred back to the count data section of this chapter.

3. Because the counts must be complete before the u chart can be constructed, all the data must be gathered before the chart is commenced. This means that the u chart always looks back at how a process performed over a given period of time.

Equations

n = sample size, which can vary with each observation.

u = the number of errors, nonconformances, or occurrences per sample, divided by the total number of units in that sample (sample size = n).

u-bar = The sum of the errors from all the samples, divided by the units in all the samples. (Samples include activities, projects, processes, and documents.)

s = the square root of u-bar divided by n.

UCL = u-bar + 3s

LCL = u-bar – 3s

These equations are displayed in Figure 7.18.

How It Works

Step 1. Sample size for each observation = n.

Step 2. Count the errors, nonconformances, or occurrences = c.

Step 3. Calculate u for each sample.

Step 4. Calculate the u-bar mean.

Step 5. Calculate the upper and lower control limit for each data point.

Step 6. Plot the u values, u-bar, and limits on the chart.

Step 7. Search for special causes. Any point above the UCL or below the LCL would be an SCV. The u chart gives a Poisson distribution rather than a normal distribution, and is further complicated by the variable control limit boundaries. Therefore, pattern tests are not generally used on u charts.

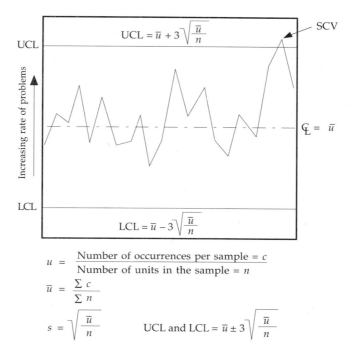

$$u = \frac{\text{Number of occurrences per sample} = c}{\text{Number of units in the sample} = n}$$

$$\bar{u} = \frac{\Sigma c}{\Sigma n}$$

$$s = \sqrt{\frac{\bar{u}}{n}} \qquad \text{UCL and LCL} = \bar{u} \pm 3\sqrt{\frac{\bar{u}}{n}}$$

Figure 7.18. *u* chart.

u *Chart Examples*

The five examples shown in Figure 7.19 illustrate when to use the *u* chart. It will be noticed that, in contrast to the *c* chart examples, these *u* chart examples track departments, projects, documents, and client occurrences. This is because each sample (project or client) varies, making it ineligible for *c* chart tracking.

Each example shows a truncated version of the full data set as a minimum of 20 points are required, and 30 or more are recommended. Each of these examples must fulfill the three conditions for *u* charts.

Worked Example

The third example in Figure 7.19 will be expanded into a case history, starting with the *u* chart check sheet shown in Figure 7.20, and concluding with the actual *u* chart in Figure 7.21. It can be observed that

Project receivables age

Samples	Number of projects	Average days late	
Department A	15	63	n = varies
Department B	30	59	
Department C	45	78	

Marketing expenses per proposal

Samples	Proposal	Proposal costs	
Prospect A	$2050.5K	$4.1K	n = varies
Prospect B	$175.0K	$2.1K	
Prospect C	$1153.7K	$3.7K	

Number of errors per document set

Samples	Documents	Number of errors	
Project C.93.021	Set of 12	7	n = varies
Project C.93.135	Set of 27	14	
Project C.92.504	Set of 16	6	

Information requests per project

Samples	Hours worked	Information requests	
Proj. A.94.063	2228 hrs.	5	n = varies
Proj. C.94.074	4531 hrs.	45	
Proj. C.94.112	3316 hrs.	22	
Proj. E.94.125	906 hrs.	17	

Rework hours per project

Samples	Billable hours	Rework hours	
Proj. A.94.063	2228 hrs.	27	n = varies
Proj. C.94.074	4531 hrs.	209	
Proj. C.94.112	3316 hrs.	104	
Proj. E.94.125	906 hrs.	123	

Figure 7.19. u chart topics.

the quality control system is stable except for a single, assignable SCV. This organization may still improve its work and quality review processes with a PIT.

Note: If the variation in sample size is small, it may be acceptable to average the sample size and use a constant UCL and LCL. This decision would be a judgment call. (See p chart, step 5 for the methodology.)

Number of errors in document sets found during quality control

	Samples	n	Errors	u	UCL	LCL	Comments
	Project	Documents per set	Non-conformance	$\frac{Errors}{n}$			
1	C.93.021	12	7	0.58	0.79	0	
2	C.93.135	27	14	0.52	0.63	0	
3	C.92.504	16	6	0.37	0.72	0	
4	C.93.178	53	16	0.30	0.53	0.08	
5	A.92.471	40	12	0.30	0.57	0.04	
6	B.92.360	12	3	0.25	0.79	0	
7	D.93.004	15	7	0.47	0.74	0	
8	B.92.125	33	12	0.36	0.60	0.02	
9	B.92.407	42	7	0.17	0.56	0.05	
10	A.93.021	9	3	0.33	0.86	0	
11	A.92.375	17	9	0.53	0.71	0	
12	C.92.221	23	8	0.35	0.65	0	
13	C.92.103	27	8	0.30	0.63	0	
14	B.93.153	25	11	0.44	0.64	0	
15	C.93.179	11	11	1.00	0.81	0	*County codes changed in*
16	C.93.111	8	2	0.25	0.90	0	*mid-project.*
17	C.92.346	33	5	0.15	0.60	0.02	
18	A.92.479	27	10	0.37	0.63	0	
19	C.92.362	17	2	0.12	0.71	0	
20	D.92.352	21	5	0.24	0.67	0	
21	C.92.109	14	2	0.14	0.75	0	
22	C.92.109	17	5	0.29	0.71	0	
23	C.93.065	37	4	0.11	0.58	0.03	
24	B.93.277	29	11	0.38	0.62	0	
25	B.93.107	32	9	0.28	0.60	0.01	
26	C.93.068	15	1	0.07	0.74	0	
27	A.93.102	25	8	0.32	0.64	0	
28	C.92.227	18	4	0.22	0.70	0	
29	C.93.199	43	14	0.33	0.56	0.05	
30	C.92.415	31	8	0.26	0.61	0.01	
	Σ	729	224	Totals			

$$\bar{u} = \frac{\Sigma \text{ Errors from all the samples}}{\Sigma\ n} = 0.31 \qquad s = \sqrt{\frac{\bar{u}}{n}} = \text{varies} \qquad UCL = \bar{u} + 3s = \text{varies}$$

$$LCL = \bar{u} - 3s = \text{varies}$$

Figure 7.20. u chart check sheet.

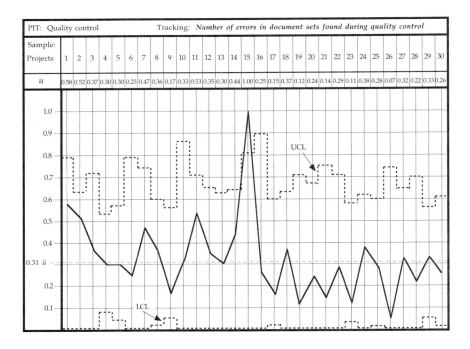

Figure 7.21. *u* chart example.

p Chart

What It Is

By identifying the fraction or percentage of the activities, processes or documents that are wrong, defective, or unacceptable, the *p* chart can demonstrate stability or instability in a system. The *p* chart works with attribute data.

How the **p** *Chart differs from* **c** *Charts and* **u** *Charts*

The *c* and *u* charts monitor the number of errors, nonconformances, or occurrences per sample. The *p* chart monitors the fraction or percentage of samples that are wrong, defective, or unacceptable.

When the p *Chart Is Used*

Four conditions must be met in order to draw a *p* chart.

1. The total number of items in each sample must be identifiable and countable.
2. The total number of items in each sample with errors, nonconformances, or instances are identifiable and countable.
3. This means that the potential for items with errors, nonconformances, or instances is finite, up to 100 percent. Readers are referred back to the attribute data section of this chapter.
4. Because the counts must be complete before the *p* chart can be constructed, all the data must be gathered before the chart is commenced. This means that the *p* chart always looks back at how a process performed over a given period of time.

Equations

n = number of readings or observations of each sample. The number n may vary from sample to sample.

p = the percentage of activities, processes, or documents per sample with errors, nonconformances, or instances.

p-bar = The sum of all the defective items in all the samples, divided by the sum of all of the items in all the samples.

s = see Figure 7.22.

UCL = p-bar + 3s

LCL = p-bar − 3s

All these equations are displayed in Figure 7.22.

How It Works

Step 1. Sample size for each observation = n.

Step 2. Note the number with errors, nonconformances, or instances.

Step 3. Calculate p for each sample.

Step 4. Calculate the mean p-bar.

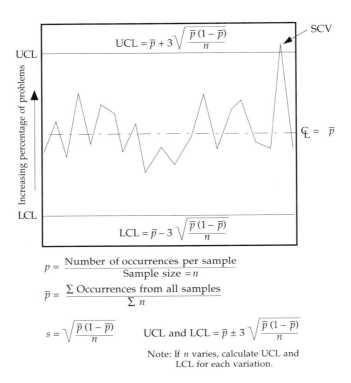

Figure 7.22. p chart.

Step 5. Calculate the upper and lower control limits. If n varies, and the variation is small, there may be no need to calculate a separate UCL and LCL for each data point. This is explained below.

Step 5a. Find the average value of n.

Step 5b. If 2.0 × average is greater than the largest value of n, and if 0.5 × average is smaller than the smallest value of n, use the average n for the UCL and LCL calculation. If not, calculate the UCL and LCL for each data point.

The PIT may elect to substitute 1.5 and 0.75 or other multipliers. Another shortcut is to use the average n for the UCL and LCL calculation if no point exceeds the average by more than 25 percent. These numbers and these shortcuts are discretionary.

Step 6. Plot the *p* values, *p*-bar, and limits on the chart.

Step 7. Search for special causes. Any point above the UCL or below the LCL would be an SCV. The *p* chart gives a binomial distribution rather than a normal distribution, and is further complicated by variable control limit boundaries. Therefore, pattern tests are not generally used on *p* charts.

p *Chart Examples*

The five examples shown in Figure 7.23 illustrate when to use the *p* chart. Each example shows a truncated version of the full data set as a minimum of 20 points are required, and 30 or more are recommended. Each of these examples must fulfill the four conditions for *p* charts.

Worked Example

The second example in Figure 7.23 will be expanded into a case history. This example starts with the *p* chart check sheet shown in Figure 7.24, and concludes with the actual *p* chart on Figure 7.25.

Discuss the chart with the project managers before starting to measure. Point out that it is not the project managers themselves that are being checked. It is the system that they are using that may need repair.

The control chart in the example exhibits statistical control, but this is not to say that things are satisfactory. The UCL is far higher than most companies would accept as an upper specification limit. This is a clear case of a system that is statistically stable, but in definite need of improvement. A PIT will find ways to positively change the system and permanently reduce the mean *p*-bar value.

A Note About np *Charts*

In cases where the sample size is constant, *np* charts are used. They are similar to *p* charts. In professional service organizations, the need to take constant-sized samples from large attribute data sets is not commonly encountered. In these environments, it is not inconvenient to count all the data. Hence, the recommended use of *p* charts for attribute data.

Number of errors per document set

Samples	Sheets	Sheets with errors	p	
Set A	16	3	18.7%	*n* = varies:
Set B	53	5	9.4%	16, 53, 29
Set C	29	11	37.9%	UCL and LCL will vary.

Project overruns

Samples	Projects	Projects with overruns	p	
January	27	5	18.5%	*n* = 23.93 for
February	26	17	65.4%	30 samples passes the average
March	27	12	44.4%	test.

Number of invoices with errors

Samples	Invoices	Invoices with errors	p	
January	39	11	28.2%	*n* = 38.7 average
February	47	16	34.0%	passes the average test.
March	30	9	30.0%	

Number of permit applications refused

Samples	Applications	Refusals	p	
Quarter 1	13	2	15.4%	*n* = 23.5 average
Quarter 2	29	6	20.7%	passes the average test.
Quarter 3	19	0	00.0%	
Quarter 4	33	7	21.2%	

Number of proposals short listed

Samples	Proposals	Short listed	p	
Quarter 1	9	5	55.6%	*n* = varies:
Quarter 2	14	2	14.3%	9, 14, 35, 21
Quarter 3	35	9	25.7%	UCL and LCL
Quarter 4	21	7	33.3%	will vary.

Figure 7.23. *p* chart topics.

	Samples	n	Errors = c	p	UCL	LCL	Comments
	Month	Projects	Overruns	$\frac{Errors}{n}$			
1	January	27	15	55.6%			
2	February	26	17	65.4%			*Computers down for three*
3	March	27	12	44.4%			*days.*
4	April	27	13	48.1%			
5	May	24	11	45.8%			
6	June	25	9	36.0%			
7	July	25	8	32.0%			
8	August	26	7	26.9%			
9	September	26	8	30.8%			
10	October	27	11	40.7%			
11	November	27	9	33.3%			
12	December	23	8	34.8%			
13	January	23	12	52.2%			
14	February	23	12	52.2%			
15	March	23	9	39.1%			
16	April	24	14	58.3%			*Five projects denied permits.*
17	May	24	14	58.3%			*Five projects denied permits.*
18	June	24	11	45.8%			
19	July	26	11	42.3%			
20	August	26	9	34.6%			
21	September	21	11	52.4%			*Four PMs sick for 3, 6, 8, and*
22	October	21	11	52.4%			*17 days*
23	November	21	8	38.1%			
24	December	19	7	36.8%			
25	January	18	7	38.9%			
26	February	22	7	31.8%			
27	March	22	5	22.7%			
28	April	22	9	40.9%			
29	May	23	9	39.1%			
30	June	26	9	34.6%			
	Σ	718	303				Totals

$$\bar{p} = \frac{\Sigma \text{ Errors from all the samples}}{\Sigma\, n} = 42.2\% \qquad s = \sqrt{\frac{\bar{p}\,(1-\bar{p})}{n}} = 0.101 \qquad UCL = \bar{p} + 3s = 72.5\%$$

$$n\,(av) = 23.93 \qquad\qquad\qquad\qquad\qquad\qquad\qquad\qquad\qquad LCL = \bar{p} - 3s = 11.9\%$$

Figure 7.24. p chart check sheet.

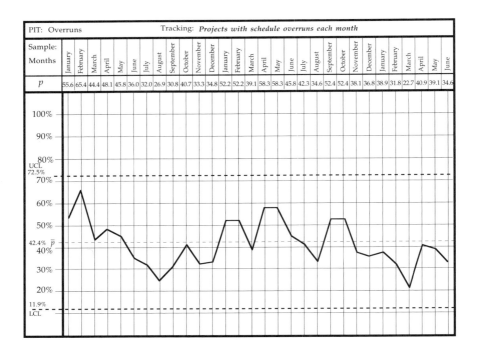

Figure 7.25. *p* chart example.

X-bar and R Chart

What It Is

The X-bar and R chart works with variable data, and is one of the most widely used SPC charts. This tool is actually comprised of two separate charts, each tracking a different facet of a process. Unlike the c, u, and p charts, the X-bar and R chart can be used to continuously monitor a process and plot data points in progress. With sufficient data points, usually a minimum of 30, control limits may be calculated.

X-bar Chart

This chart notices and can monitor a shift in the process centerline. A sample X-bar chart is shown at the top of Figure 7.26. X-bar denotes the average or mean of a sample of data points, and is also known as the central tendency. The X-bar chart has its own mean value, known as X-double bar, and its own set of upper and lower control limits.

R *Chart*

This chart notices and can monitor the process range or dispersion, which is a display of the variability of a set of data.

A sample R chart is shown at the bottom of Figure 7.26.

$$R = \text{(the maximum data value)} - \text{(the minimum data value)}$$

This is also known as the spread. The standard deviation measures the square root of this spread and is an effective way to track the dispersion. The further apart the spread, the less stability is present. The R chart has its own mean value, known as R-bar, and its own set of upper and lower control limits.

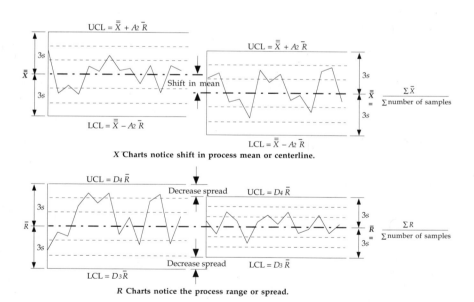

Figure 7.26. $\overline{X}$ and R charts.

How the X-bar Chart Works

Step 1. Sample size = n. Usually n = 3–6, but it may vary from 2–12. The sample size denotes the number of observations taken for each sample. Be careful not to observe potential disparate effects. For example, a weekly observation taken from five different departments would give n = 5, but the control chart may not be valid if some departments have stable systems and others have unstable systems.

Step 2. Calculate X-bar, the average of the data points, for each sample.

Step 3. Calculate R, the difference between the largest and smallest data points, for each sample.

Step 4. Calculate R-bar, the sum of all the R's, divided by the total number of all the samples.

Step 5. Calculate X-double bar, the sum of all the X-bars, divided by the total number of all the samples.

Step 6. Use the table shown in Figure 7.27 to find A_2.

Step 7. Calculate and draw the upper and lower control limits:

$$UCL = X\text{-double bar} + (A_2 \times R\text{-bar})$$
$$LCL = X\text{-double bar} - (A_2 \times R\text{-bar})$$

Step 8. Plot and link the X-bar data points and draw the X-double bar centerline on the chart.

How the R Chart Works

Step 9. Use the table shown in Figure 7.27 to find D_4 and D_3.

Step 10. Calculate and draw the upper and lower control limits:

$$UCL = D_4 \times R\text{-bar}$$
$$LCL = D_3 \times R\text{-bar}$$

Step 11. Draw the R-bar centerline, found in step 4.

Step 12. Plot and link the R values on the chart.

Step 13. If the R chart is unstable, investigate the reason.

Step 14. If the R chart is stable, examine the X-bar chart for stability.

n	A_2	D_3	D_4
2	1.880	0	3.267
3	1.023	0	2.574
4	0.729	0	2.282
5	0.577	0	2.114
6	0.483	0	2.004
7	0.419	0.076	1.924
8	0.373	0.136	1.864
9	0.337	0.184	1.816
10	0.308	0.223	1.777
11	0.285	0.256	1.744
12	0.266	0.283	1.717

n = number of observations per sample

Minimum 20–30 samples are recommended.

Sample size, the number of observations of each sample n, is 12 or less.

In practice, sample size is usually 3–6.

Source: Table adapted from "Factors and formulas for control charts for variables," ANSI/ASQC A1-1987. Published with permission.

Figure 7.27. Values for variables charts.

Either chart is unstable if it has out-of-control points or if it exhibits nonrandom effects by failing the zone pattern tests shown in Figure 7.13.

X-bar and R Chart Examples

The three examples shown in Figure 7.28 illustrate X-bar and R chart situations. Each example shows a truncated version of the full data set as a minimum of 30 points or more are recommended.

Worked Example

The first example in Figure 7.28 will be expanded into a case history as shown in the X-bar and R chart check sheet in Figure 7.29. The system in the X-bar chart is unstable. A PIT should find ways to reduce the mean overrun hours and should find ways to decrease the spread of the data points.

Schedule overrun at project milestones			
	30% complete	60% complete	90% complete
Project A	16 hours	10 hours	14 hours	$n = 3$
Project B	30 hours	23 hours	18 hours
Project C	43 hours	30 hours	22 hours

Time to pay four random sample invoices			
	Invoice 1	Invoice 2	Invoice 3	Invoice 4
January	32 days	35 days	51 days	65 days	$n = 4$
February	26 days	62 days	44 days	68 days
March	71 days	53 days	40 days	32 days

Errors on four random sample document pages			
	Sample 1	Sample 2	Sample 3	Sample4
Project A	10 errors	0 errors	7 errors	11 errors	$n = 4$
Project B	9 errors	3 errors	16 errors	5 errors
Project C	3 errors	20 errors	0 errors	7 errors

Figure 7.28. $\bar{X}$ and R chart topics.

X and Moving Range Chart

What It Is

The X and moving range chart works with variable data, and while less sensitive, may be more practical than the X-bar and R chart in many professional service applications. This is because it may take a long time to gather data from samples, such as projects, and these charts operate with a sample size equal to one. Like the X-bar and R chart, this tool is comprised of two separate charts, each continuously monitoring a different facet of a process in progress. This tool is also useful when data point variation is so small that the UCL and LCL on an X-bar chart would be very close together. A minimum of 30 data points is recommended; 50 or more are preferred.

X Chart

The X chart, like the run chart, plots raw observed values. The X chart has its own mean value, known as X-bar, and its own set of upper and lower control limits.

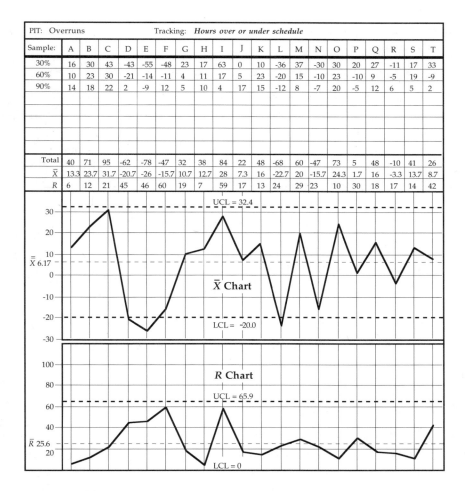

PIT: Overruns						Tracking: *Hours over or under schedule*													
Sample:	A	B	C	D	E	F	G	H	I	J	K	L	M	N	O	P	Q	R	S	T
30%	16	30	43	-43	-55	-48	23	17	63	0	10	-36	37	-30	30	20	27	-11	17	33
60%	10	23	30	-21	-14	-11	4	11	17	5	23	-20	15	-10	23	-10	9	-5	19	-9
90%	14	18	22	2	-9	12	5	10	4	17	15	-12	8	-7	20	-5	12	6	5	2
Total	40	71	95	-62	-78	-47	32	38	84	22	48	-68	60	-47	73	5	48	-10	41	26
$\bar{X}$	13.3	23.7	31.7	-20.7	-26	-15.7	10.7	12.7	28	7.3	16	-22.7	20	-15.7	24.3	1.7	16	-3.3	13.7	8.7
R	6	12	21	45	46	60	19	7	59	17	13	24	29	23	10	30	18	17	14	42

Figure 7.29. $\bar{X}$ and R chart example.

Moving Range Chart

This chart records the differences between consecutive pairs of X values. The smaller value in the pair is always subtracted from the larger, regardless of their positions on the check sheet. The range cannot be calculated until the first two observations have been obtained. The moving range chart has its own mean value, known as R-bar, and its own set of upper and lower control limits.

How the X Chart Works

Step 1. Sample size $n = 1$.

Step 2. Calculate X-bar, the average of the data points, for the sample.

Step 3. Calculate R, the difference between the largest and smallest data points for each consecutive set of two samples. Always subtract the smaller from the larger value.

Step 4. Calculate R-bar, the sum of all the Rs, divided by the total number of all the R values. There will always be one less R value than the sample values because there will be no R value for the first observation.

Step 5. Calculate and draw the upper and lower control limits:

$$\text{UCL} = X\text{-bar} + (2.66 \times R\text{-bar})$$
$$\text{LCL} = X\text{-bar} - (2.66 \times R\text{-bar})$$

Step 6. Plot and link the X data points and draw the X-bar centerline on the chart.

How the R Chart Works

Step 7. Calculate and draw the upper and lower control limits:

$$\text{UCL} = D_4 \times R\text{-bar} = 3.267 \times R\text{-bar}$$
$$\text{LCL} = D_3 \times R\text{-bar} = 0$$

Step 8. Draw the R-bar centerline, found in step 4.

Step 9. Plot and link the R values on the chart.

Step 10. Because of the way that moving range charts are constructed, they are not sensitive to pattern tests. So the only useful stability test is the control limits. If any moving range chart data points exceed these limits, investigate the reason.

Step 11. Examine the X chart for control limit stability. Unlike the moving range chart, the X chart may be examined for pattern test stability.

X *and Moving Range Chart Examples*

The two examples shown in Figure 7.30 illustrate X and moving range chart situations. Each example shows a truncated version of the full data set as a minimum of 30 points or more are recommended.

Number of client contacts required to capture a client

Client 1	3 contacts	$n = 1$
Client 2	11 contacts	
Client 3	6 contacts	

Project write-offs

Project A	$2763	$n = 1$
Project B	$14119	
Project C	$9204	

Research hours

Project A	47	$n = 1$
Project B	29	
Project C	116	

Figure 7.30. X and moving range chart topics.

Worked Example

The first example in Figure 7.30 will be expanded into a case history. The X and moving range chart check sheet in Figure 7.31 exhibits only CCVs. The reasons for the numerous contacts with prospective clients 12, 13, and 14 should be reviewed. Were these emotional pursuits, or was there a solid rationale to support this amount of activity?

Scatter Diagram

What It Is

The scatter diagram shows the linear relationship between two sets of data. The relationship can be positive, negative, strong, or weak. This tool is also known as a scatter plot, paired chart, and correlation diagram.

When It Is Used

This tool may be used when it is suspected that one action or activity influences a second action or activity. Should a cause-and-effect

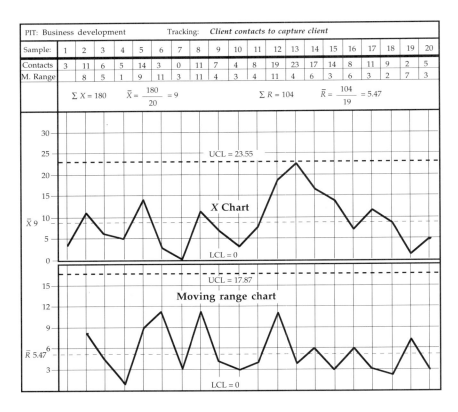

Figure 7.31. *X* and moving range chart example.

correlation be found, adjustment to one set of data will influence the second set of data.

Caution: Identifying a correlation indicates a possible relationship, but does not prove that a relationship exists. This would need to be investigated.

How the Scatter Diagram Works

Establish the axes and plot the data. Search for correlation clusters as shown in Figure 7.32. The complex methods that statisticians use for curve fitting and testing for correlation and stratification of data may be unnecessarily detailed for most professional service applications. The visual appearance of a suspected correlation could be investigated with one of the cause-and-effect analysis tools or with a Pareto cause analysis. Conversely, the conclusions reached by one of the analysis tools could be measured and plotted to verify correlation.

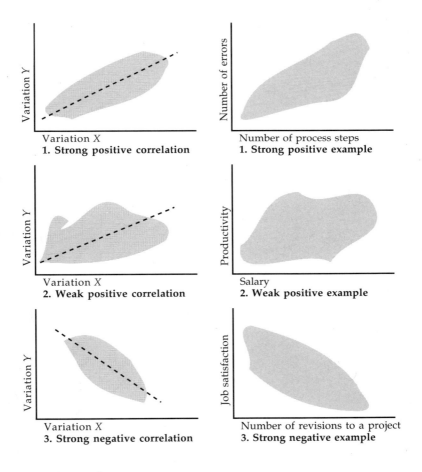

Figure 7.32. Scatter diagrams.

PART IV

Professional Service Applications

Overview

Each and every activity undertaken in a professional service firm is subject to examination and improvement. Continuous improvement must be synchronized so that refinements in one area do not overburden other areas.

Readers will notice that this part of the book does not have a chapter on continuous human resource improvement. This is because the topic of human resources is so broad, it infuses virtually all aspects of an organization and all aspects of improvements. Specific human resource ideas will be found in the operations, training, and partnering chapters. This final part of the book follows section 5 of the Shearer model.

CHAPTER 8

Continuous Improvement

Strategic Planning Improvement

Without strategic planning an organization will drift on the seas of uncertainty. While the waters may be calm and the winds be fair, one cannot know what lurks beneath the surface, nor what storm may be brewing beyond the horizon.

Strategic planning requires the guidance of leadership, and the leadership must share the process to enable others to become stakeholders in the plan. Without this buy-in, strategic planning becomes a one-person band—lots of noise, not much variety, a limited repertory, and minimal opportunities for continuous improvement.

Components of Strategic Planning

Strategic planning needs to contain much more than a mission statement and goal setting. It focuses on future markets, competitive climate, and market opportunities. Then it turns inward to look at internal strengths and weaknesses so that the perceived opportunities can be grasped. In encompassing everything from marketing to operations and from training to budgets, strategic planning provides the framework for all aspects of a professional practice. This chapter does not attempt to provide an exhaustive look at strategic planning. The focus is on some of the elements that are subject to continuous improvement.

Typical Problems

This author's dictum that "Differences of opinion will weaken firms already weak, and will strengthen firms already strong" applies equally to nations, companies, and families. With balanced TQM/CI, strengths are built up uniformly and differences of opinion will fuel strategic planning, not destroy it. Some of the strategic planning problems encountered are

- Getting managers to buy in to the strategic planning process and the plan
- Trying to assess the strengths and weaknesses of the competition
- Trying to identify the niches that will expand and grow
- Trying to identify the niches that have reached their peak and are in decline
- Having a responsive marketing system
- Having the necessary talent to take advantage of opportunities
- Getting staff to help with the implementation
- Integrating ownership transition into the strategic plan

Performance Indicators and Strategic Plan Development Ideas

Step 1. Share Visions, Directions, and Objectives

Vision statements made and set at the start of planning can be very detrimental. While it is good to have a vision, it must be subject to continuous improvement through the planning process. As market research results emerge, as historical project data are uncovered, as business development realities surface, and competitive assessments are made, the vision may need to be fine-tuned. So instead of hotly debating the details of a vision statement, reach a compromise and wait for more data to shape the final vision. Then the vision statement will become a mission statement that sums up the ethos and direction of the organization. This is best written after the strategic plan is complete, to mirror its contents, otherwise the tail may be wagging the dog.

Tools: The problem statement tool, in conjunction with brainstorming and priority voting, may be adapted to create a vision statement.

Step 2. Improve Market and Service Assessments

It will be rare to find data that exactly match the needs of the strategic planning group. Therefore, a custom market research effort or a survey may be required. What are the changes currently occurring or impending, including client industry changes, demographic shifts, financial and banking changes, legislative changes, regulatory changes, and technological developments? Data interpretation is an art and must be addressed with caution. That is why milestone validations and reference to past data are important.

Tools: Pareto charts can be used to display data, and control charts may give a sense of order to the information gathered. Wherever possible, brainstorm to uncover the story behind the data.

Step 3. Assess Practice and Proposal Histories

A study of the past three to five years of projects and proposals is usually very revealing. The following suggestions represent a small sample of the information that could be gathered, internally benchmarked, and continuously improved.

- The ratio of new clients to repeat clients each year
- Total billings for each project subgroup, such as hospitals, retail organizations, or schools
- Total billings for each service subgroup, such as research, design, reports, studies, and plans
- Average billings per client for each project subgroup
- Average billings per client for each service subgroup
- Profit breakout for each project subgroup
- Profit breakout for each service subgroup
- The percentage, broken down per project subgroup, of projects that met the budget versus those that went over budget
- The percentage, broken down per project subgroup, of projects that met the schedule versus those that went over schedule
- A breakout of write-offs per project subgroup
- Percentage of clients that produced billings greater than a target threshold

- Proposal hit rates, broken out per project subgroup
- Proposal hit rates, broken out per service subgroup

Tools: Pareto charts can be used to display the breakouts. Analysis tools such as the cause-and-effect diagram will help to understand some of the surprises that will emerge from the data. Scatter diagrams will assist in illustrating the influence of two sets of data on each other, and control charts will provide the basis for internal data monitoring and continuous improvement.

Step 4. Improve Competitive Benchmarking

Other than publicly owned companies, hard benchmark data regarding the competition may be difficult to obtain. So, aside from data collection, this aspect of the strategic plan may not be subject to continuous improvement. Use the competition evaluation to bring a sense of market share reality to the plan.

In today's business climate, yesterday's competition can become tomorrow's alliance partner or even merger partner. Strategic thinking must be used to assess these opportunities. Alliances undertaken as a marriage of short-term convenience are rarely profitable. Mergers and acquisitions undertaken with short-term thinking are often disastrous.

Tools: Brainstorming, together with a few trusted outside advisors, subconsultants, and contractors can be useful. It must be made clear at the outset that confidential information is not sought. Perceptions gathered and confirmed from a number of sources will facilitate useful conclusions.

Step 5. Improve Risk Assessment, Budgeting, and Milestone Goal Setting

A strategic plan will require a budget to implement. A risk assessment must be made to increase the chance that the investment in time, money, and effort will be rewarded. Does diversification make sense at this time? Is an acquisition being made for valid long-range reasons? Is a geographic expansion being considered for an emotional or a logical reason? What data back up the logic? What is the source of the data and how reliable is it? Risk assessments must also evaluate the consequences of results so that mitigation steps can be preplanned.

Projections and decisions can be made using the information from steps 2 and 3 so that these decisions can be made rationally and soundly.

While traditional TQM eschews goals, they are indispensable in strategic planning. What is important is not the goal as a finish line, rather the goal as a milestone. There is no end to the road of strategic planning. Sometimes a milestone is reached a little earlier, sometimes a little later than anticipated. The only danger of this concept is that one must ensure that a milestone represents progress to prevent going around in circles.

Tools: Agreement on issues such as abandoning an unprofitable project subgroup and setting milestone goals can be difficult. These goals are made much easier, however, by going through the data breakout and competition assessment steps. Tools such as the force field analysis, priority voting, comparison matrix, and the benefit/LOE analysis may be useful. The milestones themselves may be monitored with control charts.

Step 6. Establish an Implementation Plan

A milestone goal without an implementation plan is like a beautiful automobile with no engine. It looks wonderful, but it is not going to go anywhere. An honest appraisal of past implementation successes and failures can form a baseline. The plan needs names, dates, and clearly expressed steps. The people involved in implementation should never be presented with a *fait accompli.* Their input should be obtained in fine-tuning the plan.

Tools: The steps of the plan can be mapped out as a system flowchart to ensure cohesion and practicality. Agreement on tactics can be facilitated with the benefit/LOE analysis, force field analysis, priority voting, and comparison matrix.

Step 7. Track and Report Continuous Improvement

This discussion deals not so much with the form of tracking, as with the effort needed to record information, assemble it, communicate it, compile it, and interpret it for signs of continuous improvement. Be practical about the measurements tracked. Too much data may mean paperwork overload and an interpretation nightmare. What are the critical measurements to take? How will this information be used? Schedule the involvement of each individual.

Tools: Create company-wide templates for tracking and reporting. Individual branches and divisions may adapt these to suit their environments, but the format should remain uniform. The templates may be customized, or they may be standard SPC tools.

Operations Improvement

Operations planning generally boils down to a few key ideas.

1. Recognizing operations as an entity whose sole purpose is to serve the organization's global activities.

2. Establishing a well-structured organizational framework.

3. Finding ways to streamline the links between tasks and the links between people.

Operations should be almost transparent in serving the different facets of the organization. When invisible, chances are that operations are running smoothly and effectively. When visible, chances are that operations are bottlenecking, or worse, blocking. This results in inefficiencies, frustration and waste.

Components of Operations Planning

Operations planners generally focus on financial and staff utilization data. This data tells one what happened, but rarely what will happen. So this information is like a mirror reflecting the past. The past can be useful as a performance indicator, especially when used as a benchmark for future performance. This section will focus on only a few of the data aspects that form part of the Shearer TQM/CI model.

- Productivity tracking
- Management information systems
- Staff planning, hiring, and reduction practices
- Staff communication and administration
- Financial management and structure
- Accounts payable and receivable systems

- Contract administration
- Operational quality reviews

Typical Problems

- Low productivity
- Missed communication and misunderstandings
- Inconsistencies in communication, procedures, and documentation
- Long cycle times between steps
- Undocumented poor supplier performance
- No standard hiring protocols or personnel database
- Nonexistent or inadequate human resource management
- Scattered management information systems
- No workload leveling reviews to prevent layoffs in one group while another group is working weekends
- Too much or too little financial reporting
- Inefficient accounts payable and receivable systems
- Excessively risky contractual processes
- No overall monitoring of operational performance
- No exit interviews

Performance Indicators and Measurement Ideas

The following operational tracking ideas supplement the dozens of financial indicators that accountants can track.

- Cost of stagnation decrease
- Net earning gains attributed to eliminating waste
- Net earning gains attributed to system and process refinement
- Staff survey results compiled year by year
- Exit interview trends
- Rates of improvement in staff retention
- Rates of on-time payment improvement

Tools: These indicators can be explored with the cause-and-effect diagram or the I/O cause-and-effect diagram. Work paths can be analyzed and continuously improved with a breakout of step-by-step activities in an IPO audit. Process breakouts can be displayed on a Pareto chart, and explored with the Pareto cause analysis. Trends can be displayed with scatter diagrams to search for correlations, and control charts can be used to monitor events and search for special causes.

Project Management Improvement

Project managers are problem solvers, that is part of their job description. Unfortunately, most of the problems tackled are internal, such as how to overcome a crisis, how to get back on schedule, how to get adequate staff resources, and how to manage with a poor job tracking system. This is unacceptable. Improved systems and processes will allow project managers to focus all their talents on solving clients' problems instead of their own.

Accepting that continuous improvement can be applied to strategic planning and operations, how can it possibly help projects when no two projects are alike? Processes such as estimating, scheduling, coordination, production, and job tracking can be improved and made more consistent. Therefore, they are subject to continuous improvement.

Components of Project Management

The Shearer model lists the following areas to continuously improve.

- Work plan management
- Teaming and coordination
- Schedule control
- Budget control
- Documenting, tracking, and reporting
- Standard operating procedure compliance
- Quality reviews

Flowing out of these topics, there are four broad goals for project managers.

1. Exceed the client's expectations.
2. Keep the staff happy.

3. Keep the company out of litigation.

4. Make a profit.

With the assumption that the right kind of work is being pursued by the marketing department, three internal activities make or break these expectations. These will be further explored in the next sections.

- Planning the work
- Doing the work
- Quality reviewing the work

Planning the Work

Seven vital planning steps to be used when commencing projects and during projects are as follows:

1. Assess the current status of the project.

2. Develop a vision of the most likely future scenario based on the scope, the status, the project history to date, and past similar histories.

3. Develop budget and schedule breakouts and track procedures.

4. Establish a detailed staffing work plan.

5. Set up workable team communication and coordination procedures.

6. Assess risks and prepare a contingency plan by asking What if types of questions.

7. Identify the early warning signs that may trigger the contingency plan.

When a TV commercial is being created it is storyboarded. The storyboard is a series of images depicting the story line as it is developed. In project management, the storyboard concept is very useful as it asks the project manager to think through and plan the phases, stages, and steps of the project. This forces the project manager to see what the project components will look like before they are actually created.

- What will comprise the final contract documents?
- What needs to be done now to ensure that they can be produced on time?

- What lead time will be required in order to meet deadlines?
- Who needs to be contacted now to ensure smooth sailing later?
- Map out the information flow.

Examples of information to be made available to the team include a list of project participants and their roles, scope of work breakouts, scope of work boundaries, and design standards. In addition, the whole team, including technicians and support personnel, should be made aware of client expectations and the explicit expectations of their managers for the successful completion of their assignments. Feedback must flow along an unblocked, two-way channel in discussing these expectations.

Doing the Work

Doing the work can be consistently successful if the planning has been done. The wild card is work overload that can result in stress-induced errors and omissions. Problems can often be traced back to poor planning or a communication root cause. During a project there is no time for an IPO audit and new QA guidelines. But once the audits have been performed and the QA system is in place, project processes will be more efficient.

Quality Reviewing the Work

This occurs in conjunction with, and parallel to, doing the work. The concept of self-checking guided by clear QA checklists is illustrated in Figures 4.5 and 6.12.

When QRs occur, quality output becomes the next step's quality input. The work is transferred to the next person in line without errors compounding errors. This is especially important when conditions, specifications, information, or team members change midstream on a project. TQM/CI can foolproof the transfer of information.

Project managers should be encouraged to stop the action to investigate an emerging issue that has the potential to result in major downstream problems. By taking a short time-out to repair the dike, an enormous flood of subsequent disruption and expense may be prevented. When this approach becomes a standard operating procedure, people will pull together to solve issues upstream.

Self-checking also promotes professional pride in a job well done. This in turn fosters a coaching-mentoring environment, which opens the door to an enduring management by partnership culture.

Typical Problems

- No historical estimating data per project subgroup, such as theaters, hotels, and so on
- Inadequate research of owners' concerns, project constraints, and community-political minefields
- No protocols and steps for work planning
- No project kickoff to review the project with the team
- No clear communication lines for problem solving with clients, in-house team members, subconsultants and prime consultants, contractors, subcontractors, and regulatory agencies
- Waiting too long for an issue to be resolved
- Tolerating poor performance by a team member without coaching feedback
- No delegation, or ineffective delegation of tasks
- Excess perfection syndrome, trying to be perfect when perfection is neither in the scope, nor in the budget
- Inflexibility when flexibility is needed
- Flexibility when toughness is needed
- Disregarding early upstream warning signals
- Uncooperative attitudes
- Politics and power plays
- No IPO agreements or QA guidelines established to enable QRs to take place during the work
- Quality control after project documents are complete
- Quality control after project documents submitted
- No constructability evaluations before the detailed design phase begins
- Not getting the client more involved in decisions and phase sign-offs

The root cause of project management problems is often found in the following:

- Ambiguous scopes of work and assumptions
- Accepting tight schedules without negotiating
- Accepting changes without negotiating
- Lack of adequate project planning
- No partnering agreements with
  —internal team members
  —external team members
  —contractors
  —owners

Readers will notice that all of these causes are upstream issues.

Performance Indicators and Measurement Ideas

Project managers need data to track their projects, to spot emerging problems, and to make minor course corrections. The project tracking sheets should contain the critical success factors for the project and not a mass of statistics buried within a dump truck load of paperwork. These will relate to budget, scope, hours, deadlines, and client expectations.

It is also important to have a system that collects red flags. Whenever a problem occurs, its solution should be recorded. This speeds up the learning curve for all project managers, allowing them to learn from the experiences of their colleagues. A task team could create an easily accessed red flag tracking system.

Tools: The process flowchart and the IPO audit may be used to map out project steps and identify key information transfer needs. This will reduce the need for revisions and rework. Backward flips might be beautiful in gymnastics, but in project management they are nightmares. Check sheets can collect history of occurrence data to encourage management by facts, and to bolster supplemental service agreement negotiations. The comparison matrix and benefit/LOE analysis will facilitate decision making, especially when used with client input.

A standardized postproject debriefing form, based on the problem statement format, will help to identify trends and needed improvements. On small and medium-sized projects a lunchtime brown-bag debriefing will be useful. On large projects, three debriefings could be held.

1. An internal debriefing.

2. A debriefing with team members and contractors.

3. A debriefing with the owner. This might occur in conjunction with the second debriefing.

Marketing Improvement

Getting to the top of one's profession can be bad news! Success breeds complacency, because once at the top, there is a tendency to relax and keep doing whatever it was that brought one to the top. Sooner or later this stand-still attitude will result in decay because markets, business environments, and targets change. With continuous marketing improvement, organizations at the top will not experience decay, nor will those striving to get to the top.

Components of Marketing

Marketing has a much grander role to play than assistance in client retention and new client pursuit. Marketing can be right in the center of the continuous improvement spiral, actually stimulating change through surveys and publicizing improvements. Three examples are given.

1. It may become evident through informal feedback or through a market survey that clients are unhappy with project management inefficiencies. Marketing may then work hand-in-hand with management to identify specific improvements, and subsequently highlight project management in the marketing materials.

2. A debriefing on an unsuccessful proposal might highlight a training need. Once this has been accomplished, the marketing department gets back into the loop to inform the markets about the comprehensiveness of the new or improved skills, knowledge, and abilities.

3. Perhaps research will identify a market niche opportunity. Should management decide to act on this information, the new focus will be reflected in the marketing materials.

So it is evident that marketing can both stimulate continuous improvement and act as the voice of continuous improvement.

Typical Problems

- Market planning not done so workload reacts to the peaks and valleys of the marketplace
- Opportunities missed because everybody is too busy doing the work to notice
- Projects not summarized resulting in inadequate write-ups when a rush proposal goes out
- Inefficient proposal preparation giving a poor image
- Shotgun submittals
- Winning projects that lose money
- Unplanned and unrehearsed presentations resulting in presentation embarrassments and lost work
- Newsletters produced inconsistently or inefficiently
- Business development by the seat-of-the-pants method
- Win-lose tracking and project debriefing not done resulting in unimproved submittals

Performance Indicators and Measurement Ideas

The following discussions expand on the Shearer model.

Improvement 1: Market Planning

The market plan should be built within the framework of the strategic plan. The strategic plan sets up the vision, directions, and the milestones, and the market plan translates the plan into the nuts and bolts of marketing. In some cases, organizations will build the market plan right into the strategic plan. In any event, the strategic plan should launch the market plan. Most strategic plans include an assessment of current market conditions and a projection for the future.

Improvements can be made in the research methodology to efficiently yield pertinent information. Questionnaires can be refined after feedback and improvements made in the way that the data are analyzed. Brainstorming and priority voting can be helpful in trimming down a lengthy list of questions.

Measurement will lead to numerical predictions, with supporting data. These predictions can be plotted and tracked for accuracy. No one expects the marketing staff members to suddenly become expert forecasters, but with time, accuracies will improve and the reasoning behind the predictions will become more substantial.

Improvement 2: Opportunity Research

The market plan will list targets to pursue, but new opportunities will crop up from time to time. There must be a process that gathers, collects, channels, analyzes, and acts on this information.

Gathering and Collecting. This could include regular targeted market research, a clipping service, reading the business press and trade journals, and encouraging staff to network. Information gathering can usually be made more efficient and less random. A problem statement can help to define what exactly is being pursued and information sources that produce the best leads. Links to the most productive networks can be identified with a Pareto chart.

Channeling. Few organizations have an efficient way of sorting and categorizing data, so this is an area ripe for improvement via a PIT. Improving the channeling system will stimulate the involvement of more people in research reporting.

Analyzing. Some of the information will point to trends that must be tracked while other information will demand a quick response. The actual analysis of trends is both an art and a science and is subject to continuous improvement when results are monitored. Also, the frequency of analysis can be adjusted.

Acting on the Information. Functioning links between senior management, marketing, and the implementers is required. Assessments must be made rationally. A go/no-go template will help to provide the logic to back up emotional decisions and logical reasons to restrain irrational decisions. A practical go/no-go process might be available, but if decisions are not being acted upon, or are acted upon too late, the system needs improvement. A lot of dollars wasted on no-hope opportunities might encourage the use or improvement of a go/no-go system.

Improvement 3: Project and Client Tracking

Computerized tracking systems that can sort, find, and report are best. There are also numerous, dedicated software programs that will track prospects, projects, and clients. There is nothing wrong with these programs. The problems stem from inadequate or incorrect data that are given to the data processor, or from good output that is not used. The number of times that incorrect information is given, or the number of times that searches have to made for missing data could become an interesting baseline. Dramatic measurable improvements could be built off this baseline.

Improvement 4: Proposal Preparation Processes

Efficient proposal preparation requires a database, easy ways to access past proposals, and a quick way to assemble a first draft. Most inefficient proposal preparation processes occur in firms that have a good system, but are hampered by a bottleneck. Examples of bottlenecks include delays or indecision in making a go/no-go assessment; delays in teaming decisions; word processors who are overloaded; outdated software; project managers who delay gathering and writing up information; impulsive changes at the last minute; involving too many reviewers; and reviewers who are not available.

Other problems include poor estimates; omitted information; unresponsive content; pages missing, mislocated, or sent upside down; typographical errors; and poor grammar. These may occur very infrequently, but still need to be totally eliminated. After establishing performance measures, tracking will spot negative trends so that they may be eradicated by PITs.

Improvement 5: Presentation and Interview Processes

Efficient presentation preparation requires a schedule of preparation tasks. This may include additional data gathering, presentation outline planning to discuss roles and visuals, and a rehearsal. The barriers to success need to be found and eradicated. This too will require tracking to recognize the problems. A frequent complaint is the lack of time to prepare adequately. In some instances this is a veil to cover up presentation anxiety, or it hides an unwillingness to accept the fact that a particular individual is not a great presenter.

Presentations themselves are also an art, but this art form can be continuously improved. This ties into training.

Improvement 6: Marketing Materials

Advertising results can be tracked, but getting brochure, newsletter, or announcement feedback is difficult. Perhaps the best one can do is to refine the segmentation of the mailing list and send very targeted pieces. Data-gathering and production processes can be continuously improved in order to become more cost efficient.

Once the PITs are operating, the marketing department should compose a short statement on the firm's quality management process. This can be used in proposals and statements of qualification. The statement might contain the following:

- The quality mission statement
- The continuous improvement structure, including how issues are approached, how teams are managed, and how processes and solutions are documented
- How quality reviews are performed
- Current issues being examined by PITs
- Measurable successes to date

While the organization's quality story needs to be a part of marketing, it is with continuous improvement where the real focus must lie.

Improvement 7: Business Development Planning and Tactics

This area is ripe with opportunities for continuous improvement. Performance measures include the following:

- The frequency of contacts per department
- The number of follow-up letters mailed
- The number of lunches that resulted in a proposal within three or six months
- The number of staff members that belong to client-oriented associations
- The number of hours devoted to business development per market area versus the gains in business in that market area
- The ratio of visits leading to engagements
- The number of engagements that came from referrals, repeat clients, reacquired clients, and new clients
- The root sources of clients, broken down by market area
- The number of visits to a trade show booth that resulted in an engagement or a referral
- The percentage of repeat assignments before and after a client retention program is established

Technical quality has only a 10 percent impact on acquiring clients. New clients are more interested in the following:

- On-time work
- Budget management
- Communication skills of the project manager
- Responsiveness of the team
- Cost-effective services
- Ability to assist with regulatory agencies
- Practical and realistic recommendations
- Low-risk or risk-free recommendations

These are the areas to continuously improve. They are also the areas that marketing must continue to sell.

Improvement 8: Business Development Activity Tracking

If market plans are well designed and implemented, if opportunities are spotted and pursued in time, if data gathering is well administered, if publications are well targeted, and if proposals and presentations are excellent, win-lose tracking is just a way of keeping score. If things are poorly run, if systems are not in place or not used, if proposals and presentations are regularly lost, and if nobody cares about business development, win-lose tracking can become a driving force for change.

Tools: The entire marketing operation could be drawn as a structure flowchart to clarify links and tasks. Activities such as opportunity research and proposal preparation could be diagrammed with a system flowchart, and all interfaces with marketing could undergo an IPO audit. In addition, project management improvements can be depicted on a system flowchart and used selectively for marketing. The cause-and-effect tools can point to necessary marketing improvements, and the most effective business development tactics can be shown on a Pareto chart. Check sheets can collect win-lose histories to be displayed on a control chart, and relationships can be shown on a scatter diagram.

Training Improvement

Lack of training shows up frequently on cause-and-effect diagrams. In some cases, it is a root cause, and in others a contributor to an ineffective process. It is a mistake, however, to leap to the conclusion that with more training, everything automatically gets better. Nevertheless, integrating training into the workplace, with a focus on continuous improvement, will provide a great return on investment.

Comprehensive Staff Training

Training serves the strategic plan by establishing the groundwork for success through people. Training includes the following:

- New staff orientation
- TQM/CI training
- Leadership and management training
- Project management training
- Client relation skills
- Meeting skills
- Time management skills
- Presentation skills

- Financial management training
- Health and safety training
- Regulatory update training
- Computer training
- Human resource management training

- Communication skills
- Writing skills
- Telephone skills
- Technical skills
- Conflict resolution skills

The instructor-pupil model provides less value per hour of training. A facilitated workshop setting is much better. The best type of learning takes place in an on-the-job setting, provided in a coaching-mentoring environment, supported by well-designed workshops.

TQM/CI Training

The continuous improvement process must have effective team facilitators. Keeping everything moving, preventing disruptions by difficult people, sidestepping disputes and digressions can be learned through observation and practice with an experienced facilitator.

Some consultants recommend intensive team leader and participant training before TQM is started. This is is usually unnecessary for organizations that utilize project management teams. They have no lack of leaders and potential leaders. Too much emphasis in trying to improve leadership skills sidetracks the implementation of continuous improvement that must involve everybody. Private coaching sessions for a team facilitator with a top-notch guide will help with conflict resolution skills, before and after the PIT meetings. By carefully following the PIT guidelines given in chapter 4, however, there may be no need to spend hundreds of hours training facilitators. That is the beauty of the PIT step-by-step process given in this book. Not only does it get results, but team facilitators also become more effective by using the structured Shearer model. Chapter 3 provides additional detail on TQM/CI training.

Typical Problems

The lack of an effective training program can have serious side effects. The following list portrays some typical problems

- No overall training plan
- No link between advancement and training

- No rational method to identify gaps in skills
- No link between staff reviews and training opportunities
- No staff input regarding training needs
- Haphazard approval process for training requests
- Frustration caused by a lack of opportunities
- Talent undeveloped without training
- No prior audit or evaluation of training programs
- No debrief or evaluation after training is complete
- Poor facilitation leading to inefficient meetings
- Skills learned at training programs not applied at work
- Trained staff frustrated because workload can't be shared with untrained staff
- Errors resulting from inequitable workload and work overload
- Client dissatisfaction and liability exposure resulting from untrained staff errors

Performance Indicators and Measurement Ideas

Some professional service firms spend heavily on training, but it is not the dollar amount that is important. It is the return on investment in money and in developing human potential that counts. Worthwhile programs should be identified and attended by as many people as necessary to implement the ideas learned. New ideas often need a critical mass of people behind the idea in order to effect change.

It is difficult to ascribe direct performance indicators for training, because training is a tool to enhance all other aspects of a professional practice. Readers are referred to Figure 2.7 as training is an important component in preventing stagnation. So the results of training are reflected in continuous improvement throughout the organization.

Tools: Training needs can be compiled by creating an assessment matrix based on staff feedback. A brainstorm session followed by priority voting or the comparison matrix could then be used to select the topics. The content of different training programs can be studied using the system overlap matrix. The benefit/LOE or force field analyses can be used to assess the realistic likelihood of in-house implementation. All training sessions should have an evaluation form handed out at the conclusion of the program, and the evaluations could be plotted on a control chart to establish the boundaries of effective training. Management must ensure that there are equal training opportunities and that these opportunities link to a cohesive professional development program. Evaluating training and monitoring its implementation are task team issues.

Partnering

Nobody works in a vacuum. Organizations are structures that link systems; systems link processes; and processes link inputs and outputs. Partnering enhances all of these links.

Some firms have a narrow view of TQM. They believe that partnering is TQM and that "if only we could all get along everything would be just fine." Partnering is an essential component of TQM/CI, but it is merely the charger upon which the knight of continuous improvement rides.

Partnering reduces paperwork, litigation, posturing, and rework. It results in seamless interactions between diverse elements of professional service teams. This is not always easy to achieve. Diversity can be dangerous or beneficial to internal or external partnerships. Readers will recall that diversity weakens a weak team and strengthens a strong team. So, diverse ideas that originate within a strong partnership are a cement for team bonding.

Partnering and team building are well-explored concepts, with enough articles, papers, and books written to fill a library wall. The next sections will not investigate the concepts nor the techniques, but will instead look at a few of the benefits, difficulties, measurements, and tools associated with partnering.

Internal Partnering

Internal partnering includes the following from the Shearer model.

- Information sharing between management and staff
- Performance recognition
- Reviewing and coaching

- Employee well-being
- Encouraging personal improvement

In order for internal partnering to succeed, management and staff must build two-way loyalty and must communicate. Cross-training will produce flexible and adaptable staff members who are well equipped to respond to internal and external client needs. This starts with managers who take the time to mentor and coach their staff, five minutes at a time. Multiple dividends include skill building, morale enhancement, job satisfaction, and managers having more confidence in delegating tasks to their newly coached team members. An important by-product is joint staff-management stakeholding in process improvement.

All of these activities will eliminate the ultimate barriers to partnership—one-way communication and lack of trust. Staff members will work very hard to meet their commitments if they feel a part of their team, if they trust their manager, and if they have even a tiny role in setting their task goals. This will translate into improvements on projects as early feedback always pays dividends downstream.

External Partnering

External partnering includes people working *with* each other, and *for* each other. Potential partners include the following:

- Subconsultants
- Suppliers and vendors
- Contractors and subcontractors
- Accountants and attorneys
- Regulatory agencies
- Clients

Changes in Relationships

Under the old way of doing business, executives were usually acquaintances who teamed frequently. This often led to an excellent working relationship and effective communications. Sometime in the 1960s this started to change. Today, many team members are selected on price, affirmative action status, being a super specialist, giving a marketing advantage to a team, or because the client insists on their inclusion. No wonder adversarial situations frequently arise!

The clue to the future lies in the past, with relationship-oriented partnering. When clients want partnering, they are looking for the assurance that their teams are comprised of real partners, not just a conglomeration of experts assembled to chew on pieces of a project. Clients will be part of this team. Partnering relationships must have

- Trust built up on nonadversarial attitudes

- Compatibility of communication and working style

- A mutual desire to work together toward quality results

Subconsultants and subcontractors, including disadvantaged businesses, must be seen as part of the solution, rather than part of the problem. A partnering charter will bring out the best in the relationship.

When to Commence A/EC Partnering

The A/EC world poses a special partnering challenge. Partnering has usually commenced when the contractor comes on board. Yet, in most cases, the journey is half over by this time. Partnering should start even before day one on each and every project.

- Recognizing that a nonadversarial alliance between the owner and the project design team will be best for all, a partnering charter is formed. This defines communication and documentation ground rules, and has a written understanding of roles and responsibilities to decrease the risk of misunderstandings.

- Procedures are mapped out together with the client, using a system flowchart.

- The IPO audit clarifies interactions and outcomes for all project entities.

- Reviewing project approaches with regulatory agencies before project commencement, with a view to early identification of impending rule changes, code interpretations, red flags, preferred formats, and new permitting processes, is advised.

- Even using an experienced construction manager, or a construction consultant who takes a role as the voice of the contractor, to give a fresh, unbiased opinion during the early stages of conceptual design and design development may be useful.

Typical Difficulties

Partnering will be further explored from the perspective of the A/EC industry. Before the concept of partnering, project participants traditionally started a project with their own mission statement, agenda, and processes.

Planning Specific Communication Links

With partnering, all players can start with a joint understanding about the project's mission, and agree upon a partnering agenda that coalesces their individual agendas and processes. The next step will prevent the warm initial feelings from cooling and will keep the trust from freezing. This is the establishment of the actual nuts and bolts of the working relationship, which is especially important to make partnering successful in competitive bid situations.

This entails a thorough roll-up-your-sleeves examination of who will do what, when it will be done, and how. This could include the following:

- Clear lines of communication
- Scope risks and opportunities
- Joint project mobilization planning
- Dispute avoidance and issue elevation steps
- Documentation formats and procedures
- Requests for information and shop drawing processing
- Schedule change processing
- Contractual revisions and change orders
- Safety planning

Unpredictable issues inevitably arise during projects. Looking at what could go wrong, and assessing project unknowns and potential changes are great ways to start an honest partnering relationship.

Compose a detailed conflict avoidance action plan with a hot line for issue elevation and resolution of disagreements. These details will result in a joint buy-in to the success of all other stakeholders. Consider a charter renewal meeting at some point during long projects to reaffirm agreements and possibly fine-tune the processes.

Solving Immediate Difficulties

Although having a voice of the contractor during the design and document production stages may eliminate a number of constructability flaws in the documents, there may still be differences of opinion before the construction partnering session commences. This can lead to an adversarial situation in spite of partnering. Perhaps the successful contractor may complain because there is a cheaper way to construct the project. If these concerns are tackled before the partnering charter is in place, feelings may become emotional. If these concerns are put on hold until after the partnering session is over, the meeting may not proceed smoothly because everybody knows that a crisis is in the wings. So it may be best to incorporate the concerns into the agenda without attempting to negotiate a solution. Then start the partnering session and address the communication links that will be established to deal with the contentious issues, without attempting to solve them. When the partnering session is over the issues can be tackled using the agreed-on pathways. The partnering facilitator may assist in this negotiation by helping the teams stay on track and by dealing with facts and not opinions. In this way, not only does the partnering occur, but a difficult issue also gets resolved right afterward. This establishes a positive track record and solidifies the charter.

Penalties

If a win-win partnership has a win-lose hidden agenda, partnering will not work. Partners who just play the game, using partnering as a ploy to gain advantage over other team members, should be penalized. The antidote is to apply the penalty, not in a court of law as happens so frequently today, but in a spirit of professionalism linked to the agreements in the charter. It is best if the penalty is something simple, yet something significant to pride. This could include making a donation to a charity, buying a case of wine, or a loss of points in a game to see who hosts the party at the end of the project. These penalties form part of the ground rules in the charter. When respect is the goal, loss of professional pride is more important than loss of money.

Performance Indicators and Measurement Ideas

Partnering is a value-added, waste-elimination, upstream improvement activity that embodies the continuous improvement spirit. The wide variety of issues that could be measured include the following:

- The number of days taken to return reviewed shop drawings
- The number of times a document is resubmitted for approval
- The number of days that it takes to get a response to a request for information
- The number of joint meetings that end on time
- The number of items on a punch list
- The number of safety infractions on a job site
- The number of times that meeting agendas are predistributed
- The number of disputes that are resolved without elevation to a supervisory or managerial level
- Partnering time versus the estimated time saved on the project

These types of measurements should be tracked, not in the spirit of proving a point, but rather in the spirit of a professional challenge to see what can be accomplished.

External partnering between project team members can be tracked using the same criteria that were reviewed in the project management section. It might take time for external partnering to get off the ground, because systems and processes must be aligned. This often requires modifications and changes in the way that the work is done, as well as a willingness by the participants to find the time to make changes.

Camaraderie and morale cannot be directly measured, but can be felt. If the data trends are down and there is an air of tension, root causes must be sought and addressed.

If the partnership is seen as a short-term or as a stop-gap alliance, the energy and willingness will most often be absent, and the alliance may be unprofitable and eventually dissolve. At worst, it may lead to litigation. The more effort that is put into the partnership and a belief in a positive outcome, the greater the return that will flow back. This alignment cannot be done effectively while the teams are faced with project pressures and deadlines. The pathways must be established beforehand, so that projects will run smoothly and the payoff in terms of team spirit, profit, and client delight will be considerable.

Tools: As partnering is linked to all other aspects of a professional practice, all of the tools in this book are valid, depending on the issue being examined. Partnering process solving can utilize the task team steps shown in Figure 4.2. Some examples are given in the following sections.

Relationship Building

Brainstorming, priority voting, the comparison matrix, or the benefit/LOE tool could be used to establish ground rules and determine priorities. A modified system overlap matrix showing teams and project goals can help to identify and resolve conflicts and coalesce mutual concerns. The problem statement can be used to guide the formation of the partnering charter, and the partnering structure can be created with the structure flowchart.

Teamwork

The details of the partnership can be identified using an IPO audit, with the resulting interactions linked into a system flowchart. Ideas may be banked and the idea bank assessment used.

Semantics

The phrase *problem solve* may have a negative connotation as the word *problem* is emotive and should be avoided in partnering. Preferred phrases are *resolve issues, address situations, work to resolve a question,* or *take care of a concern.* The Pareto or cause-and-effect tool families are unemotional ways to find causes.

Tracking

It is essential for the partnering charter to specify a uniform tracking methodology. One partner tracking a process with a scatter diagram and another using a run chart may run into interpretation difficulties. It is best that they either use a common tool, or that they agree on how, when, and where their individual data methods will be assessed, and who will be responsible for integration and interpretation.

Mind-Set

An adversarial mind-set leads to contract documents written from the perspective of the eventual court case. These will be applied and interpreted in the field to help support a future win in court. Submittals will be treated as exhibits and evidence, and everything will be documented with a view to the future legal discovery process.

Here the root cause is the mind-set. This must change, and change can occur through partnering. It is not easy to give up the legal security blanket, but it feels so good to treat people as humans and not just as future courtroom adversaries. This is the ultimate benefit, not so much an enhancement of profit, rather a rediscovery of trust and humanity in business.

Personal Improvement

This chapter moves away from the technical side of improvement and deals with stress, frustration, irritation, anger, and personal lifetime issues. The most efficiently designed corporate process or system will not be very effective when staffed by highly stressed people. Readers interested in continuous personal improvement might pick and test drive two or three of the ideas and techniques that they find personally appealing in order to find out what works best for them.

Typical Problems

The number of potential personal problems are limitless. The lists given are some of the more common issues that occur and recur.

Time Management

- Trying to do too much by oneself
- Not being able to say no
- Work overload leading to burnout
- Personal disorganization
- Daydreaming

- Unfinished tasks
- Procrastination
- Inefficient meetings

Communication

- Poor listening habits
- Not asking for clarifications
- Not giving clarifications
- Untimely communication
- Giving incomplete instructions or information
- Invalid assumptions
- Ignoring nonverbal signals
- Overwhelming the listener with excess detail

Conflict and Morale

- Allowing emotion to surface
- Trying to solve issues while emotion dominates
- Negative criticism
- No feedback
- Not distinguishing between a complaint, a concern, and a statement
- Jumping to conclusions
- Dealing with difficult situations without a plan
- Bias

Health

- Lack of exercise
- Poor exercise technique leading to injury
- Eating unhealthy or nutritionally deficient foods
- Overeating

- Insufficient sleep
- Alcohol and substance abuse
- Smoking
- Stress

Implementing Continuous Personal Improvement

This chapter is not about solutions for these problems, since there are thousands of books that readers can access for ideas on every conceivable self-help issue. Rather, readers will see that continuous improvement processes can help them find their own answers, and effect long-wished-for personal change.

Identify a Chronic Problem

Issues and crises needing resolution come up in everyone's life. Random difficulties are not subject to continuous improvement, although the tools can be used for many one-time issues. It is the regular behaviors and occurrences that can be tackled through the continuous improvement process.

Personal Problem Statement

Personal issues are especially prone to misclassification. It is very hard to view a personal issue dispassionately. Guilt, suspension of logic, and unrealistic expectations can cloud one's vision and lead to solutions that have no bearing on the real issue. Because of this, continuous personal improvement relies heavily on a problem statement that forces a breakout of the issues into who, what, where, why, when, and how.

Before a surgeon operates, tests must be done to identify exactly where the operation needs to be performed. The surgeon wants to start off with as much prior knowledge as possible. Then the incision can be made cleanly, smoothly, and effectively. No one wants a surprise at this point. In the same way, once the problem statement has been formulated—perhaps with the help of a spouse, friend, minister, counselor, or peer—the issue is clarified, and the target for improvement becomes visible.

Personal Process Breakout

Why was an action undertaken? What statement or thought stimulated a response? How was the background to a behavior developed? The personal process breakout continues the problem statement investigation in more detail. In many instances, an adapted IPO audit will be a valuable tool as it helps to break personal interactions down into inputs, thought processes, and reactions or actions.

Personal Baseline Data

Time management can be helped by tracking tasks completed or uncompleted, distractions that occurred, or interruptions and crises that erupted. The check sheet and Pareto chart are useful tools to collect and display time utilization. The frequency of misunderstandings and conflict can be tackled as can outcomes.

Health issues yield the most direct opportunities for measurement. EEGs, EKGs, blood counts, body fat analysis, x-rays, and MRI are all used by the medical profession as diagnostic tools, and every medical and dental practitioner likes to have a baseline to compare results. There are many measurements that individuals can take on their own: exercise data such as time, distance, weight lifted or carried, and repetitions; nutritional intake such as vitamins, sodium, and fats per day; food intake in terms of calories consumed each week and weight gain and loss; hours of sleep; and the number of drinks consumed or cigarettes smoked.

One of the major stressors in life is the feeling of being out of control, of events pushing one around, and of being at the mercy of fate. By keeping a record of incidents, by noting frequencies and trends, it is possible to gain a feeling that the recording of events is just one step away from controlling events. Of course, this is an illusion, but it can nevertheless help in alleviating stress.

Thousands of events could be turned into data. While very few people would have the inclination, energy, or time to track all of the issues listed, tracking a few might allow one to regain the feeling of being in control, while reducing the anxiety linked to unpredictability.

- Days when the commute exceeded 30 minutes
- Days when the neighbors were noisy

- Frequency of angry incidents with teenagers
- Number of junk mail items per day
- Length of time the neighbor's dog barks
- Number of people who are impolite each day
- Days with rain
- Number of equipment malfunctions per month
- Number of migraines per month
- Number of hours of contact with a rude relative each month
- The time it takes to get through the checkout line at the store

These incidents could be plotted on a Pareto or control chart, correlated with other events on a scatter diagram, or simply counted on a check sheet. By turning life's random occurrences into a game, one can gain a sense of order within disorder and peace within chaos.

Analyze and Find Root Causes

The cause-and-effect diagram is a prime tool to dig into the reasons for habits and behaviors. The umbrella categories could include the following:

- Emotion
- Communication
- Finances
- Stress
- Pressure and time management
- Education

It may be necessary to perform this analysis alone, but an objective family member or friend could provide a different viewpoint. Professional therapists perform this type of analysis all the time, only they don't call it a cause-and-effect diagram. Their methods can be much more sophisticated, depending on their therapeutic approach. If the issue is serious, a visit to a counselor or therapist might be advisable.

Create and Implement the Best Trial Solution

Most personal issues are not solved overnight. Finding the best way to deal with a teenager, improve health, become a better listener, give up a bad habit, or eliminate a bias might take a while; in some cases, a long while. It is not the speed with which the solution is reached, it is the continuous improvement journey that brings the dividends. It is rare for people to embark upon a personal improvement journey working on only one aspect of life. Usually change is sought in several areas at once, and readers should not become discouraged because one improvement lags behind gains made in other areas.

Collect Data and Evaluate

Is the improvement working? Does it work in some situations and not in others? Have some gains been made? Does it feel better? An evaluation on one's own is often more subjective than objective, but it is nevertheless important. Whenever possible, supplement this evaluation with the opinion of an outsider, such as a friend, minister, or therapist, to assess gains. In instances where two or more people, such as in a family, commit to improve interactions, the group can assess gains and brainstorm further refinements. Where data are being collected, such as with health and fitness issues, gains will tend to be objective.

Standardize and Monitor

It is important not to fall back into bad habits or old, negative, destructive patterns. Data monitoring is one technique, but simpler is to ask for the support of a family member, friend, counselor, or minister to help maintain gains until a new habit structure is solidly constructed.

Additional Uses for the Tools

The sample ideas given are a potpourri of real-life situations that could be helped by the application of TQM/CI. They include the use of the standard tools for one-time issues and for long-term trends. Worries, anxieties, and fears can be crystallized and reduced in stature by breaking them down with the problem statement tool.

- Who is likely to be affected by this situation?
- Where is it happening most frequently or seriously?

- When is it happening?
- How much can it escalate if nothing is done about it?
- How often could it occur each month?
- Why have I allowed it to bother me so much?
- What is at stake?
- What is the worst possible outcome?
- If the worst outcome occurred how would I handle it?

The use of the problem statement tool in this fashion allows one to break out a worry, examine the worst possible outcome, and start to plan how to mitigate or deal with the worst, should it occur. One of the greatest stresses comes from the worry of the unknown. This method turns the unknown into the known.

- Families could brainstorm issues to gather improvement ideas. A family partnering meeting could be held to explore viewpoints, perceptions, roles, fears, and expectations. A family charter could be agreed upon and signed.

- Choices, such as a vacation spot, could be made using priority voting or the comparison matrix. Decisions such as diet choices, exercise choices, and chore selections could be evaluated with the benefit/LOE tool.

- The sources for everything from teenage behavior to heat pump breakdowns, and from feelings of anxiety to crop failure, can be explored with cause-and-effect diagrams.

- Transactions with family members, repair technicians, health care providers, and baby-sitters represent a sample of the interactions that can benefit from the IPO audit.

- Any situation that involves go/no-go decision making or choices, such as planning to build or remodel a home or planning a job or career change, can benefit from a system flowchart with alternate pathway explorations.

- The frequency of different health symptoms, the sources of traffic delays, and a variety of equipment malfunctions are examples of issues that could benefit from a Pareto chart. It may make sense out of a random jumble of occurrences.

- Many of these occurrences may also be plotted on a run or control chart to separate common cause variations from special causes. One can then visit a physician, counselor, or mechanic with a clear set of data to be assessed. As mentioned, these tools are also stress reducers, for they give a personal sense of control over issues, and make the vagaries of life seem less threatening.

Summary

Continuous personal improvement might be considered both the most difficult to accomplish, as well as the most rewarding. Those who are fixed in their personal ways and resist personal improvement will often be the same people who attempt to block corporate change. People who are open and interested in personal change are also often open to corporate change.

The chief obstacle to personal change is habit, and the glue that grips habit is emotion. The key to loosen emotion is imagination, because it can stimulate change by seeing how much better things could be. Once this gives rise to a desire for change, the battle for continuous personal improvement is half won.

Definitions for Professional Service TQM/CI

The following definitions are not meant to be universal. They reflect this author's vision of professional service terms used in this book.

A/EC   The architectural, engineering, and construction industry. Includes designers, scientists, and planners.

CI   Continuous improvement of inputs, processes, outputs, work environments, and relationships through dedicated, knowledgeable leaders, teams, and stakeholders. Continuous improvement works best when it is structured.

Data   Data illustrate and describe inputs, systems, processes, outputs, and activities. Data support evaluations and conclusions. Data are unemotional, but the conclusions usually provoke emotions.

Global TQM/CI   The practice of applying CI to all aspects of an organization.

Inputs   Written or verbal information transmitted to facilitate process performance. Inputs should comply with codes, specifications, standards, expectations, and QA checklists and guidelines.

IPO   Input-Process-Output. The building blocks of continuous improvement.

Outputs   Information or documentation given or transmitted after it has been created, translated, improved, or revised. Outputs should comply with expectations, QA checklists, and guidelines.

PIT   Process improvement team.

Process   An activity connecting one or more inputs to one or more outputs. A process has a starting point, a duration and an ending or transfer point. Several interlinked processes form a system. Processes should comply with QA checklists and guidelines.

QA   Quality assurance. Written guidelines, checklists, and standard operating procedures. A quality assurance manual should cover all aspects of a professional practice.

QC   Quality control. Often entails checking work after it is completed, or even stopping production at the end of a phase on a drawing, report, document, or activity. This is also known as off-line QC. The document is checked or inspected for compliance with a code, specification, manual, professional standard, regulation, and the scope of work. When a QC check is performed after QRs have been done, the QC check provides a final assurance of excellence.

QR   Quality reviews. Self-checks performed during the work to ensure conformance with the scope of work, quality assurance checklists, guidelines, and standard operating procedures.

Results   Results frequently have an emotional content, because of their link to a human expectation. Continuous improvement prefers objective results supported by facts and data rather than opinion. This tends to dampen emotional responses.

SC   The steering committee that administrates and links the continuous improvement teams.

SPC   Statistical process control provides a window for viewing statistical boundaries and process capabilities. It confirms stability and warns of instability.

System   A system is comprised of one, or more interlinked processes. Examples include a project management system, a marketing system, and a financial reporting system.

TSC   Trial solution component. A solution idea that combines or merges with other ideas to form a comprehensive solution. A piece of the potential solution.

TQM   Total quality management. Most often related to the improvement of the quality of products. Management theory is now adapting TQM to services.

TQM/CI   (1) The practical application of TQM for professional services. When TQM is correctly implemented in a professional service environment, it becomes TQM/CI, a continuous improvement process. (2) A TQM/CI organization is a quality affiliation of professionals practicing comprehensive CI. (3) An attitude that equates quality with excellence in all aspects of an organization or an individual's life. As part of a personal philosophy, it means being the best that one can be and continuously getting better. In a partnership context, it means people drawing out the best in each other and continuously getting better.

Quality Assurance Manual Outline

The quality assurance manual outline shown in this appendix reaches beyond the scope of most QA manuals. One might even call it a quality work practices manual, as it provides guidelines for the procedures, standards of care, due diligence, and benchmarks for all professional service activities and interactions. The following outline, developed using elements of the Shearer model, is not meant to be comprehensive in order to encourage firms to custom design their own manual. Some firms may have QA sections that are far more detailed and complex. Legal advice is always advised for contractual guidelines and in all cases where due diligence and standards of care are being established.

1. Strategic Planning

This will be a statement of vision, directions, and objectives. Market and service assessments will be utilized, and the history of project success and profitability will be documented. These may result in the following types of QA guidelines to assess, avoid, and manage acceptable risks.

- Checklists to

  —Assess prospective client risks.

  —Assess prospective project risks.

  —Improve client contact before and during projects.

- Guidelines for risks such as leases and employment contracts.

- Process to deal with nonstandard circumstances
  - —Damage control plan (spokesperson)
  - —Issues requiring professional judgment
  - —Client expectations not within recognized standard of care
- Loss prevention reduction through
  - —Continuous improvement
  - —Internal review
  - —Client debriefing
  - —Education

In addition to getting legal advice, readers are also urged to discuss these issues with their liability insurance carrier.

2. Operational Procedures

These procedures document ways to ensure that contracts are comprehensive. They set the protocols for getting signed contracts before work is completed, as well as how the exceptions will be handled.

- Examples of contracts
- A checklist for the preparation of a contract
- Clauses that must be included in every contract
- Examples of optional contract clauses and loss prevention language
- Who has signature and commitment authority
- Client needs and agenda checklist
- Project history questionnaire
- Scheduling and budgeting guidelines
- Scope of work checklist
- Negotiation guide
- Contract preparation flowchart

The procedures ensure consistency in reporting and management functions, financial management, and the governing organizational structure.

- Checklists for operational and support staff
- Skills inventory including technical champions and specialists
- Examples of operational reports, how to read them, who receives them, and actions to take
- Organizational structure chart with explanatory notes
- Interactions between operations and line management
- Library system and records management
    —Information retrieval system
    —Computer file security
    —Project filing guide
    —Archiving guide
- Accounting guidelines
    —Corporate accounting procedures
    —Accounts receivable and accounts payable procedures
    —Accounting and management links—a flowchart

The operational procedures set standards of expectations and fairness for staff.

- Hiring procedures flowchart
- Hiring, layoffs, and termination guidelines
- Job and task descriptions
- Benefits management and policies

3. Project Management and Document Production

Included here are procedural checklists and guidelines to ensure consistently excellent communications and coordination.

- Project management system flowchart
- Project planning and mobilization phase checklist
- Project kickoff and partnering guidelines
- Schedule and budget management guidelines
- Client and consultant communication and coordination guidelines
- Documentation audit trail procedures

- Internal staff member communication and coordination guidelines
  —Report and letter writing style guide with examples
- Public agency communication and coordination guidelines
- Contractor/subcontractor communication and coordination guidelines
- Field health and safety guidelines and checklist
- Change order management checklist
- Project closeout checklist
- Business development guidelines for project managers

Quality assurance and quality review guidelines to document the standard procedures include the following:

- QA/QR budget guidelines
- QA/QR procedures include the following:
  —Checklists to be used,
  —Nonconformance procedures
  —Level of review detail (link to complexity and size of project)
  —Exceptions (cases where reviews may be waived or simplified)
  —QR steps at work transfer
  —Accountability
  —QC audits to verify QR consistency
  —Documentation, record keeping guidelines, and examples
- Documentation guidelines for each project might include the following:
  —Client decisions
  —Public agency decisions
  —Standards
  —Code interpretations
  —Scope of work and assumptions
  —Budget and schedule breakouts
  —Project work and staffing planning

—Design decisions and calculations

—Correspondence

—Conversations (telecons, meetings)

—Nonconformances and corrective actions taken

- Monitoring of estimating accuracy for continuous improvement
- Model project manager guidelines, such as the following:

  —Review project with client. Identify history of the project, plus client's needs and expectations.

  —Review contractual obligations and wording.

  —Internally evaluate standards of care and discuss risks versus rewards.

  —Break out scope of work in greater detail than in proposal.

  —Establish partnering.

  —Review uncertainties and limitations with client.

  —Storyboard the project using the system flow method.

  —Customize internal and subconsultant QR procedures for each project (balance fee and risk). Use IPO audit.

  —Create a work and staffing plan.

- Additional QA/QR guidelines such as the following:

  —Discuss alternatives with client for a decision.

  —Discuss concerns and potential delays with clients.

  —Document all interactions and decisions.

  —Have periodic client approvals/sign-offs.

  —Track compliance with QA standards via checklists in QA manual.

  —Deal with problems upstream.

  —If requested, consider providing quality review reports to client.

  —Hold regular internal project debriefings (for example, post-design, post-construction, post-occupancy).

—Implement a QA red flag system to record and continuously improve frequently occurring problems.

4. Marketing and Business Development

- Standards and guidelines for market planning research
- Database guidelines for information retrieval
- Tracking procedures
- Proposal and presentation standards, methods, and checklists including the following:

  —Go/no-go worksheet

  —Materials, formats, and audiovisual guidelines

  —Project and staff experience database system

  —Documentation, records, and assembly procedures

- Government form standards and database
- Client relations guidelines, including professional staff inter-actions, follow-up, and tracking
- Business retention and acquisition processes

5. Professional Development Guidelines

- Policies for training all grades of personnel including the following:

  —In-house and outside training, including technical, communica-tion, business, marketing, conflict resolution, and risk manage-ment topics

  —Dissemination of outside training lessons learned

- Career path guidelines and counseling
- Professional library
- A system of mentors to assist new personnel

6. Partnering

- Internal partnering

  —Performance review guidelines

—Joint manager-employee goal setting (individual goals linked to team and system goals)

—Mentoring training and guidelines

—Employee welfare and equal opportunities

• External partnering

—Guidelines for establishing and conducting partnering

—Mutual QA/QR procedures

—Avenues of communication and coordination

—Avenues of issue resolution

—Documentation and record-keeping agreements

APPENDIX C

Suggested Reading

ASQC Statistics Division. 1983. *Glossary and tables for statistical process control.* 2d ed. Milwaukee: ASQC Quality Press.

Brocka, Bruce, and M. Suzanne Brocka. 1992. *Quality management.* Homewood, Ill.: Business One Irwin.

Crocker, Charney. 1986. *Quality circles.* New York: Mentor.

Crosby, Phillip B. 1979. *Quality is free.* New York: McGraw-Hill.

Deming, W. Edwards. 1986. *Out of the crisis.* Cambridge, Mass.: MIT Center for Advanced Engineering Study.

Dobyns, Lloyd. 1991. *Quality or else.* Boston: Houghton Mifflin.

Ernst & Young. 1990. *Total quality: An executive's guide to the 1990s.* Homewood, Ill.: Dow Jones-Irwin.

Feigenbaum, Armand V. 1983. *Total quality control.* New York: McGraw-Hill.

Gavin, David. 1988. *Managing quality.* New York: Free Press.

George, Stephen. 1992. *The Baldrige quality system.* New York: John Wiley & Sons.

Harrington, James H. 1991. *Business process improvement.* New York: McGraw-Hill.

Hartzler, Meg, and Jane E. Henry. 1994. *Team fitness: A how-to manual for building a winning team.* Milwaukee: ASQC Quality Press.

Imai, Masaaki. 1986. *Kaizen: The key to Japan's competitive success.* New York: Random House.

Ishikawa, Kaoru. 1982. *Guide to quality control.* Tokyo: Asian Productivity Organization.

————. 1986. *What is total quality control? The Japanese way.* Englewood Cliffs, N.J.: Prentice Hall.

Juran, J. M. 1988. *Juran on planning for quality.* New York: Free Press.

————. 1989. *Juran on leadership for quality.* New York: Free Press.

Kinlaw, Dennis C. 1992. *Continuous improvement and measurement for total quality.* Homewood, Ill.: Business One Irwin.

Lamprecht, James L. 1993. *Implementing the ISO 9000 series.* New York: Marcel Dekker.

Logothetis. 1992. *Managing for total quality.* Englewood Cliffs, N.J.: Prentice Hall.

Miller, George L., and LaRue L. Krumm. 1992. *The whats, whys, and hows of quality improvement.* Milwaukee: ASQC Quality Press.

Pyzdek, Thomas. 1990. *Pyzdek's guide to SPC. Vol. 1, Fundamentals.* Tucson, Ariz.: Quality Publishing.

Rabbit, and Bergh. 1993. *The ISO 9000 book.* White Plains, N.Y.: Quality Resources.

Walton, Mary. 1986. *Deming management at work.* New York: Putnam.

Organizations to Join

American Society for Quality Control (ASQC)
P.O. Box 3005
MIlwaukee, WI 53201-3005
800-248-1946

Association for Quality and Participation (AQP)
801B West 8th Street, Suite 501
Cincinnati, OH 45203
513-381-1959

Index

About the Author

Clive Shearer, P.E., C.Eng., founded a management consulting practice late in 1982. Since then he has provided management consulting services to more than 300 clients, of whom over 250 are professional service organizations. Shearer is a British-trained structural engineer, registered as a professional engineer in Washington, Oregon, and California, and in the United Kingdom as a chartered engineer. Shearer is also a registered counselor in Washington state. Since 1984, he has facilitated stress and anger management classes, and currently teaches at three regional health care facilities.

Since 1984, he has authored a monthly management and marketing column in the Seattle Daily Journal of Commerce, and has been published on these topics in the United States, Canada, and the United Kingdom.

Shearer is a member of ASQC and the American Society for Training and Development. He has chaired the Bellevue Chamber of Commerce's Business Development Committee, is past president of Eastside Toastmasters, and served as president of the Pacific Northwest chapter of the Institute of Management Consultants.